Alexandria (Arlington) County, Virginia
Death Records
1853-1896

Compiled by
Wesley E. Pippenger

HERITAGE BOOKS
2008

HERITAGE BOOKS
AN IMPRINT OF HERITAGE BOOKS, INC.

Books, CDs, and more—Worldwide

For our listing of thousands of titles see our website
at
www.HeritageBooks.com

Published 2008 by
HERITAGE BOOKS, INC.
Publishing Division
100 Railroad Ave. #104
Westminster, Maryland 21157

Copyright © 1994 Wesley E. Pippenger

All rights reserved. No part of this book may be reproduced or transmitted in any form or by any means, electronic or mechanical, including photocopying, recording or by any information storage and retrieval system without written permission from the author, except for the inclusion of brief quotations in a review.

International Standard Book Numbers
Paperbound: 978-1-58549-358-6
Clothbound: 978-0-7884-7716-4

TABLE OF CONTENTS

INTRODUCTION v

ABBREVIATIONS USED vii

CAUSES OF DEATH ix

ACT REQUIRING VITAL STATISTICS xv

DEATH RECORDS 1

   Not Identified 107

INTRODUCTION

The Register of Deaths for Alexandria County, 1853-1896, is kept with the Clerk of the Circuit Court, Arlington County, Virginia. This record was the only Court account of deaths in the city or county of Alexandria until the newly-created Alexandria City government began keeping an additional record there in 1869—a year previous to when most city positions and duties were clearly defined.

There are no register entries for the time just before and during the Civil War, years 1857-1864. Also, it appears that for the last entries of 1887, mismatched columns have made for incorrect information regarding parents' names, informant, and relation of the informant to the deceased. A study of the Alexandria County birth register for those who died in 1887 allowed the compiler to unravel much of the incorrectly recorded death register data for this year.

Death records for the year 1888 are missing from the original register; however, we find that there was a report returned by H.L. Holmes, Commissioner of Revenue, but it was never recorded in the register. Similarly, the register contains no entries for the years 1857-1859, but the compiler located Commissioner returns for these years as well. In total, original Commissioner returns have been found for the years 1853-1859, 1865-1868, and 1888. These original returns are found at the Library of Virginia (formerly known as the Virginia State Library), Archives Division, Arlington County records, accession #24121, bundle 182a. Entries from these original returns have been inserted in this volume.

An important point regarding how the register was made centers around the Commissioner of Revenue's task of collecting the data. It was the Commissioner that solicited from persons within his district information about any deaths which had occurred during the previous year. A review of the 1853 legislation which required the keeping of this data (see page xv) also reveals that the information was first collected in one form, then transcribed by the Clerk to another "more permanent" register format. Again, a chance for errors to have occurred.

It is unfortunate that many pages of the register are riddled with incomplete entries. Among the extant information we do find errors. Since this data was collected sometimes a considerable period after a death, informants became forgetful about specifics. Therefore, users of the register and this volume should be aware of the likelihood that other sources, such as newspapers or cemetery records, may be more reliable. It is common to find deaths reported by an overseer of the poor or a keeper of a poor house. A few of these persons were: John Stephenson (1853-1859), W.H. Lomax (1879-1880), Isaac Green (1880), Robert Monroe (1887), Laura Cox (1890), and Thornton Hyatt (1893).

The standard format for the register called for the following information and sequence: name of the deceased; if white; if colored, free or a slave; name of the owner of slave; sex; date of death; place of death; name of disease or cause of death; age in years, months and days; name of parents of the deceased; where born; occupation; consort of, or unmarried; sources of information, name of person giving information of death, and designation of informant. After each transcript of data, the compiler has added the page number on which the entry can be found in the original register. Entries which came from Commissioner returns are not followed by a page number reference.

This volume lists approximately 2,782 deaths, some of which occurred outside the county. Of the total, 2,331 are recorded in the register and 451 are contained in original Commissioner returns. The majority of these entries accounts for deaths of free colored persons, especially for the post-Civil War years. The comparatively large colored population during this period was primarily located in the southeastern portion of the county where was found "Freedmen's Village." An interesting comment of the situation, contemporary with the keeping of the death register, is found recorded by the County Board of Supervisors who petitioned the United States Congress for permission to recover excess costs through taxation [Reference: Library of Virginia, Archives Division, Accession #24121, "Exhibits," Folder 13, item 5, not dated]:

> Your petitioners, constituting the Board of Supervisors of Alexandria County, Virginia, and charged by law with the assessments of taxes, respectfully represent that the Arlington Estate of 1,100 acres is situate in our county and that since its acquisition by the United States in 1864, no taxes have been paid on it. Furthermore, immediately after the purchase of the Estate, the Government established upon it a general rendezvous of freedmen under the name of "Freedmen's Village," but soon after the war ceased to care for them, though permitting them to remain in the village, and threw upon our county many indigent persons whom our peoples have been continuously compelled to support at heavy expense.

Entries found in Common Law Order Books 1, 2 and 3, document that during the period 1853-1896, eight clerks of the Alexandria County Court were responsible for maintaining the register:
   a. Jefferson Tacey (June 1847 to December 31, 1870).
   b. George C. Seaton, colored (elected 8 NOV 1870 to serve 4 years beginning January 1, 1871, removed August 30, 1872).
   c. David M. Hunter (appointed September 2, 1872, pro tem, to December 30, 1873).
   d. John B. Syphax (elected 5 NOV 1872, turned out of office 3 FEB 1873).
   e. Louis E. Payne (elected November 4, 1873 to fill the vacancy caused by the removal from office of John B. Syphax, to March 7, 1879).
   f. Alexander Hunter (March 1879 to June 20, 1879).
   g. Benjamin Austin (July 1879, resignation September 7, 1886).
   h. Howard H. Young (September 1886 through 1896).

Information in brackets, "[ ]" has been corrected or inserted by the compiler and taken from other available sources such as tombstone inscriptions, newspaper obituaries and death notices, church records, or family bibles. Characters in the register which were not clearly legible or which conflict with others in the same entry are underscored in the text of this volume. Intriguing entries detail causes of death like "killed by cars," "doctors" or even an "overdose of laudanum," and the death for James Patton was reported by his "kept madam."

I am grateful for the assistance of Roland J. Charlebois, and David Bell, Clerk of the Circuit Court, Arlington, Virginia, for making this record available for publication.

Wesley E. Pippenger
Arlington, Virginia

ABBREVIATIONS USED

The use of abbreviations in this volume has been kept to a minimum. In most cases, the spelling and abbreviations used herein are as they are found in the original records. Only a few abbreviations are routinely used as listed below.

Alexa.	Alexandria
d	Day(s)
F	Female
(f)	Colored person, free
m	Month(s)
M	Male
p.	Register page
(s)	Colored person, slave
W	White
y	Year(s)
--	Blank item or items in the Register

DISEASES AND CAUSES OF DEATH

AGUE	Recurring chills or fits of shivering; "intermittent fever;" chills and sweats; "marsh fever."
ANTHRAX	Acute infectious disease of cattle and sheep which is transmissible to man; "tanner's disease;" "splenic fever."
APHONIA	Laryngitis; "clergyman's sore-throat."
APOPLEXY	Sudden and violent loss of bodily function due to rupture or occlusion of a blood vessel; foaming at the mouth, sweats, head pain; usually caused by cerebral stroke or cerebral hemorrhage, although could be epilepsy; paralysis.
ARTHRAGRA	Gout of the joints.
ATROPHY	Wasting away or tissues or other body parts; degeneration; "shrinking heart."
BARBER'S ITCH	Ringworm of face or beard; tinea sycosis.
BARLOW'S DISEASE	Infantile scurvy; "Moller's disease;" "Cheadle's disease."
BILIOUS FEVER	Typhoid fever; "bilious remitting fever."
BLACK TONGUE	Typhoid fever.
BLACKWATER FEVER	Fatal and contagious malarial disease; fever and chills with vomiting.
BRAIN FEVER	Meningitis.
BRAIN INFLAMMATION	Viral encephalitis; concussion; sun stroke; apoplexy; delirium.
BRIGHT'S DISEASE	Nephritis, inflammation of the kidneys; uremia.
BUBOES	Due to abuse of mercury and improper exposure; gonorrhea.
CAMP FEVER	Typhus fever.
CANINE MADNESS	Hydrophobia.
CARBUNCLE	Painful local inflammation of the skin and tissues, especially of the neck; accompanied by discharge, breakdown of surface skin, and fever.

Diseases and Causes of Death

CATARRH CATARRH FEVER	Common head cold; sinus infection; mucous discharge, "blue tongue."
CHILBLAINS	Inflammation of body extremities caused by continued damp cold, with burning and itching.
CHILDBED FEVER	Puerperal fever; bacterial infection of lacerations by instruments in child delivery.
CHOLERA CHOLERA MORBUS BILIOUS CHOLERA	Characterized by frequent and violent vomiting and purging; occurs in warm months of year; caused by bacterium which, untreated, killed half of its victims; death often occurred within several hours; sewage contaminated water supplies were often responsible for epidemics. Epidemics in Virginia 1832, 1834, 1849, 1854, and 1866; attacked blacks more frequently than whites; in Alexandria a cholera hospital was established at the northeast corner of Fairfax and Gibbon streets.
CHOLERA INFANTUM	"Summer complaint;" gastroenteritis; acute intestinal poisoning; often wrongly attributed to teething; often occurs the second summer of life or first summer off mother's breast.
CHOREA, CHOREIC	"St. Vitus's dance;" irregular, spasmodic and involuntary movement of limbs or facial muscles.
COLIC	Affection of the bowels; acute constipation; often caused by irritating or indigestible foods; "flatulent colic;" "bilious colic;" "dry gripes;" commonly refers to abdominal pain in infants; "painter's colic."
CONSUMPTION	Tuberculosis; wasting away of the lungs or intestine.
CORRUPTION	Infection of any type; easily fatal without modern antibiotics; also called "mortification."
COSTIVE	Common constipation; if seen on mortality schedule may be due to malignant colon tumor.
CRAMP COLIC	Appendicitis.
CROUP	Disease of the larynx, throat; membranous croup (diphtheria).
DIPHTHERIA	Acute, infectious and highly contagious bacterial disease; throat condition sometimes extending beyond the lips on the skin; causes blood poisoning if received in an open wound.

Diseases and Causes of Death

DROPSY	Filling of body cavities and cells of the head and body with fluid; edema; often caused by obstructions to the free return of blood to the heart; characterized by cold, disease and inactivity of the kidneys, arsenic; anasarca; ascites; hydrops.
DYSENTERY	Disease of large intestine marked by frequent watery stools; enteritis; colitis; often fatal to teething infants. Prevailed in Alexandria during the *unhealthy summer* of 1821.
DYSPEPSIA	Chronic indigestion; liver complaint; evidenced by coating on the tongue.
EURYCEPHALOUS ERYSEPHILOUS ERYSIPELAS	A highly infectious and contagious disease caused by group A strep; characterized by high fever, chills; often leads to nephritis, meningitis, or pneumonia; "St. Anthony's fire."
FALLING SICKNESS	Epilepsy.
FLUX	Dysentery; diarrhea; menstrual flow, often bloody; various causes; found in wartime conditions.
FOTHERGILL'S PAIN	Facial neuralgia, tic douloureux.
FRENCH POX	Venereal disease; syphilis.
GRAVEL	Stones in kidney, gall bladder, or bladder; strangury.
GLEET	Persistent or chronic gonorrhea, with discharge.
GRIPPE	(see "LaGrippe")
HIVES	Eruptive skin disease; if given as cause of death, probably reaction to poison or acute allergy.
HUMID TETTER	Skin disease; ringworm; eczema.
INFLAMMATION OF THE BOWELS	Dysentery.
INFLUENZA	Epidemic originating in bacteria; abrupt fever, headache, general pains, severe in joints, prostration, and sometimes a sore throat with irritating cough; catarrhal fever or quinsy; epidemics in Northern Virginia in 1815, 1831 and 1832.
JAIL FEVER	Typhus fever.

Diseases and Causes of Death

LaGRIPPE	Influenza; "Russian influenza;" characterized by headaches and stomach (bowel) pains.
LEAD COLIC	"Painter's colic;" chronic intestinal pains and constipation caused by lead poisoning.
LOCKJAW	Closure of jaw due to jaw spasms from chewing; early sign of tetanus.
MALARIA	Infectious disease characterized by bouts of chills, fever and sweating; transmitted by infected female mosquitos; "swamp fever;" "prickly heat."
MANIA À POTU	Delirium; occurs in habitual drunkards and drug addicts; horrid illusions.
MARASMUS	Infantile atrophy; gradual wasting away of the body due to insufficient or imperfect foods.
MENINGITIS	Spotted fever; called "brain fever" before 1871.
PNEUMONIA, MALARIA TYPHO-MALARIA	Given as cause of death when intermittent or alternating fever of unknown origin was found.
PALSY	"Shaking palsy;" "St. Vitus dance;" probably what is now known as "Parkinson's disease."
PARALYSIS, PARALYTIC	Loss of voluntary motion of muscles.
PARSONS [DISEASE]	"Grave's disease;" disease of thyroid; hyperthyroid.
PELLAGRA	Skin disease; inflammation of the mucous membranes, gastrointestinal disorders; due to lack of sufficient protein and niacin.
PHTHISIS	Wasting away; pulmonary tuberculosis.
PILES	Hemorrhoids.
PLEURISY	Inflammation of the lungs; with or without a liquid effusion.
PRICKLY HEAT	Malaria.
PUERPERAL FEVER	Childbed fever; often evolves into septicemia; infection of the placental site following delivery; Augusta County in 1850.

Diseases and Causes of Death

PUTRID FEVER PUTRID [SORE] THROAT	Diphtheria; diphtheria, mononucleosis, or strep.
QUINSY	Inflammation of the throat; strep or tonsillitis; peritonsillar abscess.
REMITTING FEVER	Malaria.
RICKETS	Disease of the bones common in children, caused by insufficient lime phosphate, calcium.
RUN ROUND	Affection of the fingers and toes; inflammation around sides and base of nail.
ST. ANTHONY'S FIRE	A form of erysipelas; believed it could be cured by intervention of St. Anthony.
ST. VITUS' DANCE	Chorea; gradually increasing abdominal pain, occasional vertigo, mood swings, confusion; generally attacks those over age 8 and under 20 years.
SCARLET FEVER	Acute and infectious virus; typically a childhood disease; frequently associated with nephritis; high fever; concentrates at the face and breast. Alexandria suffered an epidemic in 1836.
SCREWS	Rheumatism.
SCROFULA KING'S EVIL	Tuberculosis of the lymph glands; neck swelling; enlarged tonsils; sore eyes; discharge from ears; typically a childhood disease.
SCURVY	Disease caused by lack of ascorbic acid (Vitamin C); characterized by bleeding, spongy gums and general weakness.
SHIP'S FEVER	Typhus fever.
SMALL POX	Variola; acute eruptive contagious disease marked at the onset by chills, high fever, backache and headache, progressing to skin eruptions and scabs; epidemic faced Alexandria in 1872, chiefly affecting the negro population.
SPASMS	Symptom, not a disease; convulsions, may be epilepsy.
SPOTTED FEVER	Cerebro-spinal meningitis; characterized by blisters on the ankles, head and neck; victim typically succumbed in from

Diseases and Causes of Death

	three to thirty-six hours; "tic fever."
STRANGURY	Dysury; difficulty and pain in voiding urine; see "Gravel."
SUMMER COMPLAINT	See "cholera infantum."
THRUSH	"Cotton appearing" mouth and throat disease; cause is monilial bacteria; aphthae.
TIC DOULOUREUX	Facial neuralgia; "Fothergill's pain."
TOBACCO HEART	Cancer caused by smoking tobacco products.
TYPHOID FEVER	Gradually increasing fever caused by "bacillus typhosus;" often spread by food, and shell fish grown in polluted water; salmonella.
TYPHOID PNEUMONIA	Lung fever; sometimes "winter fever."
TYPHUS FEVER	Acute, infectious, contagious disease tied to filth; commonly transmitted by lice; often misdiagnosed for typhoid fever; "jail fever;" "ship fever;" "hospital fever;" "camp fever."
WHOOPING COUGH	Pertussis; contagious cough accompanied by mucous discharge, tight chest; almost exclusively a childhood disease.
WINTER FEVER	Typhoid pneumonia.
YELLOW FEVER	"Upshur's fever;" tropical viral disease transmitted by a certain type of mosquito, causing vascular congestion, frequent hemorrhages, and destruction of the liver. Outbreak in Alexandria in 1800, 1802, 1803, 1804 and 1821.

Sources

Blanton, Wyndham B., M.D., <u>Medicine in Virginia in the Nineteenth Century</u> (Richmond, Va.: Garrett & Massie, Incorporated, 1933)

Cutter, Calvin, M.D., <u>The Physiological Family Physician</u> (West Brookfield, Mass.: Merriam and Cooke, Printers, 1845)

Eli Lilly & Co., <u>Handbook of Pharmacy and Theraputics</u> (Indianapolis, Ind.: Eli Lilly & Co., 1920), "Index of Diseases With Remedies"

Rising, Marsha Hoffman, "How Did They Die? Terms of Medical Interest" <u>1993 National Genealogical Conference in the States: A Chesapeake Homecoming</u>, pp. 77-9.

Yasgur, Jay, <u>A Dictionary of Homeopathic Medical Terminology</u> (Greenville, Pa.: Van Hoy Publishers, 1992).

ACTS
of the
GENERAL ASSEMBLY
of the
STATE OF VIRGINIA

ACT REQUIRING VITAL STATISTICS

Chapter 25
An Act Concerning the Registration of Births, Marriages and Deaths, Passed April 11, 1853

Three registers to be kept by clerk.

1. Be it enacted by the general assembly, that from and after the first day of January eighteen hundred and fifty-four, the clerk of every county and corporation court shall keep three books, to be called, respectively, the register of marriages, the register of births, and the register of deaths.

Duty of ministers.

2. Henceforth it shall be the duty of every minister or other person celebrating a marriage, and of the clerk or keeper of the records of any religious society which solemnizes marriages by the consent of the parties in open congregation, at once to make a record of every marriage between white persons solemnized by or before him, and within two months after such marriage to return a certificate thereof, signed by him, to the clerk of the court of the county or corporation in which the same is solemnized.

What set forth in his record.

Such record and certificate shall set forth, as far as the same can be ascertained, the date and place of the marriage, the full names of both the parties, their ages and condition before the marriage (whether single or widowed), the places of their birth and residence, the names of their parents and the occupation of the husband.

Abstract by clerk.

3. The clerk to whom such certificate shall be returned, shall file and preserve the same in his office, and within twenty days after receiving the same, record a full abstract thereof in his register of marriages, setting out, in convenient tabular form, all the circumstances therein stated and the name of the person signing the certificate, and make an index of the names of both the parties married.

If marriage out of state.

4. It at the time of celebrating any marriage out of this state, either or both of the parties thereto be a resident or residents of this state, a certificate or statement thereof, verified by the affidavit of any person present at such celebration, may be returned to the clerk of the court of the county or corporation in which the husband resides, if he be such resident, and otherwise, of the county or corporation in which the wife resides, and an abstract thereof shall be recorded by him in the manner prescribed in the third section.

Act Requiring Vital Statistics

Penalty on minister for noncompliance.

5. If any minister who shall give bond in order to his being authorized to celebrate marriage in this state, shall fail to comply with the second section, the condition of such bond shall be deemed to be thereby broken, and he shall be subject to the penalty hereinafter prescribed for such failure.

Second section to be published; when.

6. Every such clerk of a court shall, on or before the first day of the next November term of his court, post at the front door of his courthouse a copy of the second section, with a statement of the penalties for violations thereof.

Registration of births and deaths, by whom made. When.

From what source.

7. Every commissioner of the revenue shall make an annual registration of the births and deaths in his district. When he ascertains the personal property subject to taxation, he shall ascertain the births and deaths that have occurred in the year ending on the thirty-first day of December preceding, and such circumstances as he is hereinafter required to record. He shall ascertain the births and deaths in each family from the head of such family, if practicable.

What contained in his record of births.

8. He shall record in a book to be kept by him for that purpose, so far as can be ascertained, the date and place of every such birth; the full name of the child, (if it has a name;) the sex and color thereof; and if colored, whether free or slave; also whether the child was born alive or stillborn; the full name of the mother; and if the child be free and born in wedlock, the full name, occupation and residence of the father; if the child be a slave, the name of the owner; if there be more than one child born at one birth, the fact and number shall be stated; and any other circumstances of interest relating to any birth.

Of deaths.

9. Every such commissioner shall in like manner record in a book to be kept by him for that purpose, the place and date of every death in his district during the year ending on the preceding thirty-first day of December; the full name, sex, age, condition (whether married or not,) and color of the deceased; and if colored, whether free or slave; also the occupation, if any, of the deceased, and his or her place of birth, the names of his or her parents, and (if the deceased was married) the name of the husband or wife; and if the deceased was a slave, the name of the owner; also the disease or cause of the death, so far as such facts can be ascertained.

Commissioner's affidavit.

To whom and when record returned.

10. The commissioner shall make and subscribe an affidavit, upon each of the books so to be kept by him, to the effect that he has pursued the directions in this act, according to the best of his skill; and he shall return his said books to the clerk of the court of his county or corporation on or before the first day of June.

Act Requiring Vital Statistics

Duties of clerk in relation to register of births.

11. Such clerk shall thereupon record a full abstract of the contents of the said book, containing a record of births, in his said register of births, setting forth, in convenient tabular form, all the circumstances hereinbefore required to be recorded, with references to the commissioners' books, and making an alphabetical index of the names of the free children born, and (when they have no names) of the names of the parents, and also of the names of the owners of the slaves born, placing in the index the dates of the births.

Of deaths.

12. He shall in like manner record a full abstract of the contents of the said book, containing a record of deaths, in his said register of deaths, setting forth, in convenient tabular form, all the circumstances hereinbefore required to be recorded, with reference to the commissioners' book, and making an alphabetical index of the names of the deceased and the names of the owners of deceased slaves, and placing in the index the dates of the deaths.

Commissioners' books to be filed.

13. Every such clerk of a court shall file and preserve in his office the books so deposited with him by the commissioners.

Registers transmitted to auditor, when.

14. He shall transmit to the auditor of public accounts a copy of his register of marriages during the preceding year, on or before the first day of March in each year, and a copy of his register of births and register of deaths during the preceding year, on or before the first day of August in each year.

Abstract of auditor.

When report to legislature.

15. Such copies shall be filed and preserved in the said auditor's office, and from them the auditor shall prepare an abstract annually of marriages, births and deaths in each county and corporation, and make a report upon said registrations once in every period of two years, to be laid before the general assembly.

Registers to be prima facie evidence.

16. The said books to be kept by the clerks, and copies, (or of any part thereof,) certified by the clerk lawfully having custody thereof, shall be prima facie evidence of the facts therein set forth in all cases.

Pay of clerk for copies.

17. A clerk shall be entitled to ten cents for every copy of an entry in said books relating to a marriage, birth or death, to be paid by the party requiring the copy.

How commissioner to obtain his information.

18. If a commissioner in any case cannot obtain the requisite information concerning any birth or death from the head of the family, as before required, he shall obtain the same from such persons as are hereinafter required to give it; or if that cannot be done, from any other persons, always recording the name of the person giving the information.

Act Requiring Vital Statistics

Physicians and surgeons. Their duties.

19. Every physician and surgeon shall, in a book to be kept by him, make a record at once of the death of every person dying in this state, upon whom he has attended at the time of such death, setting out as far as practicable the circumstances herein required to be recorded by a commissioner respecting deaths. He shall give to a commissioner of the revenue, whenever called on by him for that purpose, annually, a copy of such record, so far as the same relates to deaths in such commissioner's district.

Coroners; their duties.

Penalty for failure.

20. Every coroner shall keep a like record of the deaths in relation to which he acts officially, and give a copy thereof to any commissioner of the revenue, whenever called on by him for that purpose, annually, so far as the same relates to deaths in such commissioner's district. For every neglect or failure to perform any duty required of him by this section, a coroner shall forfeit twenty dollars.

Entries by commissioner.

21. The commissioner shall make such entries or corrections in his record of deaths as may be supplied or warranted by the copies so to be furnished to him by physicians, surgeons and coroners, noting the source of the information.

If head of family absent, what his duty.

Penalty for refusal to give information.

22. The head of any family, if he be not at his residence when the commissioner calls there to obtain the information required by this act to be obtained of him, shall give the same information to the proper commissioner of the revenue on or before the first day of June in the same year; and for a failure or neglect to do so, shall forfeit one dollar. If any head of a family, being lawfully requested to give any such information, shall refuse to give the same, he shall forfeit ten dollars.

Penalty of commissioner for failure of duty.

23. If any commissioner of the revenue fail to obtain any information respecting a birth or death, which he is by this act authorized or required to obtain, and which he can produce, he shall for every such failure and for every failure to record the information acquired by him respecting a birth or death, according to this act, forfeit five dollars.

For failure to perform duties in 10th section.

24. If any commissioner of the revenue fail to perform the duties required of him by the tenth section of this act, he shall forfeit fifty dollars.

Penalty of clerk for failure of duty.

25. If any clerk of a court fail to perform the any duty required of him by the third section of this act, he shall forfeit ten dollars for every such offence; and if he fail to perform any duty required of him by the eleventh, twelfth, thirteenth or fourteenth section, he shall, for every such offence, forfeit fifty dollars.

Act Requiring Vital Statistics

Fine for making false returns. 26. If any clerk of a court, commissioner of the revenue, physician, surgeon, coroner or minister celebrating a marriage, or clerk or keeper of the records of any religious society, shall, in any book, register or record, which such officer or person is by this act required to keep or make, or in any copy or certificate which by this act he is required to make or give, knowingly make any false, erroneous or fraudulent entry, record, registration or written statement, he shall for every such offence forfeit not less than one hundred nor more than five hundred dollars.

Fine for false information. 27. If any person, upon whose information or statement any record or registration may lawfully be made under this act, shall knowingly give any false information, or make any false statement to be used for the purpose of making any such record or registration, he shall forfeit not less than fifty nor more than three hundred dollars for every such offence.

Forms and instructions, how finished. 28. The auditor of public accounts shall furnish the clerk of every county and corporation court and every commissioner of the revenue with all forms and instructions which he may deem necessary or proper for carrying this act into effect.

Commencement. 29. This act shall take effect **the first day of July eighteen hundred and fifty three.**

ALEXANDRIA (Arlington) COUNTY, VIRGINIA DEATH RECORDS 1853-1896

A

ABINSHIRE, Jacob, W, M, 31 JUL 1868, Alexa., unknown, 1m14d, J. & C. Abinshire, Alexa., none, single, Jno. Abenshire, father, p.24.

ABITZ, Henry, W, M, NOV 1887, Alexa. Co., found dead, 50y, --, Germany, labor, Fredrick Holnshine, friend, p.49.

ADAM, [blank], W, F, 20 AUG 1858, Alexa., unknown, --, W.W. & Harriet Adam, Alexa., W.W. Adam, head of family.

ADAMS, Captain, W, M, [no date] 1858, Alexa., disease, 50y, pauper, John Stephenson.

ADAMS, Geo. R., W, M, 28 NOV 1884, Ballston, paralysed, 72y, Thomas & Anna, Georgetown, D.C., farmer, consort of Mary A. Adams, T.J. Adams, son, p.45.

ADAMS, John, W, M, 3 JUN 1856, Alexa., consumption, 44y6m, --, Jas. Adams, brother, p.15.

ADAMS, Mary A., W, F, 14 FEB 1893, Alexa. Co., old age, 74y, Jacob & Sarah, Alexa. Co., widow, S. Anna Hirst, daughter, p.56.

ADAMS, Thos. J., W, M, 9 JUN 1893, Alexa. Co., liver disease, 56y, Geo. R. & Mary A., Alexa., farmer, single, S. Anna Hirst, sister, p.56.

ALEXANDER, Barbra, (f), F, 11 DEC 1879, Jefferson Dist., dropsy, 35y, --, Va., housekeeping, Willis Alexander, Patsey Turner, next door neighbor, p.39.

ALEXANDER, Richard B., W, M, 25 SEP 1856, cold, 64y, --, Thos. Swann, head of family, p.17.

ALEXANDER, Robert, W, M, 2 MAY 1859, consumption, 65y, --, Pr. Wm., merchant, Chas. W. Alexander, son.

ALEXANDRIA, Annie E., (f), F, 1 APR 1878, Freedmen's Village, teething, 2y, Fannie Jones, Freedmen's Village, Fannie Jones, mother, p.38.

ALLEN, Anna, (f), F, 23 MAR 1889, Alexa. Co., dropsy, 50y, --, Va., Laura Cox, friend, p.51.

ALLEN, Anna, W, F, 4 APR 1853, Alexa., eurycephalous, 70y, A. & E. Donaldson, Alexa. Co., W. Allen, H. Donaldson, sister, p.5.

ALLEN, Catherine, (f), F, 30 JAN 1885, F. Vill[age], consumption, 28y, Henry & Nellie Gilbert, Md., housekeeping, consort of Tibbett Allen, Tibbett Allen, husband, p.47.

ALLEN, Harriet, (f), F, 8 JAN 1896, Alexa. Co., old age, 75y, --, Md., widow, Tibbett Allen, son, p.62.

ALLEN, Martha V., W, F, 10 JUN 1858, Alexa., consumption, 26y, --, Alexa., consort of James Allen, T.J. Adam, physician.

ALLEN, [blank], (f), F, 30 JAN 1885, F. Vill[age], --, 1d, Tibbett & Catherine Allen, F. Vill[age], Tibbett Allen, father, p.47.

ALLEN, [blank], (f), M, 30 JUL 1879, Jefferson Dist., --, 5d, Tibbett & Catherine Allen, Jefferson Dist., Tibbett Allen, father, p.39.

ALLEN, [not named], (f), M, SEP 1888, Arlington [Dist.], --, 3m, Tibbett & Laura V. Allen, Arlington Dist., Tibbett Allen, father.

ALLISON, Infant, W, --, 17 FEB 1857, Alexa., --, 9y, Thos. & Mrs. Allison, Alexa., mechanic.

ALLISON, Mary, W, F, MAR 1887, Alexa. Co., old age, 94y, --, Alexa. Co., widow, Samuel Shreve, nephew, p.49.

ANDERSON, Andrew, W, M, 5 SEP 1859, Alexa., unknown, 2y7m, Thos. & Mary

Alexandria (Arlington) County, Virginia Death Records, 1853-1896

Anderson, Thomas Anderson, father.
ANDERSON, Elizabeth, W, F, 21 SEP 1855, Alexa., unknown, 9m, P. & A.M. Anderson, Pr. Wm. Co., A.M. Anderson, mother, p.13.
ANDERSON, Fannie, (f), F, 24 NOV 1893, Alexa. Co., --, 1m, Geo. E. & Elizabeth, Alexa. Co., G.E. Anderson, father, p.56.
ANDERSON, Jane, (f), F, 18 MAR 1876, Georgetown Road, heart disease, 35y, Bell Fannie & Carter, Fairfax Co., housework, consort of Peter Anderson, Peter Anderson, husband, p.36.
ANDERSON, Margaret, W, F, JUN 1853, Alexa., cholera, 70y, -- Selkman, Prince Wm. Co., S. Anderson, D. Wood, son in law, p.2.
ANDERSON, Miss, W, F, 13 JAN 1857, Alexa., pneumonia, 1m10d, unknown, Alexa., unmarried.
ANDERSON, Peter, (f), M, 23 DEC 1894, Alexa. Co., --, 2m14d, Geo. E. & Elizabeth, Alexa. Co., Geo. E. Anderson, father, p.58.
ANDERSON, Susan A., W, F, 18 OCT 1865, Loudoun Co., heart disease, 51y, Catherine & Adam, Winchester, shoemaker, single, W.T. Simmons, brother in law, p.19.
ANDERSON, William, W, M, 4 APR 1856, Alexa., cold, 23y, --, Charles Co. Md., craftsman, Thos. Anderson, head of family, p.15.
APPICH, Caroline, W, F, 16 JAN 1865, Alexa., fever, 35y, unknown, Europe, unknown, consort of David Appich, David Appich, husband, p.19.
APPICH, Caroline, W, F, 7 AUG 1855, Alexa., water on brain, 7m, D. & C. Appich, D. Appich, father, p.10.
APPICH, David, W, M, 17 NOV 1855, Alexa., accident, 22y, G. & B. Appich, Alexa., G. Appich, father, p.10.
ARMISTEAD, Louisa, (f), F, NOV 1867, Alexa., dropsy, 6m, Louisa & Jno. Armistead, Alexa., none, single, Virginia Carroll, friend, p.22.
ARMISTEAD, Sarah F., W, F, 9 NOV 1867, Alexa., thrush, 1m, Jas. & Ellen Armistead, Alexa., none, single, Ellen Armistead, mother, p.22.
ARMSTEAD, Mary, (f), F, 9 OCT 1893, Alexa. Co., heart disease, 22y, --, housework, consort of Jeremiah Armstead, J. Armstead, husband, p.56.
ARNEL, James T., W, M, 22 NOV 1856, Alexa., consumption, 1y8m, C.L. & E. Arnel, C. Arnel, head of family, p.15.
ARNOLD, Alexander, W, M, NOV 1859, Alexa., paralysis, 47y, --, Pr. Wm., blacksmith, John Arnold, brother.
ARNOLD, Elvira M., W, F, 11 APR 1896, Alexa., --, 31y, --, King George, --, consort of I.D. Arnold, I.D. Arnold, husband, p.62.
ARNOLD, Jane Elizabeth, W, F, 7 NOV 1856, Alexa., consumption, 38y, --, Alexa., Wm. Arnold, Wm. Arnold, head of family, p.14.
ARNOLD, Jane, W, F, 6 NOV 1856, consumption, 38y, p.17.
ARNOLD, Mary Moore, W, F, 30 DEC 1856, Alexa., whooping cough, 1y9m, Wm. & Jane E. Arnold, Alexa., William Arnold, head of family, p.14.
ARNOLD, Mrs. Catharine, W, F, 4 DEC 1856, Alexa., neuralgia, 68y, --, Alexa., Milly Church, head of family, p.17.
ARNOLD, Susannah, W, F, SEP 1854, Alexa., paralysis, 19y, J. & C. Arnold, Alexa., W. Jinkins, bro. in law, p.7.
ARRINGTON, Ann, W, F, 11 OCT 1857, Alexa., consumption, 62y, --, consort of Washburn Arrington, John Arnold.
ARRINGTON, G.W., W, M, 4 AUG 1859, Alexa., diarrhea, 4m, Chas. & Mary Arrington, Alexa., C.W. Arrington, father.
ARRINGTON, W.T., W, M, SEP 1854, Alexa., unknown, 2y, W. & S. Arrington, Alexa., C. Arrington, aunt, p.9.
ARTHUR, Sophia, W, F, DEC 1859, Alexa., complication, 70y, --, Md., domestic,

Alexandria (Arlington) County, Virginia Death Records, 1853-1896

D.M. French, physician.
ASHBY, Boyd, W, M, 15 JUL 1855, Alexa., cholera infantum, 1y2m, T.W. & E. Ashby, Alexa., T.W. Ashby, father, p.11.
ASHFORD, Ann K., W, F, 15 DEC 1856, childbirth, 31y, consort of John Ashford, John Ashford, head of family, p.17.
ASHFORD, Hannah K., W, [F], Alexa., 30y, consort of John Ashford, John Ashford, head of family, p.15.
ASHFORD, Virginia, W, F, 3 JUL 1853, Alexa., unknown, 6m, M. & M. Ashford, Alexa., Mary Ashford, mother, p.2.
ASHTON, Smith, (f), M, MAY 1856, Alexa., consumption, 2y, H. & L. Ashton, Westmoreland Co., L. Ashton, mother, p.8.
ASHTON, [blank], (f), M, MAY 1856, Alexa., unknown, 21d, H. & L. Ashton, Alexa., L. Ashton, mother, p.8.
ASHTON, [blank], (f), M, 25 MAY 1853, Alexa., unknown, 15d, H. & L. Ashton, Alexa., L. Ashton, mother, p.4.
ATKINS, Willie, (f), M, 15 DEC 1866, Alexa., consumption, 3y, Victoria & Wm. Atkins, Alexa., single, Armstead Collins, uncle, p.20.
ATWELL, Jane, W, M, 9 OCT 1866, Alexa., unknown, 66y, Patrick & Julia Brodey, Tortuga [B.V.I.], unknown, widow, H.O. Claughton, son in law, p.20.
ATWELL, W.A., W, M, 19 JUL 1855, Warrenton, accidental, 21y, W. & J.A. Atwell, Baltimore, conductor, W. Atwell, father, p.10.
AUBINOE, Charlotte, W, F, 10 DEC 1854, Alexa., unknown, 5d, S.W. & C. Aubinoe, Alexa., S.W. Aubinoe, father, p.6.
AUGUSTA, John H., (f), M, 7 JUL 1876, East Ft. Craig, thrush, 1y, Wm. H. & Hannah Augusta, East Ft. Craig, farmer, Hannah Augusta, mother, p.36.
AUGUSTUS, Hannah, (f), F, JUN 1893, Alexa. Co., heart disease, 64y, --, Caroline Co., housework, widow, Ida Augustus, daughter, p.56.
AUGUSTUS, Lizzie, (f), F, 11 DEC 1896, Alexa. Co., killed, 27y, Wm. & Hanah, Alexa. Co., housework, single, Horace Augustus, brother, p.62.
AULD, Collin, W, M, [16] JUN 1854, Alexa., catarrh fever, 1y6m, D. & M.E. Auld, Alexa., J.A. Javins, uncle, p.7.
AULD, Mary [Elizabeth], W, F, MAY 1854, Alexa., affection of the brain, 22y, P. & H. Kidwell, Fairfax Co., David Auld, J.A. Javins, bro. in law, p.7.
AUSTIN, Edward, (f), M, 29 NOV 1881, Arlington farm, --, 50y, --, Md., farming, consort of Jane Austin, Margaret Jackson, daughter, p.42.

B

BACON, Capt. Ebenezer, W, M, 31 NOV 1867, Alexa., rheumatism, 71y, unknown, Maine, sea captain, married, Dora E. Jackson, daughter, p.22.
BACON, Susan, W, F, 15 MAR 1866, Alexa., complication of diseases, 67y, unknown, Alexa., married, Ebenezer Bacon, husband, p.20.
BAGBY, Amos, (f), M, 10 OCT 1873, Arlington Twp., whooping cough, 2y, Wash. & Jane Bagby, Arlington, --, p.33.
BAGBY, [blank], (f), F, DEC 1883, Alexa. Co., --, 1d, Washington & Sarah J. Bagby, Alexa. Co., Sarah J. Bagby, p.44.
BAGBY, [blank], (f), F, 11 MAY 1880, F. Village, --, 3d, Washington & Jane Bagby, Alexa. Co., Washington Bagby, father, p.40.
BAGGOT, John H., W, M, 18 MAY 1856, Alexa., brain fever, 16y, John & E. Baggot, Norfolk, J.H. Baggot, head of family, p.16.
BAGGOTT, A.E., W, F, 4 DEC 1853, Alexa., croup, 6y, A. & F. Baggett, Fredericksburg, Frances Baggett, mother, p.1.

Alexandria (Arlington) County, Virginia Death Records, 1853-1896

BAGGOTT, Elizabeth, W, F, 9 NOV 1866, Alexa., old age, 75y, Mary & James Caton, Alexa., widow, Saml. O. Baggott, son, p.20.
BAGGOTT, Francis A., W, --, 20 NOV 1857, Alexa., whooping cough, 8m1d, F.A. & F. Baggott, Alexa., baker.
BAGGOTT, J.T., W, M, 7 AUG 1868, Alexa., heart disease, 58y2m9d, Geo. & J. Baggett, Stafford Co., merchant, married, V. Baggott, wife, p.24.
BAGGOTT, Joseph Nevett, W, M, DEC 1853, Alexa., pneumonia, 10y, J.T. & A.V. Baggott, Fredericksburg, Joseph Nevett, gra'father, p.2.
BAILEY, Augustus, W, M, 22 JUL 1894, Alexa. Co., rheumatism, 82y, --, Va., widower, P.R. Newman, son in law, p.58.
BAILEY, Chas. C., W, M, 30 SEP 1881, Logan [Mbna.?], typhoid fever, 25y4m, Harvey & S.E. Bailey, Alexa. Co., R.R. survey, single, S.E. Bailey, mother, p.42.
BAILEY, Harriet Ward, W, F, 10 AUG 1858, Alexa., --, 10m, James P. & A.J. Bailey, Alexa., J.P. Bailey, father.
BAILEY, James, W, M, 9 NOV 1867, Alexa., erysipelas, 2y10m, Jas. & Cath. Bailey, Alexa., laborer, single, Cath. Bailey, mother, p.22.
BAILEY, Jenny, (f), F, 21 MAR 1894, Alexa. Co., --, 55y, --, Va., housekeeping, consort of James H. Bailey, Jas. H. Bailey, husband, p.58.
BAILEY, Jno., W, M, 23 NOV 1868, Alexa., natural causes, 49y, unknown, Alexa., craftsman, married, T.J. Edelin, coroner, p.24.
BAILEY, John, (f), M, 18 JUL 1875, Jefferson Mag. Dist., dropsy, 65y, Stephen Bailey, laborer, p.35.
BAILEY, Stepher, (f), M, 12 DEC 1891, Alexa. Co., old age, 80y, --, Va., labor, consort of Lilly Bailey, Lilly Bailey, wife, p.53.
BAILOR, Virginia, (f), F, 4 OCT 1878, Preston farm, whooping cough, 2y11m22d, Jas<u>h</u> H. & Virginia Bailor, Preston farm, Jas. H. Bailor, father, p.38.
BAIN, Cora, (f), F, 15 MAY 1885, Alexa. Co., consumption, 15y, Wm. & Mahalia Bain, Va., single, Wm. Bain, father, p.47.
BAKER, Chas. T.M., Sr., W, M, 2 JUL 1894, Alexa. Co., heart disease, 69y, --, Balto. Md., cooper, Chas. T.M. Baker, Jr., son, p.58.
BAKER, Eddie, (f), M, 12 OCT 1888, Arlington [Dist.], --, 9y, Simon & Emma, Arlington Dist., Emma Baker, mother.
BAKER, Fannie, (f), F, 12 OCT 1888, Arlington [Dist.], --, 3y, Simon & Emma, Arlington Dist., Emma Baker, mother.
BAKER, George, (f), OCT 1867, Alexa., summer complaint, 6m, Lewis & Minnie Baker, Alexa., none, single, Ann Baker, grandmother, p.22.
BAKER, Harriet W., W, F, --, 15 JAN 1876, old age, 80y, --, p.16.
BALDWIN, Ruth, W, F, APR 1853, Alexa., consumption, 40y, J. & R. White, Baltimore, James Baldwin, V. White, brother, p.2.
BALDWIN, W.N., W, M, 13 JUN 1856, --, 5m4d, C.A. & Mary L. Baldwin, Chas. Baldwin, head of family, p.16.
BALL, Cora May, W, F, 21 JUN 1874, Arlington, paralyzed, 21d, --, Arlington, none, p.34.
BALL, Elizabeth, W, F, 9 MAR 1872, Arlington District, consumption, 71y3m, unknown, D.C., farmer, Horatio Ball, Sr., Edwin Ball, son, p.32.
BALL, Horatio, W, M, 8 FEB 1873, Arlington Twp., old age, 88y, --, farmer, p.33.
BALL, James, (f), M, 14 OCT 1886, Arlington Dist., --, 45y, --, Va., labor, consort of Martha Ball, Martha Ball, wife, p.48.
BALL, John, Jr., W, M, 13 FEB 1854, Alexa., consumption, 38y, John & Julia Ball, hotel keeper, John Ball, father, p.6.
BALL, John, W, M, [no date] 1858, Alexa.,

Alexandria (Arlington) County, Virginia Death Records, 1853-1896

rheumatism, 75y.

BALL, Nellie, W, F, 12 NOV 1890, Alexa. Co., consumption, 32y, Chas. & Mary Shipman, Alexa. Co., labor, consort of M.T. Ball, M.T. Ball, husband, p.52.

BALL, Nettie, W, F, 21 MAY 1889, Alexa. Co., --, 5m23d, M.T. & Nettie Ball, Va., [M].T. Ball, father, p.51.

BALL, Orrigan Willson, W, M, 1 JUL 1872, Arlington Dist., cholera infantum, 9m11d, Horatio & Mary J., Arlington Dist., farmer, Horatio Ball, father, p.32.

BALL, Owen Glenn, W, M, 7 MAR 1872, Arlington Dist., congestion [of] brain, 4m24d, Edwin & Emma, Arlington Dist., farmer, Edwin Ball, father, p.32.

BALL, Samuel, W, M, 31 JUL 1889, Alexa. Co., paralysis, 69y7d, Horatio & Catherine Ball, Va., farmer, consort of Jane A. Ball, Robert E. Ball, son, p.51.

BALL, William, W, M, 10 NOV 1856, Alexa., consumption, 45y, --, Mrs. Ball, p.15.

BALLENGER, Chs. W., W, M, 14 NOV 1853, Alexa., brain fever, 4d, J.G. & C.A. Ballenger, Alexa., J.G. Ballenger, father, p.1.

BALLENGER, James, W, M, 5 SEP 1854, poor house, intemperance, 60y, -- Ballenger, Alexa., John Stephenson, keeper, p.9.

BALLENGER, S.T., W, F, 19 APR 1853, Alexa., water on the brain, 1y, P. & J. Ballenger, Alexa., P. Ballenger, father, p.2.

BALLENGER, Sally, W, F, 4 JUL 1858, Alexa., water of brain, --, Peyton & Jane Ballenger, Alexa.

BANKHEAD, Mary, (f), M, 17 FEB 1866, Alexa., cold, 3y, Thomas D. & Martha Bankhead, Westmoreland, labor, single, Thos. Bankhead, father, p.20.

BANKS, Andrew, (f), M, 18 JUL 1875, Jefferson Mag. Dist., summer sickness, --, Peter Banks, laborer, p.35.

BANKS, Annie, (f), F, 20 SEP 1877, canal basin, consumption, 1y, Eliza & Peter Banks, canal basin, Peter Banks, father, p.37.

BANKS, James, (f), M, 29 NOV 1876, Addison farm, poison, 60y, Manual & Jannie Banks, Va., farmer, husband of Mary Banks, Mary Banks, wife, p.36.

BANKS, Rose, (f), F, 10 NOV 1879, Jefferson Dist., teething, 2y, Peter & Eliza Banks, Jefferson Dist., Eliza Banks, mother, p.39.

BANKS, Rosetta, (f), F, 4 OCT 1878, near Slater's, teething, 10m, Peter & Eliza Banks, near Slater's, Peter Banks, father, p.38.

BARBER, Wm. T., (f), M, 16 MAY 1876, Freedmen's Village, 7d, Jesse & Bell Barber, Freedmen's Village, Bell Barber, mother, p.36.

BARKER, Catherine, W, F, [10] SEP 1854, Alexa., old age, 70y, --, Fairfax, Barzilla Green, friend, p.8.

BARKER, Chas. W., W, M, 8 MAY 1855, scarlet fever, 2y6m, H.S.W. & S.A. Barker, S.A. Barker, mother.

BARKER, H. Clay, W, M, 22 JUN 1856, Alexa., cholera infantum, 7m, H.C.W. & S.A. Barker, Alexa., H.C. Barker, head of family, p.17.

BARKER, Harrison Albert, W, M, 22 APR 1855, Alexa., scarlet fever, 5y, H.S.W. & S.A. Barker, S.A. Barker, mother, p.10.

BARKMAN, Edgar, W, M, MAR 1853, Fairfax Co., unknown, 2y, G.S. & M.A. Barkman, Fairfax Co., G.S. Barkman, father, p.1.

BARKMAN, Roberta, W, F, 20 OCT 1853, Fairfax Co., typhoid fever, 14y, G.S. & M.A. Barkman, Fairfax Co., G.S. Barkman, father, p.1.

BARLEY, Albert, (f), M, NOV 1895, Wash. D.C., --, Alexa. Co., Martha J. Barley, mother, p.60.

BARNER, Bessey, W, F, 6 JUL 1868, Alexa., chronic disease, 3m21d, J.R. & P.P. Banner, Alexa., none, single, J.R.

Alexandria (Arlington) County, Virginia Death Records, 1853-1896

Barner, father, p.24.
BARNES, Eli, (f), M, 28 MAY 1889, Alexa. Co., consumption, 55y, --, Va., consort of Patsy A. Barnes, Margaret Reed, mother in law, p.51.
BARNES, G.W., W, M, SEP 1855, Alexa., paralysis, 4y, G. & J.A. Barnes, G. Barnes, father, p.14.
BARNES, Julia A., W, F, SEP 1855, int. fever, 40y, J. & M. Baker, Alexa. Co., Geo. Barnes, G. Barnes, husband, p.14.
BARNNEY, Ada, W, F, 3 JUL 1857, --, water on brain, 8m5d.
BARNS, Hillery, (f), M, AUG 1881, Georgetown Road, [tisie?], 70y, --, Md., labor, consort of Maria Barns, Maria Barns, wife, p.42.
BARRETT, John W., W, M, 10 AUG 1865, Alexa., diphtheria, 2y3m, John C. & Sarah C., Alexa., mechanic, single, J.C. Barrett, father, p.19.
BARTENSTEIN, Gilbert, W, M, [no date] 1858, pauper, John Stephenson.
BARTLEMAN, Doug. W., W, M, 19 MAY 1858, Alexa., --, 9m, G.W.D. & Wilhemina Ramsay, G.W.D. Ramsay, father.
BARTLETT, John P., W, M, 26 APR 1886, Arlington Dist., gastric fever, 39y, John & Emma, N.Y., merchant, consort of Emma S. Bartlett, John Bartlett, father, p.48.
BARTLETT, John, W, M, NOV 1895, Alexa. Co., congestion of brain, 81y, --, N.Y., consort of Emma S. Bartlett, E.D. Brown, daughter in law, p.60.
BARTON, Benja., W, M, 2 MAY 1857, Alexa., dysentery, 9m, Benja. & Eliza Barton, Alexa., B. Barton.
BARTON, Franklin, W, M, 25 AUG 1853, alms house, intemperance, 55y, -- Barton, Hampshire Co., John Stephenson, poor house keeper, p.5.
BARTON, Mary, W, F, 16 FEB 1858, Alexa., old age, 88y10m, --, Ashford, England, consort of Benj. Barton, Benj. Barton, son.

BARTON, Rose, W, F, 16 JUN 1858, Alexa., --, 1m16d, --, Alexa., Benj. Barton.
BARTON, Susan Janette, W, F, 2 AUG 1854, Alexa., scarlet fever, 1y2m, B. & S. Barton, Alexa., B. Barton, father, p.6.
BARTON, Walter, W, M, 17 DEC 1865, Alexa., brain fever, 5y6m, Benj. & Eliza D., Alexa., jeweller, single, Benj. Barton, father, p.19.
BATES, William, (f), M, 19 MAY 1876, Freedmen's Village, 1y, Randle & Fannie Bates, Freedmen's Village, Randle Bates, father, p.36.
BAYLIS, Susan, W, F, 22 MAR 1893, Alexa. Co., old age, 81y, --, widow, Peter O. Newman, son in law, p.56.
BAYNE, Geo. H., W, M, 13 FEB 1858, Alexa., consumption, 48y, merchant, Mrs. Bayne, wife.
BAYNE, Geo., W, M, 28 MAR 1858, Alexa., consumption, 38y, --, consort of M.E. Bayne, M.E. Bayne, head of family.
BEACH, Adeline, W, F, 27 JUN 1865, Alexa., womb disease, 35y, John & Hall, Fairfax Co., laborer, consort of J.H. Beach, Jas. H. Beach, husband, p.19.
BEACH, Chas. S., W, M, JUN 1893, Alexa. Co., old age, 70y, --, Va., farmer, widower, W.L. Beach, son, p.56.
BEACH, Edith M., W, F, 1 FEB 1894, Alexa. Co., --, 20y25d, P.V.L. & Charlotte M., Va., housekeeping, consort of Robert O. Beach, P.V.L. Ostrander, father, p.58.
BEACH, Francis, W, F, [no date] 1865, Alexa., unknown, 1y1m, Jane & James, Fairfax Co., laborer, single, Jas. T. Beach, father, p.19.
BEACH, Ida, W, M, 29 JUL 1865, Alexa., fever, 2y, Adaline & Jas. H., Fairfax Co., laborer, single, Jas. H. Beach, father, p.19.
BEACH, Jas. A., W, M, AUG 1855, Alexa., diarrhea, 11m, J.T. & F? Beach, Alexa., M.A.E. Davis, aunt, p.13.

Alexandria (Arlington) County, Virginia Death Records, 1853-1896

BEACH, John F., W, M, 10 DEC 1857, Alexa., croup, 2y2m21d.

BEACH, Robert L., W, M, 12 FEB 1892, --, 3m, Robert O. & Edith, Edith Beach, mother, p.54.

BEACH, Solomon, W, M, SEP 1855, Alexa., chills, 54y, J. & S. Beach, Fairfax, labor, consort of Mary Beach, M.A.E. Davis, daughter, p.13.

BEACH, Solomon, W, M, 1 JAN 1856, Alexa., consumption, 55y4m, --, laborer, Wm. H. Beach, head of family, p.15.

BEADLE, Hannah H., W, F, 27 JUN 1867, Alexa., cholera infantum, 4m, H.W. & Hannah Beadle, Alexa., none, single, H.W. Beadle, father, p.22.

BEANOR, Wm. Edwd., (f), M, MAR 1867, Charles Co. Md., heart disease, 2y, S. & E. Beaner, Alexa., laborer, single, S. Beanor, mother, p.22.

BEATY, Mary A., W, F, OCT 1854, Alexa., unknown, 26y, -- Barton, Fairfax Co., consort of Robt. Beaty, E. Staunton, bro. in law, p.7.

BEATY, Robert, W, M, SEP 1854, Alexa., unknown, 34y, -- Beaty, Va., consort of Mary A. Beaty, E. Staunton, bro. in law, p.7.

BECKHAM, William, (f), M, FEB 1867, Alexa., scalded, 2y, Sallie & John Beckham, Alexa., none, single, Sallie Beckham, mother, p.22.

BECKLEY, Ernest T., (f), [M], 27 AUG 1866, Alexa., water on the brain, 10m1d, Edgar & Martha Beckley, Alexa., baker, single, Martha Beckley, mother, p.20.

BECKLEY, Hellen M., (f), F, 28 JUN 1881, Washington Road, cholera infantum, 6m, John W. & Laura Beckley, Alexa. Co., Laura Beckley, mother, p.42.

BECKLEY, [John] A., (f), M, DEC 1853, Alexa., paralysis, 48y, W. & E. Beckley, P. William Co., brick maker, consort of Sophia Beckley, Maria Waters, sister, p.4.

BEDINGER, Catharine M., W, F, AUG 1866, Alexa., general debility, 60y, Lawrence & K. Berry, King Geo. Co., unknown, widow, W.A. Taylor, nephew, p.20.

BEEVERS, Ellen, W, F, 26 JUL 1867, Alexa., suicide-drowned, 17y, -- Beavers, Alexa., laborer, single, W.W. White, T.A. Stoutenburg, Cor., p.22.

BELL, Geo. Agusta, (f), F, SEP 1891, Alexa. Co., teething, 1y, Thos. & Mary, Alexa. Co., Charlotte Chinn, grandmother, p.53.

BELL, Hillery, (f), M, 27 FEB 1880, near Col. Pike, --, 71y, --, Md., labor, consort of Maria Bell, Mary Offord, daughter in law, p.40.

BELL, James, (f), M, 5 AUG 1867, Alexa., old age, 70y, Jas. & Martha Bell, unknown, laborer, married, Lucretia sanders, daughter, p.22.

BELL, Susan, (f), F, 14 FEB 1867, Alexa., consumption, 60y, Thos. & Martha Thomas, Alexa., housekeeper, married, Lucretia Sanders, daughter, p.22.

BELL, William R., W, M, 1 DEC 1856, Alexa., consumption, 49y, Alexa., tax collector, Annie L. Ball [sic], wife, p.17.

BENEZETTE, Chas. H., W, M, 19 JUL 1872, Arlington Dist., dysentery, 2y8m, Clinton L. & Margaret, Arlington, farmer, Clinton L. Benezette, father, p.32.

BENNET, Leroe, (f), F, JUL 1889, Alexa. Co., old age, 80y, --, Va., Sarah Honesty, neighbor, p.51.

BENNET, Michl., W, M, 14 FEB 1856, cholera infantum, 1y6m, Mike & Ellen Bennet, Ellen Bennet, p.16.

BENNETT, Milly, (f), F, 5 MAR 1853, Alexa., unknown, 57y, -- & Kitty Marshall, Alexa., consort of M. Bennett, Julia Noland, daughter, p.3.

BERGEN, Martin, W, M, 24 JUN 1867, Alexa., diarrhea, 70y, Jno. & Cath. Bergen, Alexa., laborer, married, Margt. Bergen, widow, p.22.

BERKLEY, Jere., W, M, SEP 1855, Alexa., consumption, 43y, -- Berkley, Ireland, --

Alexandria (Arlington) County, Virginia Death Records, 1853-1896

Berkley, Mary Burke, friend, p.12.
BERKLEY, M., W, M, SEP 1855, Alexa., measles, 2y, D. & J. Berkley, Washington, J. Berkley, mother, p.12.
BERRIL, John, W, M, 13 FEB 1857, Alexa., suicide, 30y.
BERRY, Cath., W, F, 2 AUG 1854, Alexa., unknown, 43y, A. & M. Marlow, Md., consort of Noble Berry, N. Berry, husband, p.6.
BERRY, Henry, W, M, 14 FEB 1855, Alexa., pneumonia, 44y, B. & S. Berry, Colchester, craftsman, Geo. Berry, brother, p.11.
BERRY, John, (f), M, 30 OCT 1895, Wash. D.C., --, 40y, --, Va., labor, single, Geo. G. Crossman, employer, p.60.
BERRY, Noble, W, M, [no date] 1858, Alexa., consumption, 49y, cooper.
BERRY, Thos., Sr., W, M, 15 AUG 1855, Alexa., pneumonia, 50y, B. & S. Berry, Md., consort of Betsey Berry, N. Berry, brother, p.11.
BERRY, Wm., W, M, 20 MAR 1857, Alexa., small pox, 25y, Wm. & Palmy Berry, Alexa.
BIGGS, Hector R., W, M, 15 APR 1856, teething, 10m10d, Jas. & Elizabeth Biggs, Jas. Biggs, p.16.
BIGGS, Hector Rudolph, W, M, 20 MAY 1856, Alexa., pneumonia, 12y, Jas. & Elizabeth Biggs, Jas. Biggs, head of family, p.15.
BIGHAM, Elizabeth, W, F, 17 AUG 1853, Alexa., dysentery, 2y, A. & R. Bigham, Md., A. Bigham, father, p.1.
BINCKLEY, Samuel, W, M, 20 JUL 1859, Alexa., drowned, 30y, --, St. Mary's Co. Md., Chrisr. Neale, coroner.
BIRCH, Caleb L., W, M, 29 NOV 1884, near Saegmuller's, old age, 63y, Samuel & Carrie, Alexa. Co., farmer, widower, Jennetta Birch, daughter, p.45.
BIRCH, Caleb, W, M, 31 DEC 1858, Alexa. Co., natural decay, 80y, --, Alexa. D.C., farmer, Caleb Birch, Jr.
BIRCH, Geo. W., W, M, 25 JUN 1887, Alexa. Co., brain fever, 4m6d, Peter T. & Katie L., Alexa. Co., Peter T. Birch, father, p.49.
BIRCH, James H., W, M, 27 JUN 1857, --, shot.
BIRCH, Jas. H., W, M, 12 DEC 1892, Alexa. Co., --, 12y1m, Jacob & Ann, Alexa. Co., Ann Birch, mother, p.54.
BIRCH, John W., W, M, 14 AUG 1879, Arlington Dist., teething, 9m, Peter T. & Katie L. Birch, Arlington Dist., Peter T. Birch, father, p.39.
BIRCH, Katie L., W, F, 23 DEC 1889, Alexa. Co., sprained, 33y, Wm. H. & Eliza Graves, Va., housekeeping, consort of Peter T. Birch, P.T. Birch, husband, p.51.
BIRCH, Maria F., W, F, 4 APR 1872, Arlington Dist., childbirth, 24y, unknown, Ireland, farmer, consort of Peter S. Birch, Geo. H. Mortimore, friend, p.32.
BIRCH, Mary F., W, F, 26 JUN 1892, Alexa. Co., dropsy, 60y, --, Alexa. Co., housekeeper, consort of Randolph Birch, R. Birch, husband, p.54.
BIRCH, Mary, W, F, 1 DEC 1892, Alexa. Co., heart failure, 70y, --, Alexa. Co., widow, Ann Birch, mother, p.54.
BIRCH, Rachel, W, F, 27 MAY 1883, Alexa. Co., 70, --, Alexa. Co., consort of Samuel Birch, Samuel Birch, p.44.
BIRCH, Samuel, W, M, 30 NOV 1873, Washington Twp., old age, 84y, Joseph Birch, Washington Twp., farmer, Dr. T.B.J. Frye, p.33.
BIRCH, Sarah F.S., W, F, APR 1896, Alexa. Co., --, 3m14d, Lewis & Maggie, Alexa. Co., Lewis Birch, father, p.62.
BIRCH, Sarah Jane, W, F, 19 AUG 1891, Alexa. Co., diarrhea, 67y, Sam'l. & Ann, Alexa. Co., single, Margret A. Payne, sister, p.53.
BIRCH, Wm. H., W, M, 17 APR 1887, Alexa. Co., brain fever, 4m, Peter T. & Katie L., Alexa. Co., Peter T. Birch,

Alexandria (Arlington) County, Virginia Death Records, 1853-1896

father, p.49.
BIRCH, [blank], W, M, 4 APR 1872, Arlington Dist., birth, Peter T. & Maria, Arlington, Geo. H. Mortimore, friend, p.32.
BIRCH, [blank], W, M, 4 APR 1872, Arlington Dist., birth, Peter T. & Maria, Arlington, Geo. H. Mortimore, friend, p.32.
BIRCH, [blank], W, M, 2 AUG 1854, Alexa. Co., unknown, 1d, John & Susan Birch, Alexa. Co., Randolph Birch, brother, p.6.
BIRCH, [not named], W, M, OCT 1893, Alexa. Co., --, 2m, M.F. & Mary A., Alexa. Co., farmer, --, M.F. Birch, father, p.56.
BIRCH, [not named], W, F, [no date] 1893, Alexa. Co., --, 7m, Peter T. & Emma, Alexa. Co., farmer, Peter T. Birch, father, p.56.
BISHOP, John A., W, M, 24 OCT 1896, Alexa. Co., congestive chill, 62y11d, --, Germany, labor, widower, Caroline B. Wolf, daughter, p.62.
BITNER, Robert, W, M, AUG 1853, Alexa., dysentery, 3m, R. & B. Bitner, Alexa., R. Bitner, father, p.1.
BLACK, Mary S., W, F, 27 MAY 1858, Alexa., --, 17y, John Black, Bermuda, S.S. Masters.
BLACKBURN, Martha, (f), F, JUN 1893, Balto. Md., --, 30y, --, Caroline Co., Va., single, Nancy Jackson, mother, p.56.
BLACKLOCK, Sarah A., W, F, 13 FEB 1855, Alexa., consumption, 26y, T. & S.E. Swann, Alexa., consort of D.R. Blacklock, D.R. Blacklock, husband, p.10.
BLACKWELL, Silas, (f), M, MAY 1867, Alexa., killed, 20y, Lewis & Hannah Blackwell, Alexa., laborer, single, Hannah Blackwell, mother, p.22.
BLACKWELL, Silas, (f), M, 10 JUN 1867, Alexa., stabbed, 18y, Hannah Russell, Alexa., laborer, single, S.N. Chipley, T.A. Stoutenburg, Cor., p.22.
BLAND, James, (f), M, 21 OCT 1889, Alexa. Co., --, 50y, --, Va., single, Nana Donaldson, neighbor, p.51.
BLOCK, Mary S., W, F, 28 MAY 1858, Alexa., scarlet fever, 17y, J.S. & Susannah, Bermuda, Jas. S. Hallowell, head of family.
BLUE, Frank, (f), M, JUL 1895, Alexa. Co., killed, 15y, Jas. & Julia A., Richmond Co., Julia A. Blue, mother, p.60.
BODKIN, W.L., W, M, 27 DEC 1854, Alexa., heart disease, 42y, -- Bodkin, Bodkin, O. Fairfax, physician, p.10.
BOLDEN, Hester, (f), F, SEP 1889, Alexa. Co., --, Va., consort of Roy Bolden, Sarah Honesty, neighbor, p.51.
BOLDEN, [not named], (f), M, JUL 1889, Alexa. Co., --, 4m, Roy & Hester Bolden, Va., Sarah Honesty, neighbor, p.51.
BOLDEN, [not named], (f), F, SEP 1889, Alexa. Co., --, Va., Sarah Honesty, neighbor, p.51.
BONCE, Harriet T., W, F, 2 JUL 1856, Alexa., teething, 11m24d, John & Elizabeth Bonce, John Bonce, head of family, p.15.
BOND, Nancy, (f), F, 21 JUL 1854, poor house, old age, 90y, -- Bond, unknown, John Stephenson, keeper, p.9.
BOND, [blank], (f), M, MAR 1856, Alexa., unknown, 3d, J. & C. Bond, Alexa., J. Bond, father, p.8.
BOND, [blank], W, F, OCT 1855, Alexa., consumption, 1y, -- & Malinda Bond, N. Hicks, master, p.13.
BOOLS, Elizabeth, (f), F, NOV 1895, Alexa. Co., old age, 90y, --, King Wm. Co., widow, Flemming Pollard, son, p.60.
BOSWELL, Ada, (f), F, 10 AUG 1893, Alexa. Co., typhoid fever, 18y, George & Louisa, Alexa. Co., single, Geo. Boswell, father, p.56.
BOSWELL, Clara, (f), F, 14 OCT 1893, Alexa. Co., --, 14y, George & Louisa, Alexa. Co., single, Geo. Boswell, father, p.56.
BOSWELL, Henry, (f), [M], 10 APR 1873,

Alexandria (Arlington) County, Virginia Death Records, 1853-1896

Arlington Twp., old age, 70y, farmer, p.33.
BOSWELL, Murey, (f), M, 12 JUL 1896, Alexa. Co., consumption, 19y, Geo. & Louisa, Alexa. Co., labor, single, Geo. Boswell, father, p.62.
BOSWELL, Percey, (f), M, APR 1893, Alexa. Co., teething, 1y2m, Wallace & Florence, Alexa. Co., Wallace Boswell, father, p.56.
BOSWELL, Theodore, W, M, SEP 1853, Alexa., consumption, 32y, Mary Boswell, Washington City, editor, consort of Nancy Boswell, W. Reynolds, uncle in law, p.2.
BOSWELL, W., (s) of Elizabeth Monroe, M, AUG 1854, Alexa., consumption, 2y, -- Amanda Boswell, Alexa., C.L. Adam, master, p.6.
BOULDEN, [blank], (f), F, 12 MAR 1882, Hall's Hill, --, 1y4m, Roy & Hester Boulden, Alexa. Co., Roy Boulden, father, p.43.
BOWEN, Gertie, (f), F, 18 DEC 1881, F. Village, scarlet fever, 1y4m, John R. & Caroline Bowen, F. Village, Caroline Bowen, mother, p.42.
BOWEN, John H., (f), M, 21 DEC 1882, Col. Pike, malaria fever, 1y1m13d, John R. & Caroline Bowen, Alexa. Co., J.R. Bowen, father, p.43.
BOWEN, John R., (f), M, 23 DEC 1893, Alexa. Co., paralysis, 48y, Fielder & Rachel, Wash. D.C., labor, consort of Caroline Bowen, Caroline Bowen, wife, p.56.
BOWEN, Lavinia, W, F, SEP 1854, Alexa., unknown, 50y, P.C. Smith, Fairfax Co., slave, Charlotte Smith, W. Minor, owner, p.9.
BOWEN, Mary, (f), F, JUN 1892, Alexa. Co., --, 2y, Geo. F. & Kate, Wash. D.C., Geo. F. Bowen, father, p.54.
BOWIE, Drayton, (s), M, DEC 1855, Alexa., cold, 4m, Genny Bowie, Alexa., E.B. Addison, master, p.12.
BOWIE, Edwin, (f), M, 18 SEP 1855, Alexa., whooping cough, 10m, R.H. & C. Rowe, Alexa., Celia Rowe, mother, p.11.
BOWLER, Reuben, W, M, 9 MAY 1855, Alexa., consumption, 54y, C. & E. Bowler, Rhode Island, consort of Hannah Bowler, H. Bowler, widow, p.12.
BOWLER, Sarah Jane, W, F, 20 SEP 1867, Alexa., inflammation of bowels, 16m2d, S.W. & Mary E. Bowler, Alexa., none, single, Mary E. Bowler, mother, p.22.
BOWLES, William, (f), M, 24 OCT 1866, Alexa., accidentally shot, 14y, unknown, unknown, laborer, single, constable, coroner, p.20.
BOWMAN, Ann, (f), F, APR 1894, Alexa. Co., --, 60y, --, Md., housekeeping, consort of Samuel Bowman, Samuel Bowman, husband, p.58.
BOWMAN, Eli, (f), M, SEP 1895, Alexa. Co., --, 4y, --, Alexa. Co., Mary Wilson, mother, p.60.
BOWMAN, Mary, (f), F, 1 APR 1893, Alexa. Co., consumption, 14y, Samuel & Ann, Alexa. Co., Sam'l. Bowman, father, p.56.
BOWMAN, Mary, (f), F, JAN 1894, Alexa. Co., consumption, 15y, Samuel & Ann, Alexa. Co., Samuel Bowman, father, p.58.
BOYD, Frank, (f), M, 14 APR 1872, Arlington Dist., accidentally shot, 20y, David, Va., farmer, unmarried, David Boyd, father, p.32.
BOYD, James H., (f), M, 19 MAY 1880, Ballston, --, 23d, David W. & Mary Boyd, Alexa. Co., D.W. Boyd, father, p.40.
BOYD, [blank], (f), F, 5 OCT 1876, near Balston, 1d, David & Eliza Boyd, near Balston, David W. Boyd, father, p.36.
BOYD, [blank], (f), F, 4 OCT 1876, near Balston, 1d, David & Eliza Boyd, near Balston, David W. David, father, p.36.
BOYER, Siloam, W, F, [15] JUN 1853, Alexa., paralysis, 6y, H.L. & M. Boyer, Alexa., H.L. Boyer, father, p.2.
BOYHER, Henry, W, M, 16 JUN 1859, Alexa., mania-à-potu, 44y, --, Alexa.,

Alexandria (Arlington) County, Virginia Death Records, 1853-1896

dealer in lottery tickets, Hezh. Patton, brother in law.
BOYKIN, Rachel, (f), F, 23 JUL 1887, Alexa. Co., heart disease, 48y, Peter & Caroline, Va., housekeeping, consort of Levi Boykin, Levi Boykin, husband, p.49.
BOYNTON, Jesse Lee, W, M, 20 SEP 1867, Nelson Co., unknown, 6d, E.S. & C.E. Boynton, Nelson Co., none, single, E.S. Boynton, father, p.22.
BRADDOCK, Caroline, (f), F, 29 SEP 1866, Alexa., fever, 1y10m, Robert & Mary Braddock, Alexa., carpenter, single, Robt. Braddock, father, p.20.
BRADDOCK, Rebecca, W, F, 23 NOV 1855, Alexa., paralytic, 65y, -- Ramsey, Chas. Co. Md., Th. Braddock, G.W. Braddock, son, p.11.
BRADLEY, John H., W, M, 17 AUG 1853, Alexa., unknown, 2m, J. & J. Bradley, Alexa., J. Bradley, father, p.1.
BRADLEY, Mary J., W, F, OCT 1868, Alexa., brain fever, 1y2m, J. & Kate Bradley, Alexa., none, single, K. Bradley, mother, p.24.
BRADSHAW, Mary Jane, W, F, 1 JUN 1856, child birth, 23y, --, Alexa., H.K. Bradshaw, H.K.B., head of family, p.16.
BRADY, Mike, W, M, 1 AUG 1854, Alexa., sun struck, 40y, P. & S. Brady, Ireland, laborer, consort of B. Brady, B. Brady, p.9.
BRANDT, Francis D., W, M, 10 JAN 1859, Alexa., diarrhea, 8y10m, Jno. D. & Rosana Brandt, Alexa., John D. Brandt, father.
BRANHAM, Austin, (f), M, 9 NOV 1879, Arlington Dist., old age, 80y1m24d, Peter & Caroline Branham, Va., labor, widower, Roselee Branham, daughter, p.39.
BRANHAM, Fanny, (f), F, 20 FEB 1886, Arlington Dist., pneumonia, 26y, Guy & Sarah Henry, Alexa. Co., housework, consort of W.A. Branham, W.A. Branham, husband, p.48.
BRANNON, James, W, M, 14 AUG 1867, Alexa., teething, 13m, Jas. & Ann Brannon, Alexa., none, single, Ann Brannon, mother, p.22.
BRANNON, Thomas, W, M, [no date] 1858, --, pauper, John Stephenson.
BRANSOM, Laura, (f), F, 3 MAY 1877, Freedmen's Village, cold, 2m, Mitilda & A. Bransom, Freedmen's Village, Edith Jackson, grandmother, p.37.
BRANSON, Lewis, (s), M, 6 JAN 1855, Alexa. Co., suicide, 40y, B. Branson, Fairfax, slave, Julia Branson, Smith Miner, master, p.14.
BRANSON, Matilda, (f), F, 24 MAR 1877, Freedmen's Village, consumption, 19y, Edith & Cyrus Jackson, Va., housework, Edith Jackson, mother, p.37.
BRANSTON, [blank], (f), M, 2 DEC 1856, Alexa., born dead, Henry & Matilda Branston, Henry Branston, head of family, p.15.
BRANZELL, Benj. F., W, M, 17 JUN 1879, Arlington Dist., --, Isaac & Elizabeth Branzell, Arlington Dist., Isaac Branzell, father, p.39.
BRANZELL, Virginia, W, F, 14 SEP 1878, Rosslyn, congestive chill, 11m7d, Isaac & Elizth. Branzell, Rosslyn, Isaac Branzell, father, p.38.
BRAWNER, Mrs., W, F, 11 DEC 1858, Alexa., pneumonia, 70y.
BREEN, Alexr., W, M, 14 JUL 1856, Alexa., unknown, 7m, J. & M. Breen, Alexa., M. Breen, mother, p.8.
BREEN, Elizabeth, W, F, 25 OCT 1856, Alexa., chills, 3y, J. & M. Breen, Fairfax Co., M. Breen, mother, p.8.
BREEN, Margaret, W, F, 18 DEC 1858, consumption, 50y.
BREEN, Patrick, W, M, 20 OCT 1856, Alexa., unknown, 1d, P. & M. Breen, Alexa., M. Breen, mother, p.8.
BREEN, R.W., W, M, 19 NOV 1853, Alexa., spasms, 8d, P. & M. Breen, Alexa., Mary Breen, mother, p.3.
BREEN, William, W, M, AUG 1855, Alexa.,

Alexandria (Arlington) County, Virginia Death Records, 1853-1896

killed, 19y, P. & M. Breen, Ireland, plasterer, P. Breen, father, p.12.

BRENAN, James, W, M, 5 SEP 1857, Alexa., jaundice, 6d, Jas. & Elizabeth Brenan, Ireland.

BRENGLE, Amanda, W, F, 14 OCT 1855, Alexa., child bed, 22y, J. & F. Mankin, Alexa., C. Brengle, C. Brengle, husband, p.11.

BRENGLE, Amelia H., W, F, 11 AUG 1856, Alexa., teething, 11m, C. & A. Brengle, Alexa., C. Brengle, head of family, p.15.

BRENNER, Joseph, W, M, 15 JUL 1856, Alexa., teething, 9m, John & Julia Brenner, Alexa., John Brenner, head of family, p.14.

BRENT, [blank], (f), M, AUG 1866, Alexa., unknown, 1y, John & Elsey Brent, Westmoreland Co., Elsey Brent, mother, p.21.

BREWER, J.W., W, M, 13 JUL 1854, Alexa., dysentery, 9y, J.W. & L. Brewer, Alexa. Co., J.W. Brewer, father, p.9.

BRIGHT, Elenora, (f), F, 20 JUL 1868, Alexa., unknown, 6m, A. & E. Bright, Alexa., none, single, E. Bright, mother, p.24.

BRIGHT, [blank], (f), M, 30 APR 1866, Alexa., fits, 7d, Louisa & John Bright, Alexa., Louisa Bright, mother, p.21.

BRILL, Louis, W, M, 26 JUN 1858, Alexa., dysentery, 9m, Louis & Catherine Brill, Alexa.

BRILL, Rudolph, W, M, 18 FEB 1867, Alexa., spasms, 1m27d, Lewis & Katie Brill, Alexa., none, single, Lewis Brill, father, p.22.

BRILL, Susana E., W, F, 8 MAR 1867, Alexa., burned, 11y, Lewis & Katie Brill, Md., none, single, Lewis Brill, father, p.22.

BRISCO, Fredrick, (f), M, 30 OCT 1878, Georgetown Road, --, 55y, --, labor, W.H. Lomax, overseer of the poor, p.38.

BRISCOE, [blank], W, M, 20 AUG 1857, Alexa., --, 1y.

BROADUS, John James, W, M, 29 AUG 1857, Alexa., dysentery, 8y, J.M. & M.C. Broadus, Culpeper, J.M. Broadus.

BROADUS, Witmer, W, M, 27 AUG 1856, Alexa., 12y, James M. & Mary C. Broadus, Jas. M. Broadus, p.15.

BROADUS, [blank], W, M, 14 DEC 1856, Alexa., --, 12y, J.M. & C. Broadus, J.M. Broadus, head of family, p.15.

BRODBECK, Jacob, W, M, 15 SEP 1858, Alexa., lost in the Austria, 33y, confectioner, consort of M.A. Broadbeck, M.A. Brodbeck, head of family.

BRODERS, Willie, W, M, 27 JAN 1858, Alexa., 5m18d.

BRODERS, [blank], W, F, 9 AUG 1866, Alexa., unknown, --, John M. & Mary C. Broders, Alexa., John M. Broders, father, p.21.

BRONOUGH, Robt., W, M, 30 DEC 1858, Alexa., --, 1m, J.B. & Sarah Bronough, merchant.

BRONOUGH, Sylvanus, W, F, 11 NOV 1858, Alexa. Co., consumption, 15y, J.B. & Sarah Bronough, Washington, D.C.

BROOKS, Esau, (f), M, 27 MAY 1867, Alexa., sores, 60y, --, Pr. Wm. Co., laborer, married, Sylvia Brooks, wife, p.22.

BROOKS, Fred., (f), M, 28 JUL 1853, Alexa., unknown, 11m, F. & P. Brooks, Alexa., P. Brooks, mother, p.3.

BROOKS, George, (f), M, 1 SEP 1868, Alexa., old age, 81y, unknown, unknown, driver, married, C. Brooks, wife, p.24.

BROOKS, J.H., W, M, 15 SEP 1853, Alexa., bloody flux, 9y, J.H. & S.M.J. Brooks, Alexa., H.B. Arnold, brother in law, p.2.

BROOKS, John H., W, M, 15 MAR 1853, Alexa., liver complaint, 43y, -- Brooks, Prince George's [Co.] Md., cabinet maker, consort of M.J. Brooks, H.B. Arnold, son in law, p.2.

BROOKS, Mary Ann, W, F, JUL 1853, Alexa., dysentery, 1y7m, G. & A. Brooks,

Alexandria (Arlington) County, Virginia Death Records, 1853-1896

Alexa., G. Brooks, father, p.3.

BROOKS, Mary M., (f), F, AUG 1867, Alexa., congestion of brain, 8m, G. & Frs. Brooks, Alexa., none, single, Frances Brooks, mother, p.22.

BROOKS, Rebecca, (f), F, 26 APR 1879, Jefferson Dist., pneumonia, 14y9m, John & Laura Butler, Washington, D.C., housework, single, Laura Butler, mother, p.39.

BROOKS, Sarah, (f), F, 15 OCT 1874, canal basin, dropsy, 40y, William Shorter, St. Mary's Co., laborer, married, George Franklin, friend, p.34.

BROOKS, Sarah, W, F, 16 JUN 1859, Alexa., old age, 78y, --, Alexa., Dr. Maher, physician.

BROWN, Adolphus, (f), M, 28 OCT 1882, F. Vill[age], --, 1y6m, Albert & Bettie Brown, Alexa. Co., Albert Brown, father, p.43.

BROWN, Albert, (f), M, 3 SEP 1877, Freedmen's Village, teething, 1y, Bettie & Albert Brown, Freedmen's Village, Albert Brown, father, p.37.

BROWN, Annie (f), F, 19 OCT 1881, near Syphax's, --, 3y6m, James & Rebecca Brown, Alexa. Co., Rebecca Brown, mother, p.42.

BROWN, Edward, (f), M, JUN 1868, Alexa., teething, 9m, Hy. & J. Brown, Alexa., none, single, N. Washington, grandmother, p.24.

BROWN, Elizth., (f), F, 26 APR 1866, Alexa., inflammation, 36y, --, married, Cubit Brown, husband, p.20.

BROWN, Emily, (f), F, 19 JUN 1887, Alexa. Co., spasms, 1m, Thos. T. & Elizabeth, Alexa. Co., Thos. T. Brown, father, p.49.

BROWN, Frekins, (f), M, 30 SEP 1884, F. Vill[age], --, 1y8m, Albert & Bettie, Alexa. Co., Albert Brown, father, p.45.

BROWN, Henry, W, M, 28 OCT 1867, Alexa., consumption, 28y, Carrie & Washn. Brown, Alexa., laborer, single, Louisa Morgan, sister, p.22.

BROWN, Hiram, W, M, 14 AUG 1890, Alexa. Co., old age, 90y, Wm. & Mary, N.H., widower, J.C.H. Brown, son, p.52.

BROWN, James, (f), M, 24 DEC 1879, Arlington Dist., consumption, 40y, --, Va., labor, consort of Rebecca Brown, Rebecca Brown, wife, p.39.

BROWN, John C.H., W, M, 11 FEB 1893, Alexa. Co., pneumonia, 46y, Hiram & Mary, N.H., farmer, consort of Maggie Brown, Maggie Brown, wife, p.56.

BROWN, Lewis G., (f), M, OCT 1881, F. Village, diphtheria, 7m, Joseph & Sallie Brown, F. Village, Joseph Brown, father, p.42.

BROWN, Lucy A., (f), F, 10 JUN 1895, Alexa. Co., --, 56y, --, Va., homework, consort of Reuben Brown, Benj. Perry, brother in law, p.60.

BROWN, Olive, (f), F, SEP 1885, F. Vill[age], teething, 2y, Joseph & Sallie Brown, F. Vill[age], Joseph Brown, father, p.47.

BROWN, Samuel, (f), M, 3 MAR 1879, Arlington Dist., --, Thos. & Lizzie Brown, Arlington Dist., Lizzie Brown, mother, p.39.

BROWN, Thomas, (f), M, 20 DEC 1873, Arlington Twp., croup, 2m, Thos. E. Brown, Arlington, p.33.

BROWN, Virginia, W, F, 5 OCT 1853, Alexa., chills, 3m, R. & E. Brown, Alexa., Emily Brown, mother, p.2.

BROWN, W.F., W, M, 20 SEP 1854, Alexa., summer complaint, 1y, W.B. & S.J. Brown, Alexa., W.B. Brown, father, p.7.

BROWN, Willie C., W, F, 20 MAR 1856, cholera infantum, 9m4d, C.G. & E.D. Brown, E.D. Brown, p.16.

BROWN, [blank] (f), M, 7 AUG 1878, Rosslyn, --, 7m, Thos. & Lizzie Brown, Rosslyn, Thomas Brown, father, p.38.

BROWN, [blank], (s), F, [no date] 1855, Alexa. Co., unknown, 1y, -- & Mary Brown, Alexa. Co., labor, H.

Alexandria (Arlington) County, Virginia Death Records, 1853-1896

Daingerfield, master, p.14.
BROWN, [blank], -- M, [no date] 1857.
BROWN, [not named], (f), M, 22 OCT 1894, Alexa. Co., --, 10d, Moses & Pattie, Alexa. Co., Pattie Brown, mother, p.58.
BROWN, [not named], (f), F, JUL 1888, Arlington [Dist.], 10m, Thomas T. Brown & Lizzie, Arlington Dist., Thomas T. Brown, father.
BRYAN, John, W, M, 25 NOV 1854, Alexa., consumption, 81y, -- Bryan, Md., Ann Bryan, A. Bryan, widow, p.9.
BRYANT, Harriet A.B., W, F, 11 OCT 1855, Alexa., ague & fever, 46y, N. & -- Noland, Va., consort of J.J. Bryant, Mary E. Southern, daughter, p.11.
BRYANT, Isabella, W, F, 7 DEC 1859, Alexa., consumption, 18y, Reubin & Mary Bryant, Reubin Bryant, father.
BRYANT, R.E., W, M, JUN 1854, Alexa., water on brian, 5m, R.& E. Bryant, Alexa., E. Bryant, mother, p.7.
BUCHANAN, Ella, W, F, 16 DEC 1856, croup, 2y3m17d, R.E. & Maria, R.E. Buchanan, head of family, p.17.
BUCHANAN, Josephine, (f), F, DEC 1894, Alexa. Co., consumption, 50y, --, Alexa. Co., housekeeping, widow, Geo. Jefferson, brother, p.58.
BUCKHANAN, Mary, W, F, JUN 1853, Alexa., scarlet fever, 1y5m, R.E. & E.M. Buchanan, Alexa., R.E. Buchanan, father, p.2.
BUCKINGHAM, Thos., W, M, 21 SEP 1855, Alexa., dysp. on bowels, 25y, J. & M. Buckingham, Alexa., merchant, consort of S.E.G. Buckingham, J. Buckingham, father, p.10.
BUCKLEY, Jere., W, M, 13 NOV 1854, Alexa., consumption, 45y, -- Buckley, Ireland, laborer, consort of Bridget Buckley, B. Buckley, widow, p.7.
BUCKLEY, T.E., W, M, 12 MAY 1854, Washington, consumption, 1y9m, J. & B. Buckley, Washington, B. Buckley, mother, p.7.

BULL, Ann, W, F, [no date] 1853, Alexa., unknown, 3m, J. & V. Bull, Alexa., W.N. Brown, grandfather, p.3.
BUNCE, Mary C., (f), F, 11 JAN 1893, Alexa. Co., childbirth, 36y, --, Wash. D.C., consort of Chas. H. Bunce, Chas. H. Bunce, husband, p.56.
BURGESS, Chas. H., (f), M, 4 JUL 1892, Alexa. Co., 6m, Wm. H. & Margret A., Alexa. Co., Margret A. Burgess, mother, p.54.
BURKE, James Co., W, M, 21 AUG 1896, Alexa. Co., --, 4y, James & Sarah, Alexa. Co., --, James Burke, father, p.62.
BURKE, Julia T., W, F, 23 JUN 1854, Alexa., child bed, 29, S.P. & E. Thompson, Alexa., consort of S.W. Burke, S.W. Burke, husband, p.7.
BURKE, Nelson T., (f), M, 9 APR 1888, Arlington [Dist.], heart failure, 60y, --, Arlington Dist., messenger, John H. Burke, son.
BURLESS, Hester, (f), F, AUG 1893, Alexa. Co., --, 10m, John & Emma, Alexa. Co., J.H. Burless, uncle, p.56.
BURLESS, Jesse W., (f), M, 27 FEB 1894, Alexa. Co., pneumonia, 7m, Joseph H. & Edie, Alexa. Co., J.H. Burless, father, p.58.
BURLESS, John B., (f), M, 7 JAN 1893, Alexa. Co., paralysis, 72y, --, Fauquier Co., blacksmith, consort of Sally Burless, J.H. Burless, son, p.56.
BURLS, Sarah J., (f), F, 1 OCT 1894, Alexa. Co., paralysis, 65y, --, Fairfax Co., housekeeping, widower, Adline Butler, daughter, p.58.
BURN, Ada A., W, F, 7 JAN 1856, childbirth, 15y, Henry & Margaret Tatsapaugh, Henry Tatsapaugh, p.16.
BURNS, Catherine, W, F, MAY 1853, Alexa., consumption, 9y, E. & M. Burns, Ireland, T. O'Brien, brother in law, p.4.
BURRELL, [blank], (f), F, 30 AUG 1881, near P.H. Lane, --, 1d, Jourdan & Jane Burrell, Poor House Lane, Jane Burrell,

Alexandria (Arlington) County, Virginia Death Records, 1853-1896

mother, p.42.

BURROWS, Carrie A., W, F, 5 SEP 1880, Ballston, cholera infantum, 1y26d, W.T. & Maria L. Burrows, Alexa. Co., W.T. Burrows, father, p.40.

BURROWS, Henson G., W, M, 29 JUN 1892, Alexa. Co., --, 70y2m, Robert & Casanna, Alexa. Co., W.T. Burrows, mother [sic], p.54.

BURROWS, Maria L., W, F, 24 AUG 1880, Ballston, heart disease, 21y4m26d, Geo. H. & Louisa Mortimore, Fairfax Co., housekeeping, consort of Wm. T. Burrows, W.T. Burrows, husband, p.40.

BURROWS, Sarah A., W, F, 18 SEP 1879, Arlington Dist., consumption, 55y, --, Md., housekeeping, consort of Henson G. Burrows, Sarah L. Burrows, daughter, p.39.

BURROWS, Sarah L., W, F, 31 NOV 1881, Ballston, consumption, 29y, H.G. & Sarah Burrows, Georgetown, D.C., housekeeping, single, W.T. Burrows, brother, p.42.

BUSHBY, D., W, M, 13 SEP 1854, poor house, paralytic, 70y, -- Bushby, unknown, John Stephenson, keeper, p.9.

BUSHBY, John, W, M, AUG 1854, Alexa., dysentery, 8m, W. & L. Bushby, Alexa., B. Delphy, gra'pa., p.7.

BUSHBY, Maria, W, F, 26 OCT 1853, Alexa., child bed, 33y, J. & S. Bushby, Alexa., Elizabeth Forsith, friend, p.4.

BUTCHER, Albert (f), M, APR 1892, Alexa. Co., --, 8y6m, Wm. H. & Annie, Annie Butcher, mother, p.54.

BUTCHER, Robt., W, M, 28 SEP 1890, Alexa. Co., --, 45y, --, Alexa. Co., labor, consort of Eliza Butcher, H.R. Fish, neighbor, p.52.

BUTLER, Infant, W, --, 21 AUG 1857, Alexa., cholera infantum, 2y, Jas. & Mrs. Butler, Alexa.

BUTLER, John, (f), M, 10 MAY 1881, Washington Road, pneumonia, 40y, --, Ky., labor, Laura Butler, consort of Laura Butler, Laura Butler, wife, p.42.

BUTLER, Matilda, (f), F, 18 AUG 1885, Md., --, 25y, Andrew & Ellen Tolson, Md., housekeeping, consort of Ben Butler, Ben Butler, husband, p.47.

BUTLER, [blank], W, M, 5 AUG 1857, Alexa., teething, E. & J. Butler.

C

CAIN, Sarah A., W, F, 13 AUG 1855, Alexa., water on brain, 1y, W. & E. Cain, Warren Co., W. Cain, father, p.10.

CALDER, [blank], W, F, 27 JUN 1859, Alexa., unknown, 6m, E.A. & J.A. Calder, Alexa., John Calder, father.

CALLEN, Catherine, W, F, 12 AUG 1865, Alexa., fever, 8m, Henry & Margaret, Ireland, merchant, single, Henry Callen, father, p.19.

CALLEN, Mary, W, F, 15 SEP 1865, Alexa., croup, 4y6m, Henry & Margret, Ireland, single, Henry Callen, father.

CALLIS, W.S., W, M, JUL 1895, Alexa. Co., consumption, 56y, --, Alexa. Co., merchant, consort of S.D. Callis, S.D. Callis, wife, p.60.

CALVERT, Mary C., W, F, 7 OCT 1866, Fairfax Co., chronic diarrhea, 4y3m3d, G.W. & L.A. Calvert, Prince Wm. Co., laborer, single, Geo. W. Calvert, father, p.20.

CAMPBELL, Anna C., W, F, JUN 1858, Alexa., scarlet fever, 11y1m, W.R. & A. Campbell, Alexa., W.R. Campbell, father.

CAMPBELL, Cora, (f), F, 1 APR 1866, Alexa., diphtheria, 2y6m, Wm. & Louisa Campbell, Va., laborer, single, Wm. Campbell, father, p.21.

CAMPBELL, E.J., W, F, 30 SEP 1855, Alexa., water on brain, 2y6m, D. & S. Campbell, Alexa., D. Campbell, father, p.12.

CAMPBELL, Elizabeth, W, F, [c.JUN] 1853, Alexa., old age, 69y, D. & -- Smedley,

Alexandria (Arlington) County, Virginia Death Records, 1853-1896

Jefferson Co., W. Campbell, W. Campbell, husband, p.2.

CAMPBELL, James, W, M, JAN 1855, Alexa., consumption, 31y, J. & M. Campbell, Ireland, shoemaker, consort of Anna Campbell, D. Campbell, brother, p.12.

CAMPBELL, John, (f) of Miss Gordon, M, 19 JAN 1859, Alexa., dysentery, 75y4m6d, --, Alexa., Milly Campbell, wife.

CAMPBELL, Mary, W, F, 28 OCT 1853, Alexa., pneumonia, 34y, W. & D. Dyer, Fairfax Co., consort of J.W. Campbell, J.W. Campbell, husband, p.1.

CAMPBELL, [blank], W, M, 26 OCT 1853, Alexa., --, 1d, J.W. & M. Campbell, Alexa., J.W. Campbell, father, p.1.

CANE, Eliza, (s), F, APR 1855, unknown, 5m, A. & H. Cane, Fairfax, Harriett Keene [sic], mother, p.12.

CAREY, Falkland, W, M, 2 JUN 1856, --, 16y, Archibald Carey, Cumberland, Md., O. Fairfax, head of family, p.16.

CARLIN, [Andrew]. W.F., W, M, 28 OCT 1885, Alexa. Co., catarrh stomach, 54y, Jas. H. & Letia Carlin, Alexa. Co., farming, single, Ann E.A. Carlin, sister, pp.47, 48.

CARLIN, W.B., W, M, 15 JAN 1859, Alexa., diarrhea, 4m, Wm. H. & Francis Carlin, Alexa., Wm. H. Carlin, father.

CARLIN, William W., W, M, 20 NOV 1856, Alexa., teething, 2y6m, J.F. & Mary Carlin, Alexa., J.F. Carlin, head of family, p.14.

CARLIN, [blank], (f), F, 7 SEP 1876, upper end King Street, spasm, 14d, Thom. & Martha Carlin, upper end King Street, Martha Carlin, mother, p.36.

CARNE, Amanda, W, F, SEP 1853, Alexa., typhoid fever, 11y, R.L. & C.L Carne, Alexa., R.L. Carne, father, p.1.

CARNE, James M., W, M, 18 DEC 1856, Alexa., cold, 31y, --, laborer, S. McCuin, brother, p.15.

CARNE, Richard L., W, M, 24 AUG 1867, Alexa., suffusion of brain, 70y, unknown, --, none, married, R.L. Carne, Jr., son, p.22.

CARPENTER, Caroline, (f), F, AUG 1892, Alexa. Co., heart failure, 30y, --, consort of Mathew Carpenter, Jennie Jackson, neighbor, p.54.

CARPENTER, Matthew, (f), M, 1 JUL 1877, Washn. Dist., teething, 2y, Caroline & M. Carpenter, Washn. Dist., Mathew Carpenter, father, p.37.

CARPENTER, [blank], (f), M, 1 NOV 1887, Alexa. Co., --, 1m, Mathew & Caroline, Alexa. Co., Mathew Carpenter, father, p.49.

CARR, James, W, M, AUG 1854, Alexa., brain fever, 9m, John & M. Carr, Alexa., J. Carr, father, p.7.

CARR, Mary V., W, F, 10 JAN 1856, Alexa., scarlet fever, 1y, E. & A.E. Carr, A.E. Carr, mother, p.8.

CARROLL, Betsey, (f), F, AUG 1853, Alexa., unknown, 2y, slaves, Fairfax, Rosetta Carroll, mother, p.3.

CARROLL, Daniel, (f), M, [no date] 1880, Georgetown Road, diphtheria, 3y4m5d, Dan'l. & Martha Carroll, Alexa. Co., Daniel Carroll, father, p.40.

CARROL, Ellen, (f), F, 1 AUG 1875, Jefferson Mag. Dist., --, 1m, Sam Carrol, Alexa. Co., p.35.

CARROLL, John, (f), M, APR 1887, Alexa. Co., killed, 16y8m, Daniel & Martha, Alexa. Co., labor, Daniel Carroll, father, p.49.

CARROLL, John H., W, M, APR 1854, Alexa., burnt, 1y9m, O. & B. Carroll, Fauquier Co., O. Carroll, father, p.7.

CARROLL, Margaret, W, F, 1 MAY 1854, Alexa., unknown, 5y, O. & B. Carroll, Md., O. Carroll, father, p.7.

CARROLL, Martha, (f), F, 30 MAY 1884, near F. Vill[age], --, 40y, --, Md., consort of Daniel Carroll, Mary E. Carroll, daughter, p.45.

Alexandria (Arlington) County, Virginia Death Records, 1853-1896

CARROLL, Nellie, (f), F, 1 MAR 1876, rear of Walkers brickyard, 1m, Samuel & Malinda Carroll, near of Walkers brickyard, Nellie [sic] Carroll, mother, p.36.

CARSON, Edgar, W, M, 17 SEP 1859, Alexa., unknown, 2m, Geo. W. & Annie Carson, Alexa., Geo. W. Carson, father.

CARSON, Margaret, W, F, 28 OCT 1853, Alexa., consumption, 38y, -- & S. Lewis, Pa., consort of Geo. Carson, Geo. Carson, husband, p.5.

CARTER, Hanah, W, F, 11 APR 1889, Alexa. Co., catarrh of head, 72y, --, Va., consort of Luke Carter, Isabella Carter, daughter, p.51.

CARTER, Lucy, (f), F, 10 FEB 1866, Alexa., cramp choleic, 5y, Frank & Matilda Carter, Culpeper Co., single, Frank Carter, father, p.20.

CARTER, Margaret, (f), F, 26 AUG 1877, near Ft. Albany, childbirth, 30y, Eliza Payne, Va., housework, consort of Ed. J. Carter, Ed. J. Carter, husband, p.37.

CARTER, Matilda, (f), F, 15 MAY 1866, Alexa., fever, 43y, Harriet Mills, Culpeper Co., married, Frank Carter, father [sic], p.20.

CARTER, Moses, (f), M, 15 SEP 1866, Alexa., typhoid fever, 12y0m18d, Kate & Philip Carter, Va., laborer, single, Philip Carter, father, p.21.

CARTER, Richard, (f), M, 27 SEP 1892, Alexa. Co., congestive chill, 42y, --, laborer, consort of Alice Carter, Alice Carter, wife, p.54.

CARTER, Tenia, (f), F, MAR 1868, Alexa., consumption, unknown, J. & Fannie Carter, unknown, none, single, Ida Carter, sister, p.24.

CARTER, W.H., (f), M, 10 NOV 1857, Alexa., consumption, 30y, --, Pr. Wm. Co., --, Chas. Alexander.

CARTER, Walter, (f), M, 12 JUL 1878, near F. Village, teething, 1y, Susan Winkfield, Washington D.C., Susan Winkfield, mother, p.38.

CARTER, Wm., (f), M, DEC 1875, Jefferson Mag. Dist., hemorrhage of heart, 21y, Ned Carter, Alexa. Co., laborer, p.35.

CARTER, Wm. E., W, M, 4 OCT 1877, Loudoun Co., drowned, 36y, Cath. & W.B. Carter, grocer, husband of Lucy A. Carter, Lucy A. Carter, wife, p.37.

CARTON, Dr. James, W, M, 10 SEP 1855, Alexa. Co., old age, 83y, S. & E. Carton, Ireland, gentleman, consort of U. Carton, J.B. Carton, son, p.14.

CASH, John, W, M, 12 FEB 1853, Alexa., heart disease, 18y, -- Cash, Warrenton, druggist, J.R. Pierpoint, employer, p.1.

CASSINE, Geo. F., W, M, SEP 1892, Wash. D.C., asphyxiated, 45y, --, laborer, consort of Ellen Causine [sic], J. Goldman, neighbor, p.54.

CASTOR, Moses, (f), M, MAY 1893, Alexa. Co., --, 70y, --, consort of Martha Castor, John H. Castor, son, p.56.

CASTOR, Moses, (f), M, 17 JUN 1894, Alexa. Co., teething, 11m, John & Lucinda V., Alexa. Co., John H. Castor, father, p.58.

CATLETT, Erskine, W, M, 27 MAY 1856, suddenly, 47y, Chas. J. Catlett, Loudoun [Co.], Col. Stewart, friend, p.16.

CAWOOD, Delia, W, F, 8 APR 1855, Alexa., pneumonia, 53y, C. & -- Robinson, Md., consort of M.O.B. Cawood, M.O.B. Cawood, husband, p.12.

CAYWOOD, [blank], W, M, 30 JUN 1859, Alexa., disease of bowels, 2m, M.O'B. Caywood, Alexa., M.O'B. Caywood, father.

CAYWOOD, M.O'B., W, M, 31 DEC 1859, Alexa., apoplexy, 65y, --, Alexa., fisherman, James Vernon, neighbor.

CAZENOVE, Mary S., W, F, 28 APR 1853, Alexa., scarlet fever, 2y, W.G. & M.E. Cazenove, Alexa., W.G. Cazenove, father, p.1.

CEPHAS, [blank], (f), F, 30 AUG 1896, Alexa. Co., --, 2d, Alex. & Nanna, Alexa.

Alexandria (Arlington) County, Virginia Death Records, 1853-1896

Co., Nanna Cephas, mother, p.62.
CEPHAS, [blank], W, --, NOV 1895, Alexa. Co., --, Alex. & Nanny, Alexa. Co., Alex. Cephas, father, p.60.
CHAMBERLAIN, Ann C., W, F, 31 JAN 1858, Alexa., childbirth, 26y, --, consort of James Chamberlain, J. Chamberlain.
CHAMBERLAIN, Ella Jane, W, F, [22] AUG 1854, Powhattan Co., brain fever, 2y, J.L. & A.C. Chamberlain, Alexa., J.L. Chamberlain, father, p.6.
CHAMBERS, Jennie, (f), F, NOV 1855, Alexa., old age, 90y, no body knows, Fairfax, Jonathan, Chambers, Patsey Nelson, neighbor, p.11.
CHAPMAN, Bartley, (f), M, SEP 1866, Alexa., consumption, 17y, Bartley & Eliza Chapman, Va., laborer, single, Bartley Chapman, father, p.21.
CHAPMAN, Sarah P., W, F, 26 APR 1856, debility, 80y, p.16.
CHAPMAN, Virginia, (f), F, DEC 1867, Alexa., unknown, 16y, Charlotte & Saml. Chapman, Alexa., none, single, Eveline Chapman, sister, p.22.
CHARLTON, [blank], W, M, 18 JAN 1855, Alexa., unknown, 1d, J. & S. Charlton, Alexa., Jane Charlton, mother, p.13.
CHASE, Elisha C., W, M, 25 DEC 1853, Alexa., consumption, 23y, J. & E. Chase, Md., clerk, J.E. Chase, brother, p.1.
CHASE, Mary, (f), F, 4 SEP 1867, Alexa., fever, 7y, Elizh. & Frank Chase, Alexa., none, single, Eleanora Chase, sister, p.22.
CHASE, Rachel, (f), F, 1 FEB 1867, Alexa., congestive chills, 69y, Matilda & Peter Magruder, Alexa., housekeeper, married, Adeline Chase, daughter, p.22.
CHASE, William, (f), M, 4 MAY 1855, Alexa., consumption, 20y, S. & E. Chase, Mary Chase, sister, p.12.
CHATHAM, Henry, W, M, 31 DEC 1865, Alexa., old age, 85y, unknown, unknown, gent, widower, John Dixon, son in law, p.19.
CHESHIRE, James B., 25 APR 1895, Alexa. Co., old age, 86y, --, Pr. Wm. Co., widower, Mary Cheshire, daughter in law, p.60.
CHESHIRE, S.J., W, M, 20 MAY 1857, Alexa., --, 1y.
CHESLEY, Harriet, (f), F, 14 AUG 1867, Alexa., measles, --, Mariah & Hy. Chesley, Md., none, single, Mariah Chesley, mother, p.22.
CHILD, Norris, (f), F, [no date] 1858, --, pauper, John Stephenson.
CHILDS, Geo. W., W, M, 31 JUL 1859, Alexa., drowned, 18y, William Childs, Louisa Co., student, E.R. Price, captain of boat.
CHILDS, Martha, (f), F, 27 APR 1893, Alexa. Co., heart disease, 31y, Humphrey & Esther, --, housework, consort of R.W. Childs, R.W. Childs, husband, p.56.
CHILDS, Millie, (f), F, JUL 1893, Alexa. Co., paralysis, 71y, --, Caroline Co., housework, widow, Emma Minor, daughter, p.56.
CHINN, Chas. W., (f), M, 10 MAY 1891, Alexa. Co., shot, 38y, --, Fairfax Co., labor, consort of Charlotte Chinn, Charlotte Chinn, wife, p.53.
CHINN, Margret, (f), F, 7 AUG 1891, Alexa. Co., dysentery, 15y, Chas. W. & Charlett, Alexa. Co., Charlotte Chinn, mother, p.53.
CHISOM, Felix, W, M, MAR 1885, Alexa. Co., congestion of brain, 33y, --, Md., farming, consort of Sarah Chisom, H.D. Donaldson, father in law, p.47.
CHURCH, William E., W, M, 5 JUL 1867, Alexa., liver disease, 58y, Sarah & Gilbert Church, Alexa., farmer, married, M. Padgett, niece, p.22.
CHURCHMAN, Lewis, W, M, 27 AUG 1854, poor house, intemperance, 45y, -- Churchman, Alexa., John Stephenson, keeper, p.9.
CHURCHWILL, Emma, (f), F, 4 SEP 1883, Alexa. Co., --, 1y1m, Arthur & Fannie Churchwill, Alexa. Co., Fannie

Alexandria (Arlington) County, Virginia Death Records, 1853-1896

Churchwell, p.44.
CLAPDORE, Jacob, W, M, 15 MAY 1853, Alexa., consumption, 40y, -- Clapdore, Petersburg, fishing, consort of Mary Clapdore, M. Clapdore, widow, p.3.
CLAPDORE, L.V., W, F, OCT 1853, Alexa., unknown, 6m, J.M. & E. Clapdore, Alexa., J.W. Clapdore, father, p.2.
CLAPDORE, Susan, W, F, OCT 1855, Alexa., unknown, 2m, J.M. & E. Clapdore, Alexa., J.M. Clapdore, father, p.11.
CLARK, Andrew, W, M, 3 NOV 1855, Alexa., unknown, 1m, Geo. & C. Clark, Alexa., C. Clark, mother, p.13.
CLARK, Carolinus, (f), M, 3 APR 1853, Alexa., fever, 3y, N. & S. Clark, Alexa., Sarah Clark, mother, p.3.
CLARK, Eliza, W, F, 26 SEP 1865, Alexa., pneumonia, 66y, Amelia Brockett, Alexa., --, widower, Ferd. Knight, son, p.19.
CLARK, Frank, W, M, SEP 1892, Alexa. Co., teething, 1y6m, A.B. & Alice, single, A.B. Clark, father, p.54.
CLARK, James, (f), M, AUG 1892, Alexa. Co., killed, 45y, --, Va., laborer, consort of Lillian Clark, Lillian Clark, wife, p.54.
CLARK, Lettie, W, F, AUG 1892, Alexa. Co., typhoid fever, 16y, A.B. & Alice, single, A.B. Clark, father, p.54.
CLARK, M.E., W, F, 29 JUL 1855, Alexa., spasms, 7m, J. & M. Clark, Alexa., M. Clark, mother, p.13.
CLARK, [blank], (f), M, NOV 1856, Alexa., small pox, 1d, N. & S. Clark, Alexa., Sarah Clark, mother, p.8.
CLARKE, James, W, M, 13 APR 1857, Alexa., --, Chr. Neal, coroner.
CLARKE, Peyton, W, M, 10 AUG 1859, Alexa., consumption, 51y, --, Alexa., cigar maker, consort of Margaret Clarke, Margaret Clarke, wife.
CLARKE, Sopha, (f), F, NOV 1875, Jefferson Mag. Dist., dropsy of heart, --, wife of Denice Clarke, laborer, p.35.

CLAUGHTON, St. Clair, W, M, 26 MAR 1858, Alexa., --, 9m, H.O. & Jane Claughton, H.O. Claughton.
CLAUGHTON, Wm., W, M, 9 FEB 1856, general debility, 18y, P.C. Claughton, P.C. Claughton, p.16.
CLEM, Stewart, (f), M, 20 JAN 1879, Jefferson Dist., measles, 2y2m, Samuel & Maria Stewart, Jefferson Dist., Samuel Stewart, father, p.39.
CLEMENTS, Fannie, W, F, [22] MAR 1889, Alexa. Co., consumption, --, T.H. & Martha Sypherd, Va., housekeeping, consort of Jas. E. Clements, J.E. Clements, husband, p.51.
CLIFFIN, Eliza, (f), F, 27 NOV 1879, Arlington Dist., heart disease, 50y, Moses & Flora Brown, Surry Co., housekeeping, consort of Richard Cliffin, Nancy Carroll, daughter, p.39.
CLIFFORD, John, W, M, 10 MAR 1858, Alexa., old age, 75y, --, Alexa.
CLINKET, Julia, (f), F, 17 JUL 1895, Alexa. Co., consumption, 13y, Isaac & Mary, Alexa. Co., labor, Isaac Clinket, father, p.60.
CLINKETT, James, (f), M, DEC 1887, Alexa. Co., consumption, 60y, --, Va., labor, widow, Isaac E. Clinkett, son, p.49.
CLOSE, Edsall B., W, M, 25 MAY 1857, Alexa., pneumonia, 2m12d, Jas. T. Close, Alexa., Dr. Stabler.
CLOSE, Jas. T., Jr., W, M, 23 MAY 1857, Alexa., pneumonia, 3y10m22d, Jas. T. Close, Alexa., Dr. Stabler.
COGSWELL, Francis, W, M, [no date] 1857, Alexa., brain fever, 1y10m, J. & Delila Cogswell, Alexa.
COGSWELL, [blank], W, M, 15 SEP 1857, Alexa., water on brain, 2y.
COLE, Laura Virginia, W, F, 11 JUN 1859, Alexa., consumption, 15y, James & Mary Cole, Alexa., James Cole, father.
COLE, Mary, (s), F, MAR 1855, Alexa., dropsy, 45y, Mary Cole, Fairfax, -- Cole, J. Summers, master, p.10.

Alexandria (Arlington) County, Virginia Death Records, 1853-1896

COLE, [blank], (s), F, FEB 1855, Alexa., unknown, 7d, -- Cole, Alexa., J. Summers, master, p.11.

COLE, [blank], (s), F, AUG 1854, Alexa., overlaid, 3m, R. & M. Cole, Alexa., slave, J. Summers, master, p.7.

COLEMAN, Della, (f), F, 18 APR 1876, near Canal Basin, colic, 37y, --, Va., house work, consort of Thos. Coleman, Thos. Coleman, husband, p.36.

COLEMAN, Earnest, (f), M, 13 DEC 1888, Jefferson [Dist.], --, 5d, Thos. & Kattie Coleman, Jefferson [Dist.], Kattie Coleman, mother.

COLEMAN, Estella, (f), F, 14 OCT 1887, Alexa. Co., teething, 9m, Thos. & Kate, Alexa. Co., Thomas Coleman, father, p.49.

COLEMAN, Georgianna, (f), F, 20 AUG 1866, Alexa., spasm, 9y, Wm. & Hannah Coleman, Caroline Co., single, Hannah Coleman, mother, p.20.

COLEMAN, Humphrey, (f), M, 14 NOV 1895, Alexa. killed, 65y, --, Alexa. Co., labor, consort of Frances Coleman, F. Coleman, wife, p.60.

COLEMAN, Humphrey, (f), M, MAY 1896, Alexa. Co., killed, 60y, --, Va., labor, --, Geo. Coleman, son, p.62.

COLEMAN, Lura, (f), F, 4 OCT 1878, near F. Village, cold, 2y7m, Hamphrey & Francis Coleman, near F. Village, Hamphrey Coleman, father, p.38.

COLEMAN, Peter, (f), M, 27 AUG 1881, near Slater's, hemorrhage, 23y, Henry & Jane Coleman, Caroline Co., labor, single, Henry Coleman, father, p.42.

COLEMAN, Wm. H., (f), M, 1 NOV 1875, Jefferson Mag. Dist., --, 6y, --, Alexa. Co., p.35.

COLEMAN, [blank], (f), M, 29 JAN 1886, Jefferson Dist., --, 1m, Thos. & Kate Coleman, Alexa. Co., Thos. Coleman, father, p.48.

COLEMAN, [not named], (f), M, 3 MAR 1891, Alexa., --, 6d, Thos. & Kate Coleman, Alexa. Co., Kate Coleman, mother, p.53.

COLLINS, Chas., W, M, 24 MAY 1857, Alexa., consumption, 1y, Elijah & Mary Collins, Alexa., E. Collins.

COLLINS, Mertena, W, F, DEC 1892, Alexa. Co., old age, 98y, --, widow, Wash. Woor, son in law, p.54.

COLLINS, T. Morgan, W, M, 30 MAY 1858, Alexa., scarlet fever, 7y1m8d, W.T. & M.M. Collins, Alexa., William T. Collins, father.

COLSTON, Anthony, (f), M, AUG 1853, Alexa., cholera, 30y, F. & B. Colston, Alexa., laborer, Priscilla Colston, P. Colston, widow, p.4.

COLSTON, Betsey, (f), F, AUG 1853, Alexa., child bed, 38y, F. & B. Colston, Alexa., P. Colston, sister in law, p.4.

COLSTON, Betsey, (f), F, 16 NOV 1854, poor house, unknown, 30y, -- Colston, Alexa., John Stephenson, keeper, p.9.

COMMANDER, Rebecca, (f), F, 15 MAY 1881, canal basin, --, 3d, James & Agnes Commander, Alexa. Co., James Commander, father, p.42.

COMPTON, James William, W, M, 7 JUL 1856, Alexa., constipation on bowels, 8m, Silas & Sarah Compton, Silas Compton, head of family, p.15. [written as Williams, James]

CONNELL, Frederick J., W, M, AUG 1892, Alexa. Co., --, 2y6m, John H. & Laura C., --, J.H. Connell, father, p.54.

CONNER, Harvey, W, M, 28 SEP 1868, Alexa., fever, 1m14d, Wm. & M.E. Conner, Alexa., none, single, M.E. Conner, mother, p.24.

CONSTABLE, Mary, W, F, 2 DEC 1859, Alexa., consumption, 30y, --, Culpeper Co., consort of Dr. Constable, J.F. Latham, father.

CONTEE, Frederick, (f), M, 9 SEP 1894, Alexa. Co., dropsy, 58y, John & Amelia, Md., laborer, consort of Martha Contee, Richard Contee, son, p.58.

Alexandria (Arlington) County, Virginia Death Records, 1853-1896

CONTEE, Fredrick, (f), M, 12 MAR 1878, Georgetown Road, pneumonia, 6y5m, Fredk. & Mary Contee, Geo'town Road, Fredrick Contee, father, p.38.

CONTEE, John, (f), M, AUG 1875, Arlington Mag. Dist., rheumatism, Felon Contee, --, laborer, p.35.

CONTEE, William, (f), M, 5 JUN 1877, Washn. Forest, fever, 30y, --, Md., farmer, Bettie Robinson, friend, p.37.

CONTEE, Willie, (f), M, 1 JUN 1881, Georgetown Road, --, 4y3m, Fredk. & Martha Contee, Alexa. Co., Martha Contee, mother, p.42.

CONWAY, Euel, (f), M, 24 DEC 1892, Alexa. Co., grip, 56y, --, consort of Adlaid Conway, Adlaid Conway, wife, p.54.

CONWAY, John, (f), M, 1 OCT 1866, Alexa., consumption, 2y, John & Ann Conway, Westmoreland, laborer, single, John Conway, father, p.20.

CONWAY, Thos., (s), M, 4 APR 1855, Alexa., spasms, 33y, Jesse & -- Conway, Alexa., labor, consort of Joanna Conway, J. Conway, widow, p.12.

CONWAY, Walter, (f), M, 17 JUL 1892, Alexa. Co., --, 8m, Euel & Adlaid, Alexa. Co., Adlaid Conway, mother, p.54.

COOK, B.H., W, M, 2 MAR 1859, Alexa., cholera morbus, 54y, --, Alexa., Martha Cook, wife.

COOK, Carolina, W, F, 15 OCT 1884, Washington D.C., cancer, 62y, --, Canada, widow, F.H. Cook, son, p.45.

COOK, Emeline, W, [F], 1 JUN 1857, Alexa., cholera, 4m, L. & J. Cook.

COOK, Emeline, W, F, 28 MAY 1857, Alexa., childbed fever, 28y, --, Ireland, consort of Lemuel Cook.

COOK, Harriet, W, F, 18 APR 1854, poor house, old age, 85y, -- Cook, unknown, John Stephenson, keeper, p.9.

COOK, Ida, W, F, 4 MAY 1857, Alexa., childbirth, 24y.

COOK, Mary, W, F, 27 MAY 1857, Alexa., --, Fred & Rosa Vaccari, Alexa., grocer, consort of T.M. Cook, F. Vaccari.

COOK, R.P., W, M, 5 APR 1853, N.J., brain fever, 4y6m, G.A. & M. Cook, N.J., G.A. Cook, father, p.2.

COOK, Rebecca, W, F, 21 NOV 1866, Alexa., old age, 87y, unknown, Md., toll gate keeper, widow, Wm. Burnett, friend, p.20.

COOK, Samuel D., W, M, 3 JUL 1883, Alexa. Co., --, 64y, --, Alexa. Co., farmer, consort of Cornelia Cook, F.H. Cook, p.44.

COOK, T., W, M, 6 JUN 1857, Alexa., drowned, 52y, --, fisherman, Thos. Cook.

COOK, Theo., W, F, 4 MAR 1857, Alexa., consumption, 42y, --, Thos. Cook.

COOPER, Adelade, (f), F, 15 AUG 1866, Alexa., scarlet fever, 4y, Grafton & Sophia Cooper, Md., laborer, single, Grafton Cooper, father, p.20.

CORBETT, Emily B., W, F, 13 JAN 1880, Ballston, heart disease, 37y, Benjamin & Mary H. Moore, N.Y., housekeeping, widow, Benjamin Moore, father, p.40.

CORBETT, Mary E., W, F, 28 OCT 1876, Columbia Pike, childbirth, 29y, Sam'l. & Mary Howard, Newport R.I., postmistress, consort of Chas. F. Corbett, Chas. F. Corbett, husband, p.36.

CORDEY, Michael, W, M, 31 DEC 1858, Alexa., consumption, 50y, --, Cork, Ireland, laborer, Wm. Burley, friend.

COREY, Essex, (f), M, 10 MAR 1872, Arlington Dist., unknown, 55y, unknown, Va., laborer, widower, Geo. Mortimore, undertaker, p.32.

CORSE, Douglass, W, M, 7 JUL 1859, Alexa., cholera infantum, 2y, J.D. & R. Smith Corse, Alexa., J.D. Corse, father.

CORSE, Douglass, W, M, 3 JUL 1858, Alexa., 4d, L.D. & L.E. Corse, L.D. Corse.

CORSON, Jonny, W, M, 30 JUN 1858, Alexa., summer complaint, 6m, Job & Eliza Corson, Job Corson, head of family.

Alexandria (Arlington) County, Virginia Death Records, 1853-1896

COSTA, Mary, W, F, 10 AUG 1856, Alexa., --, cholera infantum, George & Ruth, Geo. Costa, head of family, p.15.

COSTIGAN, John, W, M, MAR 1855, Alexa., croup, 1m, J. & C. Costigan, C. Costigan, mother, p.13.

COSTOLOW, Mary, W, F, 7 NOV 1873, Washington Twp., brain fever, 1y6m, Christopher, --, Dr. T.B.J. Frye, p.33.

COUSINS, Estella, W, F, 11 SEP 1895, Alexa. Co., --, 1y5m, Claud & Laural, Alexa. Co., Laural Cousins, mother, p.60.

COX, Della, (f), M, 15 JUN 1894, Alexa. Co., Bright's disease, 17y, John & Mary E., Alexa. Co., laborer, John Cox, father, p.58.

COX, Edward E., (f), M, 12 AUG 1891, Alexa. Co., malaria fever, 14y, Elijah & Laura, Alexa. Co., Laura Cox, mother, p.53.

COX, George, (f), M, 12 DEC 1881, Hayes farm, brain fever, 6y, Toney & Maria Cox, Alexa. Co., Maria Cox, mother, p.42.

COX, James, (f), M, 17 FEB 1895, Alexa. Co., old age, 84, --, Va., Dallas Cox, son, p.60.

COX, James, (f), M, 28 JAN 1896, Alexa. Co., old age, 86y, --, Va., --, widower, Dallas Cox, son, p.62.

COX, Lawson, (f), M, APR 1886, Jefferson Dist., pneumonia, 50y, --, Va., shoemaker, widower, Mary Flemmons, daughter, p.48.

COX, Mary, W, F, 16 SEP 1855, Alexa., consumption, 1y4m, C. & C. Cox, Alexa., C. Cox, father, p.11.

COX, Polly, (f), F, 6 APR 1884, Washington Road, --, 60y, --, Rappahannock Co., consort of Lawson Cox, Lawson Cox, husband, p.45.

COX, Winnie, (f), F, 20 MAY 1895, Alexa. Co., consumption, 63y, --, Va., labor, consort of James Cox, Dallas Cox, son, p.60.

CRABB, W. Foster, W, M, 3 SEP 1855, Alexa., unknown, 9y, S. & M. Crabb, Alexa. Co., Mary Crabb, mother, p.13.

CRAVEN, J.H., W, M, 3 JUL 1853, Alexa., cholera infantum, 5m, J. & S. Craven, Alexa., J. Craven, father, p.5.

CRAVEN, J.P., W, M, 27 JUN 1853, Alexa., cholera infantum, 5m, J. & S. Craven, Alexa., J. Craven, father, p.5.

CRAVEN, John H., W, M, 22 JUL 1855, Alexa., catarrh fever, 1y, J. & S.R. Craven, Alexa., J. Craven, father, p.13.

CRAVEN, S.B., W, M, 15 DEC 1853, Alexa., aff. of the brain, 18y, J. & S. Craven, Alexa., J. Craven, father, p.5.

CRAWFORD, Daisey, (f), F, 15 AUG 1881, Col. Pike, --, 1y3m, Lemuel & Mary Crawford, Alexa. Co., Mary Crawford, mother, p.42.

CRAWFORD, Edward, (f), M, 15 APR 1878, near brick barn, --, 1d, Lemuel & Polly Crawford, near brick barn, Lemuel Crawford, father, p.38.

CRAWFORD, Mary A., W, F, 13 MAR 1854, Alexa., congestion of the brain, 2y, Chs. & M.A. Crawford, Chs. Crawford, father, p.6.

CRAWFORD, Mary, W, F, 10 JUL 1858, Alexa., water of brain, 10m, Jas. & Mary Ann Crawford.

CREDIT, Sally, (f), F, 15 MAY 1856, Alexa., consumption, 32y, James & N. Carter, Alexa., John Credit, N. Dudley, mother in law, p.8.

CRISMOND, F., W, M, JAN 1853, Alexa., spasms, 6d, W. & M. Crismond, Alexa., W. Crismond, father, p.3.

CRISMOND, Louisa, W, F, 29 OCT 1853, Alexa., scarlet fever, 2y, T. & E. Crismond, Alexa., E. Crismond, mother, p.3.

CRISMOND, Susan, W, F, 9 NOV 1853, Alexa., unknown, 26y, B. & M. Crismond, E. Crismond, sister, p.3.

CROCKETT, C.A., W, F, 2 MAY 1853, Alexa., child bed, 31y, J. & S. Webster, Alexa., consort of James Crockett, S.

Alexandria (Arlington) County, Virginia Death Records, 1853-1896

Webster, mother, p.3.
CROSSMAN, [not named], W, F, 27 NOV 1893, Alexa. Co., --, 1d, Geo. G. & Nellie, Alexa. Co., Geo. G. Crossman, father, p.56.
CROWLEY, Martha, W, [F], 22 NOV 1854, poor house, intemperance, 40y, -- Crowley, Ireland, John Stephenson, keeper, p.9.
CRUMP, John R., W, M, 6 DEC 1858, Alexa., consumption, 38y, --, Alexa., plasterer, consort of Cannon Crump.
CRYSS, Henry, W, M, 18 AUG 1855, Alexa., bilious fever, 43y, F. & Delia Cryss, Alexa., shoemaker, consort of Jane Cryss, J. Cryss, widow, p.14.
CRYSS, William Henry, W, M, 22 JUN 1855, Alexa., drowned, 15y, H. & J. Cryss, Alexa., J. Cryss, mother, p.14.
CUNNINGHAM, Harry Mc., W, M, 3 APR 1883, Alexa. Co., --, 3m, R.G. & J.A. Cunningham, Alexa. Co., R.G. Cunningham, father, p.44.
CUNNINGHAM, R.G., W, M, 21 JUN 1895, Alexa. Co., shot, --, clerk, Randolph Birch, coroner, p.60.
CUNNINGHAM, Robt. E., W, M, 26 NOV 1892, Alexa. Co., croup, 4y, R.E. & Mary E., Alexa. Co., R.E. Cunningham, father, p.54.
CURLEY, E.S.V., W, F, 14 DEC 1853, Alexa., scarlet fever, 7m, W. & J. Curley, Alexa., W. Curley, father, p.3.
CURREN, Walter, W, M, 1 AUG 1894, Alexa. Co., --, 1m19d, Joseph & Emma, Alexa. Co., Joseph Curren, father, p.58.
CURRY, John E., (f), M, AUG 1884, F. Vill[age], --, 40y, --, Va., single, Marth[a] Wildier, next door neighbor, p.45.
CURTIS, Charles, (f), M, 7 NOV 1884, F. Vill[age], killed, 45y, --, Va., labor, consort of Louisa Curtis, Louisa Curtis, wife, p.45.
CURTIS, Geo., (s) of Frobel's heirs, M, 21 APR 1855, Alexa., [drowned], 34y, slave, Fairfax, C. Neale, coroner, p.14.
CURTIS, [blank], W, F, 15 AUG 1878, Alex. Co., --, 1d, D.C. & Evelyn Curtis, Alexa. Co., D.C. Curtis, father, p.38.
CUSTIS, Laura, (f), F, 15 SEP 1855, Alexa., unknown, 30y, -- & Anna Marrs, Alexa., W. Custis, Lidia Hawkens, friend, p.12.
CUVILLIER, Effie, W, F, 10 SEP 1881, Smithson farm, congestive chill, 7y, Joseph & Mary Cuvillier, Washington D.C., Joseph Cuvillier, father, p.42.
CUVILLIER, Mary J., W, F, 5 OCT 1868, Alexa., summer complaint, 5m, S. & J. Cuvillier, Alexa., none, single, Jane Cuvillier, mother, p.24.

D

DABNEY, James, (f), M, NOV 1895, Alexa. Co., --, 2y, Russell & Mary, Alexa. Co., Mary Darby [sic] mother, p.60.
DABNEY, Mary, (f), F, NOV 1894, Alexa. Co., pneumonia, 2y, Russell & Mary F., Alexa. Co., Mary F. Dabney, mother, p.58.
DADE, George, (f), M, 24 OCT 1883, Alexa. Co., consumption, 2y5m, Peter & Caroline Dade, Alexa. Co., Peter Dade, father, p.44.
DAFFER, Allen, (f), M, MAR 1868, Alexa., old age, 111y [sic], unknown, unknown, none, married, Mariah Thornton, daughter, p.24.
DAISEY, Margaret, W, F, DEC 1854, Alexa., unknown, 11m, R. & M. Daisey, Alexa., Margaret Daisey, mother, p.9.
DAISEY, Roger, W, M, JUL 1854, Alexa., drowned, 48y, W. & B. Daisey, Ireland, consort of M. Daisey, Margaret Daisey, widow, p.9.
DANIELS, Lucy, W, F, 15 AUG 1876, near Carlin Springs, --, 4y, Fenton & Rose Daniels, Alexa. Co., Fenton Daniels, father, p.36.
DARBY, Geo. W., W, M, 12 FEB 1867, Alexa., consumption, 26y, Jas. & Mary E.

Alexandria (Arlington) County, Virginia Death Records, 1853-1896

Darby, --, bricklayer, married, Mary Darby, sister in law, p.22.
DARHORNEY, E.J., W, M, 15 SEP 1856, Alexa., water on brain, 2m, E. & C. Darhorney, Alexa., C. Darhorney, mother, p.8.
DARLEY, Minnie, W, F, 17 NOV 1867, Alexa., croup, 17m, Wm. & Mary Darley, Alexa., none, single, Mary Darley, mother, p.22.
DAUNER, Patsey, (f), F, 12 JUN 1874, Arlington, whooping cough, 30y, --, Dinwiddie, none, p.34.
DAVENPORT, Philis, (f), F, 8 NOV 1896, Warwick [Co.], dropsy, 60y, --, Va., housekeeping, consort of Lewis Davenport, Lewis Davenport, husband, p.62.
DAVENPORT, Wm. D., (f), M, [no date] 1894, Alexa. Co., --, 30y, Lewis & Phillis, Alexa. Co., laborer, Lewis Davenport, father, p.58.
DAVIDSON, Sarah V., W, F, 18 SEP 1853, Alexa., unknown, 3y3m, J. & M. Davidson, Richmond, J. Davidson, father, p.3.
DAVIES, Anna, W, F, 20 APR 1854, Alexa., cholera, 35y, P. & M. Egerson, Scotland, consort of F. Davies, F. Davies, husband, p.9.
DAVIES, Walter E., W, M, 9 MAR 1895, Alexa. Co., --, 6y, Percival & Nellie, Alexa. Co., P. Davies, father, p.60.
DAVIS, Ann, W, F, 8 DEC 1859, Alexa., old age, 70y, --, England, D.M. French, physician.
DAVIS, Augustus, (f), M, 6 JAN 1888, Arlington [Dist.], --, 65y, --, Va., labor, consort of Lucy Davis, Lucy Davis, wife.
DAVIS, Daniel, (s) of Sally Griffith, M, 11 NOV 1856, Alexa., accident, 87y, J. & E. Davis, Westmoreland Co., slave, consort of Betsey Davis, Burns Hall, daughter, p.8.
DAVIS, Florance, (f), F, SEP 1868, Alexa., unknown, unknown, G. & M. Davis, Alexa., none, single, Alfred Coy, friend, p.24.
DAVIS, Inda, (f), F, 26 DEC 1855, poor house, old age, 95y, -- Davis, J. Stephenson, keeper poor house, p.14.
DAVIS, Indiana, (f), F, 13 NOV 1878, near Wm. Gray's, --, 10d, H.W. & Mary F. Davis, near Wm. Gray's, Mary F. Davis, mother, p.38.
DAVIS, Jennette, W, F, 19 JUL 1853, Alexa., catarrh fever, 5m, W. & M. Davis, Alexa., W. Davis, father, p.4.
DAVIS, Julian, W, M, 10 FEB 1858, Alexa., cold, 1m6d, T. & Julian Davis.
DAVIS, T.F., W, M, 9 AUG 1853, Alexa., unknown, 12d, W. & S. Davis, Alexa., S. Davis, mother, p.4.
DAVIS, [blank], (s), F, MAY 1855, Alexa., unknown, 4d, Maria Davis, Alexa., Henry Miffleton, hirer, p.11.
DAVIS, [blank], (s), F, MAY 1855, Alexa., unknown, 4d, Maria Davis, Alexa., Henry Miffleton, hirer, p.11.
DAVIS, [blank], (s), M, MAY 1855, Alexa., unknown, 4d, Maria Davis, Alexa., Henry Miffleton, hirer, p.11.
DAVIS, [blank], W, --, 20 SEP 1857, Alexa., --, Edwd. & Mrs. Davis, Alexa., police officer.
DAW, S.J., W, M, 28 AUG 1855, Fairfax Co., dysentery, 2y, F. & M. Daw, F. Daw, father, p.13.
DAWSON, Thos. B., W, M, 3 JUN 1895, Alexa. Co., old age, 80y, Wm. & Elizth., Md., consort of Elizabeth Dawson, E. Dawson, wife, p.60.
DAWSON, William, W, M, 15 MAR 1859, Alexa., consumption of bow., 16y, Thos. B. & Emily Dawson, Thos. B. Dawson, father.
DAY, Caroline, (f), F, 18 DEC 1867, Alexa., burned to death, 5y, Ellen & Richard Day, Culpeper, none, single, Ellen Day, mother, p.22.
DAY, Henson, W, M, 4 DEC 1859, Alexa., bilious fever, 57y, --, ship carpenter, Jno. Thompson, neighbor.

Alexandria (Arlington) County, Virginia Death Records, 1853-1896

DAY, James Henry, W, M, 24 JUN 1856, New Orleans, consumption, 25y, Hanson & M. Day, Alexa., ship carpenter, H. Day, father, p.8.

DEARBOURN, Mary, W, F, JUL 1854, Alexa., brain affection, 7m, Geo. W. & M.L. Dearbourn, G.W. Dearbourn, father, p.6.

DEBILIN, Edward, W, M, FEB 1868, Potomac River, Alexa., murdered or drowning, 33y, unknown, New York, soldier, single, Jas. T. Burnette, coroner, p.24.

DEEBLE, Elison H., W, M, 27 AUG 1879, Washington Dist., consumption, 22y, Ed. S.K. & Elizth. Deeble, Washington Dist., farming, single, Silas W. Deeble, brother, p.39.

DEEBLE, [blank], W, M, 8 JUL 1857, Alexa., --, 2y, -- Deeble, Alexa.

DEEBLE, [not named], W, M, 16 NOV 1889, Alexa. Co., --, S.W. & Anna Deeble, Va., S.W. Deeble, father, p.51.

DEEGANS, Isabella, W, F, 4 JUL 1854, Alexa., consumption, 33y, unknown, Ireland, B. Deegans, B. Deegans, husband, p.6.

DEEGANS, Mary, W, F, 19 JAN 1854, Alexa., unknown, 6y, B. & J. Deegans, Alexa., B. Deegans, father, p.6.

DEETON, Catherine, W, F, OCT 1856, Alexa., consumption, 50y, -- Edmonds, Westmoreland Co., consort of Richd. Deeton, Mary Deeton, daughter in law, p.8.

DEEVERS, John, W, M, 1 OCT 1853, Alexa., unknown, 5y, C. & M. Davis, Fairfax Co., M. Davis, mother, p.4.

DEMAIN, Jane, W, F, 11 NOV 1859, Alexa., old age, 75y, --, unmarried, W. Price, neighbor.

DEMAIN, Julia, W, F, MAY 1855, Alexa., unknown, 1y2m, John & E. Demain, Alexa., John Demain, father, p.13.

DEMAIN, Julian, W, F, 1 AUG 1858, Alexa., cholera infantum, 2m, Wm. & E. Demain.

DENNIS, John, (f), M, 10 AUG 1879, Arlington Dist., cramp, 40y, --, Va., labor, consort of Maria Dennis, Maria Dennis, wife, p.39.

DEUTERMAN, Edward, W, M, 9 APR 1874, Arlington, asthma, 40y, --, Germany, farmer, p.34.

DEUTERMAN, George, W, M, 22 DEC, Arlington Twp., cramps, 2m, Edward & Emma Deuterman, Arlington, p.33.

DEUTERMAN, Inez O., W, F, 16 OCT 1892, Alexa. Co., typhoid fever, 24y, J.H. & Laura Whitehead, Alexa. Co., housekeeper, consort of E.M. Deuterman, E.M. Deuterman, husband, p.54.

DeVAUGHN, D.B., W, M, JUN 1853, Alexa., s. fever, 15m, S.H. & H.A. DeVaughn, Alexa., S.H. DeVaughn, father, p.1.

DeVAUGHN, Edgar, W, M, 25 JAN 1859, Alexa., consumption, 15y, Wm. H. & Sarah A. DeVaughn, Alexa., Wm. H. Devaughn, father.

DeVAUGHN, Henry Franklin, W, M, FEB 1854, Alexa., brain fever, 1y8m, J.H. & E. DeVaughn, Alexa., J.H. DeVaughn, father, p.6.

DeVAUGHN, J.W., W, M, 14 SEP 1853, Alexa., scarlet, 1y2m, J.T. & J. DeVaughn, Alexa., J.T. DeVaughn, father, p.2.

DeVAUGHN, John T., (f), M, 8 AUG 1892, Alexa. Co., heart failure, 50y, --, Va., laborer, Levi DeVaughn, brother, p.54.

DeVAUGHN, John, W, M, 27 SEP 1867, Washington, D.C., paralysis, 72y, Saml. & Anna DeVaughn, Alexa., shoemaker, married, W.H. DeVaughn, son, p.22.

DeVAUGHN, Joseph T., W, M, 15 SEP 1856, Alexa., lock jaw, 23y, --, R. McCuin, friend, p.15.

DeVAUGHN, Joseph, W, M, 15 SEP 1856, lock jaw, 22y, Harrison Kirk, head of family, p.17.

DeVAUGHN, Nancy A., (f), F, 23 DEC

Alexandria (Arlington) County, Virginia Death Records, 1853-1896

1895, Alexa. Co., heart disease, 60y, --, Va., labor, consort of Joshua DeVaughn, J. DeVaughn, husband, p.60.

DEVERS, Mary, W, F, FEB 1855, Alexa., unknown, 2y, N.H. & M.A.E. Deevers [sic], Fairfax, M.A.E. Davis [sic], mother, p.13.

DEWNEY, Rubie, W, F, [no date] 1894, Fairfax Co., --, 2m24d, Alton J. & Sarah F., Fairfax Co., Sarah F. Dewney, mother, p.58.

DICKSON, Bettie, (f), F, 12 MAY 1876, Alexa., heart disease, 21y, Thos. & Edmonia Dickson, Cumberland Co., housework, single, Edmonia Dickson, mother, p.36.

DIETZ, Catherine, W, F, 14 JUL 1859, Alexa., decline, 61y, --, Germany, consort of Jacob Dietz, Dorathy Dietz, daughter.

DIGGS, Charles, (f), M, 10 AUG 1878, Georgetown Road, --, 10d, Dennis & Cathern Diggs, Georgetown Road, Dennis Diggs, father, p.38.

DIGGS, James, (f), M, 1 SEP 1887, Alexa. Co., rheumatism, 70y, --, labor, consort of Susan Diggs, W.P. Hall, friend, p.49.

DIGGS, James A., (f), M, NOV 1884, near F. Vill[age], thrush, 1y15m, Dennis & Catherine, Alexa. Co., Dennis Diggs, father, p.45.

DIGGS, Joseph, (f), M, 15 OCT 1882, Georgetown Road, thrush, 4m, Dennis & Catherine Diggs, Alexa. Co., Dennis Diggs, father, p.43.

DIGGS, Mary C., (f), F, 15 JUL 1887, Alexa. Co., --, 5m, Dennis & Caroline, Alexa. Co., Dennis Diggs, father, p.49.

DIGGS, Matthews, (f), M, 11 JUL 1882, Georgetown Road, thrush, 1d, Dennis & Catherine Diggs, Alexa. Co., Dennis Diggs, father, p.43.

DIGGS, Rebecca, (f), F, 15 JUL 1881, Georgetown Road, whooping cough, 3m15d, Dennis & Catherine Diggs, Alexa. Co., Dennis Diggs, father, p.42.

DILLON, Catharine, W, F, 13 MAR 1867, Alexa., --, 47y, Mike & Mary A. Brannon, Alexa., housekeeper, married, Ann M. Doran, daughter, p.22.

DIX, Thos., W, M, 11 FEB 1857, Alexa., consumption, 47y, --, Alexa., cooper.

DIXON, Ada G., W, F, DEC 1868, Alexa., water on the brain, 18m, Jno. A. & T.C. Dixon, Alexa., none, single, Jno. A. Dixon, father, p.24.

DIXON, George Chatham, W, M, 24 JUL 1858, Alexa., scarlet fever, 5y3m, John & Fannie Dixon, John A. Dixon, head of family.

DIXON, John J., W, M, 25 NOV 1858, Alexa., measles, 1y6m, John & Fannie Dixon, John A. Dixon, head of family.

DIXON, Julia, (f), F, 21 OCT 1896, Alexa. Co., abscess, 60y, Coleman & Clara, Hanover Co., housekeeping, consort of Albert Dixon, Albert Dixon, husband, p.62.

DIXON, Willm. Morris, W, M, 30 JAN 1865, Alexa., dropsy, 5y3m, John & Fannie, Alexa., mer., single, John Dixon, father, p.19.

DODFREY, Toleman, W, F, 1 MAY 1873, Arlington Twp., old age, 76y, Parker Dodfrey, Mass., farmer, p.33.

DOGAN, Bridget, W, F, 16 SEP 1853, Alexa., unknown, 6y, J. & A. Dogan, Fauquier Co., A. Dogan, mother, p.5.

DOLPHEN, John, W, M, NOV 1858, Alexa., fits, 11m, Wm. H. & Mary E. Dolphen.

DONALDSON, Alfred, W, M, SEP 1854, Alexa., unknown, 58y, A. & E. Donaldson, farmer, Saml. Donaldson, brother, p.9.

DONALDSON, Cleveland, W, M, 30 OCT 1886, Washington Dist., drowned, 2y, Geo. W. & Fanny, Va., G.W. Donaldson, father, p.48.

DONALDSON, Cornelia E., W, F, 24 JUN 1880, Oliver Cox's farm, 3m, W.E. & Mary L. Donaldson, Alexa. Co., W.E. Donaldson, father, p.40.

Alexandria (Arlington) County, Virginia Death Records, 1853-1896

DONALDSON, Earnest, W, M, 10 SEP 1879, Washington Dist., water on the brain, 7m, Henry D. & Cornelia Donaldson, Washington Dist., H.D. Donaldson, father, p.39.

DONALDSON, Elizabeth, W, F, 9 JUL 1885, Alexa. Co., old age, 86y, --, Alexa. Co., widow, Geo. F. Marcey, grandson, p.47.

DONALDSON, Fanny, W, F, 30 OCT 1886, Washington Dist., drowned, 33y, Jas. & Titia Shoter, Va., housework, consort of Geo. W. Donaldson, G.W. Donaldson, husband, p.48.

DONALDSON, H.F., W, M, 26 JUN 1877, Washn. Dist., fall from a tree, 29y, Ella & Robt. H. Donaldson, Va., farmer, unmarried, Webster Donaldson, brother, p.37.

DONALDSON, Jane, W, F, 11 OCT 1855, Alexa., child bed, 42y, J. & Skidmore, Alexa. Co., consort of James Donaldson, J. Donaldson, husband, p.14.

DONALDSON, John, --, [no date] 1896, John & Bell, Alexa. Co., Matilda Donaldson, mother, p.62.

DONALDSON, John, W, M, 19 FEB 1895, Alexa. Co., consumption, 22y, H. Dorsey & Cornelia, Alexa. Co., single, Elizth. Donaldson, sister, p.60.

DONALDSON, Mary, (f), F, 23 OCT 1896, Alexa. Co., --, 1m, Henry & Matilda, Alexa. Co., E.D. Jones, neighbor, p.62.

DONALDSON, Robt. H., W, M, 25 AUG 1884, near. Geo. Reed's, fall, 72y, William & Nancy, Fairfax Co., farmer, widower, W.C. Donaldson, son, p.45.

DONALDSON, Samuel, W, M, 7 JUN 1896, Alexa. Co., rupture, 63y, Sanford & Elizabeth, Va., labor, consort of Emma Donaldson, Emma Donaldson, wife, p.62.

DONALDSON, Stropher, W, M, 30 OCT 1886, Washington Dist., drowned, 3y, Geo. W. & Fanny, Va., G.W. Donaldson, father, p.48.

DORSEY, Benjamin, (f), M, [no date] 1867, Alexa., --, 38y, Nace & Elizh. Dorsey, --, laborer, married, Ursula Dorsey, mother in law, p.22.

DORSEY, Cecelia, (f), F, MAY 1855, Alexa., teething, 5m, -- & S. Dorsey, Julia York, aunt, p.12.

DORSEY, Pearline, (f), F, 9 AUG 1895, Alexa. Co., --, 9y, --, Alexa. Co., H. Dorsey, father, p.60.

DORSEY, Sarah, (f), F, MAR 1855, Alexa., heart disease, 16y, N. & E. Dorsey, Julia York, sister, p.12.

DORSEY, Willie, (f), F, 12 OCT 1886, Washington Dist., --, 13y4m, Hezekiah & Luvenia, Alexa. Co., single, Hezakiah Dorsey, father, p.48.

DORSEY, Wm. H., (f), M, 3 DEC 1879, Washington Dist., --, 7y11m15d, Hezekiah & Lavenia Dorsey, Washington Dist., Hezekiah Dorsey, father, p.39.

DORSEY, [blank], (f), F, 15 JUN 1895, Alexa. Co., --, 2m, Hezekiah & Luvenia, Alexa. Co., --, H. Dorsey, father, p.60.

DORSEY, [not named], (f), F, 15 JUL 1894, Alexa. Co., --, 1m6d, Hezekiah & Livenia, Alexa. Co., H. Dorsey, father, p.58.

DORSEY, [not named], (f), M, 25 NOV 1891, Alexa. Co., --, 1d, Hezekiah & Luvenia, Alexa. Co., H. Dorsey, father, p.53.

DOUGHERTY, Kate S., W, F, 2 FEB 1865, Alexa., brain fever, 14y6m, Margaret & John, New Jersey, U.S. Officer, single, John Dougherty, father, p.19.

DOUGLAS, Anthony, (f), M, 15 JUL 1891, Alexa., diphtheria, 11m, John & Elizabeth, Alexa. Co., Elizabeth Douglas, mother, p.53.

DOUGLAS, Frederick, (f), M, 11 APR 1891, Alexa., --, John & Elizabeth, Alexa. Co., Elizabeth Douglas, mother, p.53.

DOUGLASS, Margaret, W, F, 28 JUN 1856, --, 8m, Jas. S. & H.F. Douglass, James S. Douglass, p.17.

DOUGLASS, Maria, (f), F, AUG 1853,

Alexandria (Arlington) County, Virginia Death Records, 1853-1896

Alexa., consumption, 34y, -- Redman, Alexa., A. Douglass, P. Hopkins, neighbor, p.3.

DOUGLASS, Saml., W, M, 19 JAN 1857.

DOUGLASS, Wm. J., W, M, 25 DEC 1888, Arlington [Dist.], pneumonia, 67y, --, Washington, D.C., farmer, widower, M.F. Douglass, son.

DOVE, Laura S., W, F, 26 OCT 1894, Alexa. Co., consumption, 25y, --, Fairfax Co., housekeeping, consort of C.F. Dove, C.F. Dove, husband, p.58.

DOVE, Lucy, W, F, 8 AUG 1880, Raub's farm, chill, 46y, Henry & Matilda Nally, Md., housework, widow, George Batts, friend, p.40.

DOWELL, Jane, W, F, [no date] 1855, Alexa., spinal affection, 55y, J. & E. Rudd, P. William, J.H. Rudd, brother, p.10.

DOWELL, Jas. E., W, M, 4 FEB 1855, Alexa., consumption, 20y, J. & S. Dowell, P. William Co., machinist, S. Kidwell, mother, p.13.

DOWNEY, Thos., W, M, 6 MAY 1858, Alexa., bronchitis, 2y3m6d, Geo. & Mary.

DOWNS, Mary, W, F, 13 OCT 1858, Alexa., old age, 98y, --, Md., Ezekial Jones.

DOWNS, Mrs. Sarah, W, F, 11 MAR 1859, Alexa., chronic, 62y1m11d, --, Thos. Downs, son.

DROWNS, Ella V., W, F, 14 AUG 1867, Alexa., brain fever, 14m, Jas. & Mary Drowns, Alexa., plasterer, single, Mary Drowns, mother, p.22.

DRUMMOND, Henry, (f), M, 30 AUG 1881, Windsor's yard, had a fall, 1y1m, Henry & Elizth. Drummond, Alexa. Co., Henry Drummond, father, p.42.

DRUMMOND, Henry, (f), M, 1 MAR 1880, Windsor's brickyard, cold, 8m, Henry & Isabella Drummond, Alexa. Co., Henry Drummond, father, p.40.

DRUMMOND, Henry, (f), M, 27 FEB 1892, Alexa. Co., consumption, 48y, --, Md., laborer, consort of Isabella Drummond, Wm. Ford, friend, p.54.

DUCKETT, Richard, W, M, [no date] 1858, --, pauper, John Stephenson.

DUDLEY, Ella, W, F, 15 NOV 1858, Alexa., scarlet fever, 1y9m, Benj. & Mary Dudley, Benj. Dudley.

DUDLEY, James, W, M, 17 JUL 1867, Alexa., rheumatism, 30y, Jas. & Margt. Dudley, Alexa., none, single, Mary Whitemore, sister, p.22.

DUFFEY, Susanna, W, F, 12 JUL 1868, Alexa., consumption, 28y6m1d, S. & A. Duffey, Alexa., none, single, S. Duffey, father, p.24.

DUFFIELD, Sarah, W, F, 5 OCT 1854, Alexa., consumption, 50y, -- Territt, Pa., Dr. H. Duffield, J.E. Newton, son in law, p.9.

DULANEY, Alcy, (s), F, DEC 1855, Alexa., dropsy, 45y, slave, Md., Phillip Dulaney, J.B.T. Perry, master, p.12.

DULANEY, S.B., (f), M, 10 MAY 1855, Alexa., spasms, 1d, H. & C. Dulaney, Alexa., C. Dulaney, mother, p.12.

DUNCAN, Ann, W, F, 21 JUN 1882, Poor House Lane, --, 50y, --, Ireland, housework, consort of James Duncan, James Duncan, husband, p.43.

DUNCAN, James, Jr., W, M, 6 MAY 1882, Poor House Lane, --, 20y9m, James & Ann Duncan, Alexa. City, telegraph operator, single, James Duncan, father, p.43.

DUNCAN, John, W, M, 13 AUG 1896, Alexa. Co., --, 65y, --, Ireland, gardening, consort of Martha Duncan, E.D. Duncan, son, p.62.

DUNCAN, Virginia, W, F, 17 FEB 1854, Alexa., child bed, 28y, -- Blacklock, Alexa., consort of W.A. Duncan, W.A. Duncan, husband, p.7.

DUNCAN, [blank], W, F, 23 OCT 1866, Alexa., unknown, --, Wm. & Isabella Duncan, Alexa., single, Isabella Duncan, mother, p.21.

Alexandria (Arlington) County, Virginia Death Records, 1853-1896

DUTCHER, Jemima, (f), F, 10 SEP 1853, alms house, consumption, 50y, --, unknown, John Stephenson, poor house keeper, p.5.

DUVALL, J.C., W, M, SEP 1853, Alexa., teething, 8m, W. & S. Duvall, Alexa., Sarah Duvall, mother, p.4.

DUVALL, W.M., W, M, 15 AUG 1855, Alexa., unknown, 3y, W. & S. Duvall, Alexa., W. Duvall, father, p.11.

DWYER, Thos. M., W, M, 2 JUL 1894, Alexa. Co., teething, 1y4m, Thos. & Hattie May, Alexa. Co., Thos. Dwyer, father, p.58.

DYE, Alvin, W, M, 26 AUG 1894, Alexa. Co., convulsions, 2y7m, John R. & Margaret A., Alexa. Co., John R. Dye, father, p.58.

DYE, Fannie, W, F, 18 SEP 1873, Washington Twp., brain fever, 8m, Hampton Dye, Washington Twp., farmer, Dr. T.B.J. Frye, p.33.

DYE, Hampton, W, M, 30 SE 1896, Alexa. Co., consumption, 52y10m, Henry & Mary, Alexa. Co., labor, consort of Sarah E. Dye, Mary E. Hembank, daughter, p.62.

DYE, Henry, W, M, [no date] 1854, Alexa., dysentery, 1y6m, H. & J. Dye, Alexa., H. Dye, father, p.9.

DYE, Henry, W, M, 1 JUL 1857.

DYE, John L., W, M, 15 OCT 1879, Washington Dist., --, 2y8m23d, Hampton & Sarah C. Dye, Washington Dist., Hampton Dye, father, p.39.

DYE, Miss, W, F, [no date] 1857.

DYE, Mrs. Ida, W, F, NOV 1875, Alexa. Co., typhoid fever, 60y, mother of H. Dye, p.35.

DYER, Josephine, W, F, 17 JUL 1853, Alexa., sore throat, 7m, J.W. & E. Dyer, Alexa., J.W. Dyer, father, p.4.

DYSON, Margaret, W, F, 30 OCT 1855, Alexa., old age, 67y, J. & M. Davis, Md., consort of Saml. Dyson, J.L. Dyson, son, p.10.

E

EACHES, Mary, W, F, 22 JAN 1858, Alexa., consumption, 25y, Joseph Eaches, consort of F.A. Marbury, F.A. Marbury.

EACHES, William, W, M, 26 FEB 1856, consumption, 25y, --, merchant, Joseph Eaches, p.16.

EASTER, Emlie, (f), M, 24 JAN 1885, Alexa. Co., froze, 23y, --, Va., labor, consort of Winnie Easter, Winnie Easter, wife, p.47.

EASTER, Matilda, (f), F, [no date] 1886, Jefferson Dist., typhoid fever, 1y, Emlie & Winnie, Va., Cyrus Jackson, grandfather, p.48.

EASTER, Matilda, (f), F, FEB 1885, Alexa. Co., --, 3y, Emlie & Winnie Easter, Alexa. Co., Winnie Easter, mother, p.47.

EASTLACK, R.W., W, M, 24 JUL 1853, Alexa., scarlet fever, 7y2m, A.W. & P. Eastlack, Alexa., A.W. Eastlack, father, p.1.

ELDRIDGE, Francis S., W, F, 23 JUL 1856, Alexa., cholera infantum, 11m, M. & S.H. Eldridge, [M. Eldridge, head of family], p.15.

ELDRIDGE, Geo. Howard, W, M, 18 JUN 1858, Alexa., scarlet fever, 5y3m, Manchester & Sybill Eldridge, M. Eldridge.

ELDRIDGE, George M., W, M, --, Alexa., scarlet fever, 5y3m, M. & S.H. Eldridge, J.H. Eldridge.

ELEMS, Rachel, (f), F, 12 MAY 1877, near cemetery, childbirth, 30y, Jane & Adam Richardson, Middlesex Co., housework, consort of Paul Elems, Paul Elems, husband, p.37.

ELLIOTT, Edna M., W, F, 7 NOV 1896, Alexa. Co., --, 6m, Joseph & Anna, Alexa. Co., John E. Elliott, father, p.62.

ELLIOTT, Eliza J., W, F, 15 JAN 1886, Washington Dist., consumption, 19y6m, Chas. W. & Mary Shipman, Va., housework, consort of John Elliott, Chas.

Alexandria (Arlington) County, Virginia Death Records, 1853-1896

W. Shipman, father, p.48.

ELLIOTT, Emma, W, F, AUG 1855, Alexa., dysentery, 2y, J. & J. Elliott, Jefferson Elliott, father, p.13.

ELLIOTT, Emma W., W, F, 20 AUG 1854, Alexa., dysentery, 2y, J. & J. Elliott, Washn. D.C., Ann Elliott, mother, p.9.

ELLIOTT, Wm. L., W, M, 2 FEB 1866, Alexa., consumption, 28y, Joseph & Jane Elliott, Va., laborer, married, Jeff. Elliott, father, p.21.

ELLIS, Susan, W, F, AUG 1855, Alexa., old age, 78y, -- Ellis, Md., -- Ellis, Jas. Dabbs, friend, p.12.

ELLIS, William, W, M, 18 JUN 1853, Alexa., cat. fever, 5m, S. & L.A. Ellis, Alexa., L.A. Ellis, mother, p.4.

EMERSON, Ellen, W, F, 27 FEB 1855, Alexa., pneumonia, 67y, T. & E. Violett, Fairfax Co., W.D. Emmerson, W.C. Emmerson, son, p.10.

EMMERSON, A.E., W, F, 24 MAR 1859, Alexa., dropsy, 60y, --, Alexa., doctress, S.S. Emmerson, stepson.

EMMERSON, Prudence, W, F, 5 JUN 1856, bilious fever, 7y, J.P. & Prudence Emmerson, Alexa., J.P. Emmerson, head of family, p.16.

ENGLAND, Elizabeth, W, F, 23 DEC 1856, Alexa., consumption, 33y, M. & E. Sulevan, Stafford Co., mantra maker, consort of Geo. England, Orpha Treslow, sister, p.8.

ENGLEBRECHT, Chs., W, M, 3 SEP 1854, Alexa., apoplexy, 44y, -- & Elizabeth Englebrecht, Germany, hotel keeper, consort of M.A. Englebrecht, M.A. Englebrecht, widow, p.6.

ENGLISH, Maria Seabury, Alexa., F, 13 DEC 1853, Alexa., pneumonia, 37y, A. & M. Baldwin, Litchfield, Conn., consort of J.A. English, J.A. English, husband, p.1.

ENTWISLE, Emma, W, F, 28 DEC 1855, Alexa., typhoid, 8y, I. & P. Entwisle, Alexa., Isaac Entwisle, father, p.13.

ENTWISLE, James, W, M, 28 JUN 1856, teething, 1y3m, Jas. & Emily, Jas. Entwisle, head of family, p.17.

ENTWISLE, James, W, M, 26 JAN 1856, Alexa., cholera infantum, --, Jas. & Emily M. Entwisle, Alexa., Jas. Entwisle, head of family, p.15.

ENTWISLE, W.B., W, M, 10 DEC 1859, Alexa., fever, 33y, --, Alexa., painter, consort of Mary Entwisle, Mary Entwisle, wife.

ENTWISTLE, Isaac, W, M, 14 JUL 1866, Alexa., infant dyspepsia, --, Jas. & Elizabeth Entwistle, Alexa., apothecary, single, Jas. Entwistle, Jr., brother, p.20.

ESKRIDGE, Caroline, (f), F, DEC 1867, Alexa., old age, 85y, unknown, --, housekeeper, married, Caroline Thornton, daughter, p.22.

ESMAN, Margaret, W, F, SEP 1853, Alexa., scarlet fever, 5y, H.D. & S. Esman, Petersburg, S. Esman, mother, p.5.

EVANS, Charles, W, M, 4 JUN 1873, Arlington Twp., consumption, 35y, --, N.Y., farmer, p.33.

EVANS, James C., (f), M, 28 DEC 1856, Alexa., unknown, 20d, J. & M.F. Evans, Alexa., M.F. Evans, mother, p.8.

EVANS, Minette, W, F, 1 JUN 1858, Alexa., consumption, 30y, consort of Louis Evans, Louis Evans.

EVANS, R.H., W, M, 22 AUG 1854, Alexa., dysentery, 7m, R. & M. Evans, Alexa., M. Evans, mother.

EVERET, Edward, W, M, 2 JUL 1856, Alexa., teething, 11m, Wm. Everet & Virginia, W. Everet, head of family, p.15.

EVERETT, E.D., W, M, 28 FEB 1881, East Falls Church Station, eurycephalous, 70y, S. & T. Everett, Mass., consort of Mary Everett, S.S. Everett, son, p.42.

EVERETT, Walter W., W, M, 13 OCT 1881, East Falls Church Station, --, 5m, S.S. & Emma J. Everett, Alexa. Co., S.S. Everett, father, p.42.

EWELL, [blank], (f), M, DEC 1867, Alexa., --, 7d, A. & N. Ewell, Alexa., none,

Alexandria (Arlington) County, Virginia Death Records, 1853-1896

single, Nancy Ewell, mother, p.24.

F

FADELEY, Ann, W, F, 22 JUL 1854, Alexa., diarrhea, 42y, -- Robinson, Md., consort of Jas. Fadeley, Jas. Fadeley, husband, p.7.

FADELEY, Bailey, W, F, 26 DEC 1858, Alexa., cold from exposure, --, James Fadeley, Jas. Fadeley.

FAIRFAX, Jane D., W, F, 27 OCT 1880, Mt. Ida, --, 40y, Fredk. & H.M. Baker, N.Y., housekeeping, consort of Herbert C. Fairfax, H.M. Baker, mother, p.40.

FANNON, Mary, W, F, 11 OCT 1868, Alexa., consumption, 35y, unknown, Ireland, unknown, consort of Mike Fannon, M. Fannon, husband, p.24.

FARLEY, Martin, W, M, [no date] 1858, --, pauper, John Stephenson.

FARMER, Arthur, (f), M, 16 JUN 1891, Alexa. Co., sun stroke, 2y9m, Jas. & Lucy, Va., Jas. Farmer, father, p.53.

FARMER, Florince, (f), F, DEC 1893, Alexa. Co., consumption, 9y, James & Lucy, Md., James Farmer, father, p.56.

FARRALL, Charles, W, M, 2 APR 1856, cholera infantum, 9m, Nancey & Charles, Charles Farrall, head of family, p.15.

FAUSTER, Jacob, (f), M, 8 MAY 1875, Arlington Mag. Dist., --, 1m3d, Jacob Fauster, Alexa. Co., p.35.

FEBREY, Amanda, W, F, 12 AUG 1882, at J.E. Febrey's, cancer of stomach, 65y, --, Alexa. Co., widow, J.E. Febrey, son, p.43.

FEBREY, Henry W., W, M, 5 MAR 1881, Washington, D.C., cancer, 52y3m, Nicholas & Elizth. Febrey, Alexa. Co., farming, consort of M.A. Febrey, W.N. Febrey, son, p.42.

FEBREY, John E., W, M, 27 MAY 1893, Alexa. Co., cancer of liver, 62y, Nicholas & Belinda, Alexa. Co., farmer, consort of Mary F. Febrey, M.F. Febrey, wife, p.56.

FEBREY, Louis B., W, M, 10 MAR 1894, Wash. D.C., diphtheria, 11y2m, W.N. Febrey, Alexa. Co., W.N. Febrey, father, p.58.

FEBRY, Belinda, W, F, 26 SEP 1858, Alexa., consumption, 63y, --, consort of Nicholas Febry, N. Febry, husband.

FEDDEN, Cath. Frances, W, F, 5 OCT 1865, Alexa., bilious, 38y, Willm. & Nancy, Westmoreland Co., farmer, consort of John Fedden, John Fedden, husband, p.19.

FENLEY, Olivia, W, F, 1 SEP 1859, Alexa., consumption, 64y, --, Jno. C. Chrisman, son in law.

FERGUSON, Blanch A., (f), F, 2 NOV 1887, Alexa. Co., malaria, 4y4m, Robt. E. & Ellen D., Alexa. Co., Robt. E. Ferguson, father, p.49.

FERGUSON, Clarence E., (f), M, 9 APR 1883, Alexa. Co., --, 3y9m, Robert E. & Ellen Ferguson, Fairfax Co., Robt. E. Ferguson, father, p.44.

FERGUSON, John W., W, M, 25 NOV 1856, consumption, 36y, Martha Ferguson, p.17.

FERGUSON, Mary E., (f), F, 7 MAY 1893, Alexa. Co., --, 1m, Robt. E. & Nellie, Alexa. Co., Nellie Ferguson, mother, p.56.

FIELDS, Charles, (f), M, 8 JUL 1894, Alexa. Co., teething, 2y, Daniel & Charity, Alexa. Co., Daniel Fields, father, p.58.

FIELDS, Mary A., W, F, 23 JUL 1894, Alexa. Co., consumption, 77y, Hezakiah & Catherine, Md., widow, J.W. Fields, son, p.58.

FIELDS, Winnie, (f), F, 17 MAY 1866, Alexa., weakness, 32y, Harriet Mills, Culpeper Co., married, Frank Carter, bro. in law, p.20.

FIELDS, [not named], (f), F, SEP 1894, Wash. D.C., --, 6d, Daniel & Charity, Alexa. Co., Daniel Fields, father, p.58.

Alexandria (Arlington) County, Virginia Death Records, 1853-1896

FISH, Alberta, (f), F, SEP 1890, Alexa. Co., --, 4y, H.R. & Margret, Alexa. Co., H.R. Fish, father, p.52.

FISH, Jennie, (f), F, NOV 1886, Washington Dist., --, 52y, --, Alexa. Co., housework, consort of Samuel Fish, Roy Bolden, son in law, p.48.

FISH, Josephine, (f), F, MAR 1894, Alexa. Co., --, 17y, H.R. & Margaret, Alexa. Co., housekeeper, H.R. Fish, father, p.58.

FISH, Sam'l. E., (f), M, JUL 1891, Va., fits, 17y, Henry R. & Margret, Alexa. Co., Margret Fish, mother, p.53.

FISHER, Sarah, (f), F, 27 NOV 1887, Alexa. Co., consumption, 19y, Solomon & Henrietta, Northumberland Co., single, Solomon Fisher, father, p.49.

FISHER, Walter, (f), M, MAY 1895, Alexa. Co., brain fever, 20y, Solomon & Henrietta, Alexa. Co., labor, single, Sol. Fisher, Jr., brother, p.60.

FITZGERALD, Mary, W, F, 2 JAN 1890, Alexa. Co., heart disease, 65y, --, Ireland, household work, consort of Patrick Fitzgerald, P. Fitzgerald, husband, p.52.

FITZPATRICK, Martha D., W, F, 2 APR 1856, consumption, 29y, --, James Fitzpatrick, p.16.

FLEET, Doretha, (f), F, 14 FEB 1896, Alexa. Co., --, 2y6m, Eddie & Mary, Alexa. Co., E.C. Fleet, father, p.62.

FLEET, Dorotha, (f), F, [no date] 1895, Alexa. Co., --, 2y9m, Edward C. & Mary, Alexa. Co., Edward Fleet, father, p.60.

FLEET, Hiram, (f), M, 11 NOV 1875, Jefferson Mag. Dist., --, 13d, Hiram Fleet, Alexa. Co., laborer, p.35.

FLEET, Howard, (f), M, 7 AUG 1896, Alexa. Co., killed, 16y, Harian & Ellen, Alexa. Co., labor, single, Ellen Fleet, mother, p.62.

FLEMING, Ruth, W, F, 22 APR 1855, Alexa., old age, 74y, -- Gibson, Loudoun Co., J. Flemming, R.C. Barton, son in law, p.12.

FLEMMING, M.W., W, F, 20 MAY 1853, Alexa., consumption, 11y, A. & M. Fleming, Alexa., Alcinda Moss, aunt, p.4.

FLETCHER, Ann C., W, F, 5 JUL 1866, Alexa., paralysis, 65y, Jas. & Elizth. Wilson, Alexa., married, E.C. Fletcher, husband, p.20.

FLETCHER, Elizabeth, W, F, 2 SEP 1873, Arlington Twp., consumption, 26y, --, Va., housekeeper, p.33.

FLOOD, F.J., W, M., [no date] 1853, Alexa., unknown, 2d, J. & N. Flood, Alexa., M. Flood, mother, p.4.

FLOOD, Stacy Ann, W, F, 6 JAN 1856, Alexa., constipation on bowels, 7m, John & Stacy Ann, John Flood, head of family, p.15.

FLOYD, Samuel, (f), M, JUL 1882, Frazier's farm, --, 60y, --, Md., labor, widower, Mary Jones, daughter, p.43.

FOLEY, Margaret, W, F, JUL 1853, Alexa., brain fever, 2y, B.R. & M. Foley, Alexa., B.R. Foley, father, p.3.

FOLMER, Chs., W, M, 19 APR 1855, Alexa., unknown, 23y, D. & S. Folmer, Germany, C. Folmer, brother, p.11.

FONES, Bernard, W, M, 3 JUN 1853, Alexa., thrush, 1m, J. & F. Fones, Alexa., F. Fones, mother, p.4.

FONES, Francis, W, M, 1 MAR 1857, Alexa., childbirth, 25y, --, Alexa., John Fones, brother.

FONES, James M., W, M, 14 OCT 1865, Alexa., consumption, 45y, unknown, Westmoreland Co., laborer, widower, John Fones, head family, p.19.

FONES, Laura, W, F, 13 SEP 1868, Alexa., summer complaint, 1y2m, T. & S. Fones, Fairfax Co., none, single, Thomas Fones, father, p.24.

FONES, Nancy, W, F, 24 NOV 1865, Alexa., don't know, 65y, unknown, Richmond, widow, John Fones, son, p.19.

FOOLE, William, W, M, 31 JUL 1856, --, 25y, Frederick Foole, Prince William, p.17.

FORD, E.H., W, M, 28 DEC 1855, Alexa.,

Alexandria (Arlington) County, Virginia Death Records, 1853-1896

whooping cough, 1y2m, J. & M.F. Ford, Josiah Ford, father, p.12.

FORD, French, (f), F, 23 DEC 1858, Alexa., pneumonia, 2y1m, John & Cecelia Ford, John Ford.

FORD, Hester J., W, F, 13 SEP 1853, Alexa., dysentery, 1y3m, J. & M.F. Ford, Alexa., J. Ford, father, p.2.

FORD, Joseph Amile, W, F, 28 AUG 1858, Alexa., scarlet fever, 3y1m, Jos. & Jane E. Ford, Jos. Ford.

FORD, W.F., W, M, 9 APR 1855, Alexa., cong. of brain, 5y, J.W. & J.E. Ford, Chs. Town, S.C., J.W. Ford, father, p.10.

FORNSHILL, John Lewis, W, M, 11 OCT 1858, Alexa., scarlet fever, 3y, John & Ruth Fornshill, John Fornshill.

FORNSHILL, Willie T., W, M, 18 OCT 1858, Alexa., scarlet fever, 5y, John & Ruth Fornshill, John Fornshill.

FORREST, Julia, W, F, MAY 1867, Alexa., suicide by drowning, 39y, unknown, --, housekeeper, *supposed to be married*, Jas. F. Walsh, T.A. Stoutenburg, coroner, p.22.

FOSTER, Francis, W, M, 19 MAY 1855, Alexa., unknown, 35y, stranger, Alexa., C. Neale, coroner, p.14.

FOSTER, Hettie, (f), F, 1 OCT 1881, Georgetown Road, --, 60y, --, Va., widow, Julia Scott, daughter, p.42.

FOSTER, Isaac, (f), M, 1 FEB 1878, Freedmen Village, teething, 2y, Jacob & Ellen Foster, F. Village, Jacob Foster, father, p.38.

FOSTER, Lucy, (f), F, 30 NOV 1885, Alexa. Co., consumption, 19y, Jacob & Ellen Foster, Alexa. Co., single, Jacob Foster, father, p.47.

FOSTER, Virginia, (f), F, 16 SEP 1885, Alexa. Co., diphtheria, 3y, Jacob & Ellen Foster, Alexa. Co., Jacob Foster, father, p.47.

FOSTER, [blank], (f), M, 21 SEP 1880, F. Village, --, 21d, Jacob & Ellen Foster, Alexa. Co., Jacob Foster, father, p.40.

FOUCH, B.W., W, M, SEP 1853, Alexa. bilious dysentery, 13y, A. & E.L. Fouch, Loudoun Co., clerk, H.S.W. Barker, employer, p.2.

FOWLE, Ella Hooe, W, F, 20 AUG 1855, Alexa., bilious fever, 23y, W.H. & E.T. Fowle, Alexa., W.H. Fowle, father, p.14.

FOWLE, George D., W, M, 18 FEB 1866, Alexa., complication, 46y, Wm. & Esther Fowle, Alexa., merchant, married, P.B. Hooe, brother in law, p.21.

FOX, Infant, W, --, 2 OCT 1857, Alexa., cholera infantum, 2m, Patrick & Mrs. Fox, Alexa.

FOY, Monica, W, F, 17 FEB 1857, --, old age, 80y, consort of Patrick Foy.

FRACTIONS, Hampshere, (f), M, 28 OCT 1888, Jefferson [Dist.], paralysis, 70y, Wm. & Nancy, Clarke Co., plasterer, consort of Rachel Fractions, Silvey Jones, daughter.

FRACTIONS, Joseph, (f), M, 9 AUG 1881, Four Mile Run, typhoid fever, 13y, H. & Maria Fractions, Alexa. City, H. Fractions, father, p.42.

FRANCE, M.J., (f), F, 20 APR 1853, alms house, unknown, 38y, -- France, unknown, John Stephenson, poor house keeper, p.5.

FRANCIS, Joseph, W, M, 24 JUL 1858, Alexa., summer complaint, 1y2m, Joseph & Mary Francis, Jos. Francis.

FRANCIS, Mary Ann, W, F, 18 AUG 1867, Alexa., brain fever, 9m, Amanda & Peter Francis, Alexa., none, single, Amanda Frances, mother, p.22.

FRANKLIN, James W., W, M, AUG 1868, Alexa., summer complaint, 7m, J. & M.L. Franklin, Alexa., none, single, Lucinda Jones, grandmother, p.24.

FRANTUM, Chas. E., (f), M, 8 APR 1854, Alexa., whopping cough, 6m, S. & L.A. Frantum, Alexa. Co., M.A. Frantum, sister, p.9.

FRAZIER, Joseph, (f), M, 15 APR 1854, Alexa., pneumonia, 21y, J. & -- Frazier, Alexa., cartman, O. Fairfax, physician,

Alexandria (Arlington) County, Virginia Death Records, 1853-1896

p.10.

FRAZIER, Joseph, (f), M, 20 APR 1858, Alexa., old age, 75y.

FRAZIER, Leticia, (f), F, 23 DEC 1853, Alexa., burnt, 65y, --, Prince Wm. Co., consort of Joseph Frazier, J. Frazier, husband, p.3.

FRAZIER, Parmelia, W, F, 26 SEP 1859, Alexa., decline, 60y, --, Alexa. Co., consort of Anthony Frazier, Anthony Frazier, husband.

FREEMAN, Emily, (f), F, APR 1867, Alexa., --, 8y, Thos. & Sallie Freeman, Rappahannock, none, single, Thos. Freeman, father, p.22.

FREEMAN, John, (f), M, 4 APR 1866, Alexa., cold, 1y, Sallie & Thos. Freeman, Alexa., Thos. Freeman, father, p.21.

FRENCH, Geo. D., W, M, JUL 1853, Alexa., unknown, 2m, G.E. & V.C. French, Alexa., G.E. French, father, p.1.

FRINKS, Aretta, W, F, 28 DEC 1884, near Goings', --, 13y6m, Charles & Sarah C., Fairfax Co., Charles Finks, father, p.45.

FUGITT, Fannie May, W, F, 3 MAR 1859, Alexa., teething, 2y, B.F. & Hattie Fugitt, Alexa., B.F. Fugitt, father.

FUGITT, Francis, W, F, 14 JUN 1854, Alexa., consumption, 25y, H. & J. Emmerson, Fairfax, consort of Benj. Fugitt, B. Fugitt, husband, p.9.

FUGITT, James, W, M, 31 JAN 1856, suddenly, 58y, --, Gazette, p.16.

FUGITT, Joseph, W, M, JUN 1853, Alexa., diarrhea, 2y, B. & F. Fugitt, Alexa., B. Fugitt, father, p.4.

FUGITT, Lewis, W, M, 30 MAR 1866, Alexa., consumption, 8y2m27d, Benj. & Harriet Fugitt, Winchester, Harriet Fugitt, mother, p.21.

FUGITT, Mary, W, F, JUN 1853, Alexa., diarrhea, 4y, B. & F. Fugitt, Alexa., B. Fugitt, father, p.4.

FUGITT, William, W, M, 7 AUG 1853, Alexa., gravel, 80y, G. & H. Fugitt, unknown, laborer, consort of Harriet Fugitt, G. Brooks, son in law, p.3.

G

GADDIS, Mary J., (f), F, 20 MAY 1867, Alexa., consumption, 25y, Mary & Thos. Gaddis, Warrenton, housekeeper, married, Mary Brown, mother in law, p.22.

GAFNEY, Patrick, W, M, 4 MAY 1868, Brown's farm, Alexa. Co., murdered, 32y, unknown, Ireland, farmer, single, F. J. Edelin, coroner, p.24.

GAHAN, James R., W, M, 8 AUG 1853, Alexa., dysentery, 5d, W. & M.A. Gahan, Alexa., M.A. Gahan, mother, p.3.

GAHAN, W.S., W, M, AUG 1856, Alexa., diarrhea, 1m, W. & M. Gahan, Alexa., M. Gahan, mother, p.8.

GAHAN, William A., W, M, 19 AUG 1856, --, 6m14d, Walter & Mary A., Walter Gahan, head of family, p.17.

GAINES, Richard, (f), M, 12 JUL 1879, Jefferson Dist., spasms, 1y, Phillip & Rose Gaines, Jefferson Dist., Phillip Gaines, father, p.39.

GAINES, [blank], (f), F, 28 MAY 1885, Alexa. Co., --, John S. & Charity Gains, Alexa. Co., Charity Gains, mother, p.47.

GALAWAY, Solomon, (f), M, 15 JAN 1880, Rosslyn, croup, 11m, Moses & Leuvenia Galaway, Alexa. Co., Moses Galaway, father, p.40.

GALE, R. Morgan, W, M, 22 APR 1867, Alexa., --, 3m, Jas. & Anna Gale, Alexa., none, single, Anna Gale, mother, p.22.

GALLIGAN, Mike, W, M, 7 FEB 1859, Alexa., intemperance, 47y, --, Ireland, Dr. Maher, physician.

GALLION, Mary, W, F, AUG 1854, Alexa., teething, 1y, J. & E. Gallion, Alexa., J. Gallion, father, p.7.

GARDINER, Nancy, (f), F, 15 SEP 1873, Arlington Twp., croup, 6m, --, Arlington, p.33.

GARDNER, David, (f), M, 20 DEC 1872,

Alexandria (Arlington) County, Virginia Death Records, 1853-1896

Arlington Dist., consumption, 22y, Oliver & Molley, Va., laborer, married, Mary Gardner, wife, p.32.

GARDNER, Patsey, (f), F, 6 JUL 1877, near Ft. Whipple, teething, 3y, Myra & Jos. Gardner, near Ft. Whipple, Jas. Gardner, father, p.37.

GARICK, Patrick, W, M, [no date] 1857, Alexa., congestion [of] brain, 50y, unknown, Ireland, grocer, married.

GARRISON, Lottie A., W, F, 19 OCT 1887, Alexa. Co., brain fever, 6m, --, Va., John N. Garrison, father, p.49.

GARROLL, Elizabeth, W, F, 6 DEC 1855, Alexa., cancer, 46y, -- Conn, Fairfax, Jas. Garroll, J. Garroll, husband, p.12.

GASKIN, Hellen V., (f), F, JUN 1892, Alexa. Co., --, 8m, Henry & Virginia, Alexa. Co., Henry Gaskins, father, p.54.

GASKINS, Ada, (f), F, 6 JAN 1867, Alexa., --, 11y, Frank & Roxana Gaskins, Alexa., none, single, Frank Gaskins, father, p.22.

GASKINS, Adelia, (f), F, 24 MAR 1894, Alexa. Co., catarrh stomach, 5y9m, Henry & Virginia, Alexa. Co., Henry Gaskins, father, p.58.

GASKINS, [blank], (f), F, 21 SEP 1880, near Ft. Strong, --, Kate Gaskins, Alexa. Co., W.H. Lomax, overseer of the poor, p.40.

GASTON, Ann, W, F, 4 SEP 1881, chain bridge, old age, 72y, --, widow, P.C. Harrison, son in law, p.42.

GATES, W., W, M, 1 JAN 1855, Alexa., unknown, 55y, stranger, --, C. Neale, coroner, p.14.

GAVIN, Margaret, W, F, 8 NOV 1856, old age, 79y2m4d, --, p.17.

GEDNEY, S.A., W, F, 26 OCT 1855, Alexa., unknown, 11m, S. & S. Gedney, Alexa., capt. s. boat, S. Gedney, father, p.10.

GEMINY, A. Marion, W, F, 2 AUG 1858, Alexa., scarlet fever, 11y10d, Richard & Margaret Geminy, Alexa., Richard Geminy, father.

GEMINY, Albion, W, M, 18 AUG 1856, cholera infantum, 2m10d, Richard & Margaret, Richard Geminy, p.17.

GEMINY, Albion, W, M, 10 AUG 1857, Alexa., cholera infantum, 2m10d, Richd. & Martha Geminy, Alexa., R. Geminy.

GEMINY, Richard, W, M, 30 SEP 1858, Alexa., scarlet fever, 10m11d, Richard & Margaret Geminy, father.

GENZBERGER, Michael, W, M, 5 JAN 1859, Alexa., scarlet fever, 5y, Leopold & Bettie Genzberger, Alexa., L. Genzberger, father.

GERMAN, A.E., W, F, JUN 1855, Alexa., unknown, 3m, M. & C. German, Alexa., M. German, father, p.10.

GERMAN, Elizabeth, W, F, 1 JAN 1854, Alexa., unknown, 4y, M. & C. German, Alexa., M. German, father, p.6.

GERMAN, Hannah, W, F, 4 JUL 1853, Alexa., dysentery, 4m, M. & C. German, Alexa., C. German, mother, p.3.

GERMAN, John Henry, W, M, 9 OCT 1856, Alexa., cholera infantum, 1m, John & Mary King, Alexa., John King, head of family, p.15.

GERMAN, Mary E., W, F, 30 DEC 1853, Alexa., pneumonia, 6y10m, M. & C. German, Alexa., C. German, mother, p.3.

GHEEN, Mary F., W, F, DEC 1867, Alexa., consumption, 35y, Wm. & Elizh. Gheen, Chester Co., Pa., housekeeper, married, John R. Gheen, father in law, p.22.

GIBSON, Elizabeth, W, F, 10 JUL 1859, Alexa., old age, 99y, --, Alexa., W.S. Peach, nephew.

GIBSON, Herbert L., (f), M, 19 NOV 1894, Alexa. Co., --, 2m7d, Henry & Sarah, Alexa. Co., Sarah Gibson, mother, p.58.

GIBSON, Jefferson W., W, M, 16 MAR 1876, Washington Road, scarlet fever, 1y6m, Wm. & Sarah Gibson, Washn. Road, Sarah Gibson, mother, p.36.

GIBSON, Sarah N., W, F, 25 AUG 1853, Alexa., spleen, 40y, M. & S. Smith, Loudoun, Bro: W. Gibson, A.G. Newton, landlord, p.5.

Alexandria (Arlington) County, Virginia Death Records, 1853-1896

GIBSON, Thomas, (f), M, 14 AUG 1881, Mt. Ida Lane, consumption, 61y, --, Orange C.H., labor, consort of Nancy Gibson, Nancy Gibson, wife, p.42.

GIBSON, [blank], W, M, 20 OCT 1857, Alexa., --, 3y, Dr. Gibson, Alexa., doctor.

GILAND, Margret, W, F, 7 OCT 1887, Alexa., old age, 60y, John N. & Annie E., Alexa. Co., Sam'l. Javins, neighbor, p.49.

GILBERT, Henry, (f), M, 20 OCT 1877, Freedmen's Village, teething, 1y, Catherine Gilbert, Freedmen's Village, Cath. Gilbert, mother, p.37.

GILLAND, John, W, M, 25 APR 1882, Mid Pike, consumption, 70y, --, Ireland, consort of Margret Gilland, Margret Gilland, wife, p.43.

GILROY, Mark, W, M, 14 MAY 1853, Alexa., cholera, 40y, -- Gilroy, Ireland, laborer, M. McCormick, friend, p.4.

GLASSCOCK, Ada, W, F, 29 JUN 1853, Frederick Co., dysentery, 14m, W.R. & A.E. Glasscock, Alexa., W.R. Glasscock, father, p.1.

GLOVER, Elizabeth, W, F, 20 SEP 1855, Alexa., bilious fever, 23y, S. & M. Causin, Alexa. Co., consort of Tho. Glover, T. Glover, husband, p.14.

GLOVER, Joseph H., W, M, 27 OCT 1853, Alexa., typhoid fever, 38y, W. & J. Glover, Va., shoemaker, consort of Jane E. Glover, J.E. Glover, widow, p.4.

GLOVER, [blank], W, M, 13 SEP 1855, Alexa., thrush, 1m, T. & E. Glover, Alexa. Co., T. Glover, father, p.14.

GOGGIN, Michael, W, M, [no date] 1858, --, pauper, John Stephenson.

GOING, Calvin, W, M, 27 AUG 1875, Jefferson Mag. Dist., old age, 80y, consort of Susan Going, Alexa. Co., p.35.

GOING, Carolin, W, F, 16 APR 1875, Jefferson Mag. Dist., croup, --, Cary Goings, Alexa. Co., p.35.

GOING, Edner, W, F, 18 JUL 1880, Mid Pike, --, 2m28d, Carey & Lucy Going, Alexa. Co., Lucy Going, mother, p.40.

GOING, James, W, M, 7 SEP 1890, Alexa. Co., consumption, 58y, Chas. & Jane, Alexa. Co., farming, single, Mrs. Cary Going, sister in law, p.52.

GOINGS, Calvin, W, M, JUL 1853, bilious fever, 17y, -- Goings, Fairfax Co., pump maker, John Hart, employer, p.4.

GOINGS, Earnest, W, M, 28 MAR 1882, Mid Pike, --, 11m, Carey & Lucy Goings, Alexa. Co., Carey Going, father, p.43.

GOINGS, Susan, W, F, 23 MAY 1884, near Mid Pike, old age, 76y, James & Nancy, Alexa. Co., widow, Mrs. Hall, daughter, p.45.

GOINGS, [blank], W, M, 12 SEP 1884, near Mid Pike, --, 1d, John H. & Louisa, Alexa. Co., J.H. Goings, father, p.45.

GOLDMAN, Harrison, (f), M, 26 APR 1882, F. Vill[age], small pox, 35y, Stephen & Kate Goldman, Va., labor, consort of Priscilla Goldman, Priscilla Goldman, wife, p.43.

GOLDMAN, Mary, (f), F, 26 APR 1895, Alexa. Co., consumption, 45y, --, labor, widow, Fanny Goldman, daughter, p.60.

GOLDMAN, Nellie, (f), F, 23 APR 1879, Jefferson Dist., cold, 21d, Harrison & Pricilla Goldman, Jefferson Dist., Harrison Goldman, father, p.39.

GOLDMAN, Step[h]en, (f), M, 2 AUG 1880, Hunter's farm, --, 60y, Abraham, & Sokey Goldman, Richmond Co., labor, consort of Kate Goldman, Stephen Goldman, son, p.40.

GOODHAND, Mary G., W, F, 27 MAY 1856, bilious fever, 16y, --, Nathaniel & Catherine, Alexa., Nathl. Goodhand, head of family, p.16.

GOODRICH, Frank, W, M, 26 MAY 1857, Alexa., 3y.

GOODWIN, James R., W, M, 11 APR 1859, Alexa., consumption, 39y, --, shoemaker, James Patterson, friend.

GOODWIN, James, W, M, 29 AUG 1854, Alexa., unknown 2y, J.R. & M.F. Goodwin, J.R. Goodwin, father, p.6.

Alexandria (Arlington) County, Virginia Death Records, 1853-1896

GORDON, Wm. W., W, M, 25 FEB 1889, Alexa. Co., paralysis, 60y, --, Va., M.E. Gordon, daughter, p.51.

GORHAM, Alice F., W, F, 3 APR 1881, near Nelson, childbirth, 20y, Wm. & Mary E. Gorham, C[harlottes]ville, single, M.E. Gorham, mother, p.42.

GORHAM, Richard, W, M, OCT 1881, Rosslyn, chills, 6m, Alice F. Gorham, Alexa. Co., M.E. Gorham, grandmother, p.42.

GORMAN, Johana, W, F, [no date] 1853, Alexa., cholera, 9y, E. & B. Gorman, Ireland, B. Gorman, mother, p.5.

GORMAN, [blank], W, M, 26 SEP 1857, Alexa., chronic dysentery, 1y, --, Alexa.

GORMOND, Franklin, W, M, JUN 1853, Alexa., scarlet fever, 8m, J. & S. Gormond, Alexa., J. Gormond, father, p.2.

GOSSUM, [blank], W, M, 21 JUL 1857, Alexa., bilious fever, 70y, --, Va., farmer.

GOTT, Ann G., W, F, 16 MAR 1880, near Falls Church, asthma, 68y, Wm. & Rebecca Gordon, Va., widow, Dr. L.E. Gott, son, p.40.

GOTT, Richard, W, M, 16 NOV 1879, Arlington Dist., neuritis, 70y, --, Md., farming, consort of Ann Gott, Dr. L.E. Gott, son, p.39.

GOULD, James, W, M, 1 DEC 1894, Alexa. Co., Bright's disease, 80y, --, England, consort of Jane Gould, Jane Gould, wife, p.58.

GOULDS, Dicey, (f), F, 20 MAY 1881, F. Village, old age, 70y, --, Va., Manda Ray, daughter, p.42.

GOVER, S.P., W, M, 30 MAR 1858, Alexa., dropsy, 39y, --, mail agent, consort of E. Gover, Mrs. Dobey, friend.

GRAMMER, Wm. Henry, W, M, 3 AUG 1858, Alexa., consumption, 19y, G.G. Grammer, Washington, Thomas Maher, physician.

GRANT, [blank], (f), M, 25 NOV 1880, F.E. Corbett's farm, burnt to death, --, Sandy Grant, Alexa. Co., W.H. Lomax, overseer of the poor, p.40.

GRAVET, [blank], (f), M, 17 AUG 1892, Alexa. Co., --, 1d, Alex. & Alice, Alexa. Co., Alice Gravet, mother, p.54.

GRAVETT, Joseph, (f), M, 4 MAY 1893, Alexa. Co., --, 9m, Alex. & Alice, Alexa. Co., Alice Gravett, mother, p.56.

GRAY, Ella, (f), F, 30 OCT 1881, Pimmitt's Run, --, 15y, John & Sarah Gray, Alexa. Co., Sarah Gray, mother, p.42.

GRAY, Emma, (f), F, [no date] 1895, Alexa. Co., --, p.60.

GRAY, Harry, (f), M, 9 JUL 1893, Alexa. Co., cholera infantum, 5m10d, Harry & Martha, Alexa. Co., Harry Gray, father, p.56.

GRAY, Laura, (f), F, 22 DEC 1876, Pleasant View, 50y, --, Va., housework, William Gray, husband, p.36.

GRAY, Nancy Maria, (f), F, MAY 1866, Alexa., dysentery, 11y, Fred & Cecelia Gray, Alexa., laborer, single, Celia Gray, mother, p.21.

GRAY, Peter C., W, M, 20 JUL 1859, Alexa., overdose laudanum, 40y, --, Scotland, watchmaker, Geo. Duffey, friend.

GRAY, Richard H., (f), M, 28 JUN 1877, Pimmitt's Run, shot, 13y, Sarah & John Gray, Washn. Dist., Sarah Gray, mother, p.37.

GRAY, Sarah, (f), F, 28 NOV 1866, Alexa., old age, 82y, unknown, unknown, widow, Jas. Cartwright, son in law, p.20.

GRAY, Selena, (f), F, 11 SEP 1892, Alexa. Co., --, 35y, Thornton & Selena, Alexa. Co., Thornton Gray, father, p.54.

GRAY, William, (f), M, OCT 1853, Alexa., disease of the heart, 48y, Ramy Gray, Alexa., Wm. Gray, nephew, p.4.

GRAY, Wm., (f), M, 11 MAY 1891, near Alexa., bladder trouble, 68y, --, Alexa., butcher, consort of Amanda Gray, A. Peters, nephew, p.53.

GRAY, Dr. Wm. H., W, M, 29 SEP 1890,

Alexandria (Arlington) County, Virginia Death Records, 1853-1896

Alexa. Co., paralysis, 54y, --, Pa., physician, consort of Sarah J. Gray, S.J. Gray, wife, p.52.

GRAYSON, (stranger), W, M, AUG 1857, Alexa., --, Chr. Neal, coroner.

GRAYSON, Walter, (f), M, 14 JUL 1854, poor house, old age, 80y, -- Grayson, unknown, John Stephenson, keeper, p.9.

GREEN, Ann V., W, F, 3 AUG 1853, Alexa., scarlet fever, 2y6m, B. & M. Green, Alexa., B. Green, father, p.1.

GREEN, Annie, (f), F, JUL 1887, Arlington Dist., --, 3y, Benj. & Rose, Alexa. Co., Benj. Green, father, p.48.

GREEN, Emanuel, (f), M, 14 MAR 1892, Alexa. Co., consumption, 15y, Isaac & Mary A., Va., Isaac Green, father, p.54.

GREEN, Frances, (f), F, 28 JAN 1892, Alexa. Co., pneumonia, 54y, --, Va., consort of Harrison Green, H. Green, husband, p.54.

GREEN, George, (f), M, 14 SEP 1887, Alexa. Co., consumption, 38y, --, Alexa. Co., labor, consort of Jennie Green, Jennie Green, wife, p.49.

GREEN, Harding, (f), M, 1 SEP 1873, Arlington Twp., teething, 6m, Francis Green, Arlington, p.33.

GREEN, Hattie, (f), F, AUG 1881, F. Village, --, 1y, Maggie Green, Alexa. Co., J. Crutchfield, grandfather, p.42.

GREEN, Ines, (f), F, 6 JUL 1876, Ft. Berry, colic, 8m, Wm. & Fannie Green, Alex. Co., Wm. Green, father, p.36.

GREEN, J. Carson, W, M, 17 NOV 1855, accidental, 26y, E. & A. Green, merchant, Edwd. Green, father, p.10.

GREEN, James, W, M, 13 NOV 1859, Alexa., unknown, 60y, --, Md., baker, consort of Martha Q. Green, Martha Q. Green, wife.

GREEN, Joseph, (f), M, JUL 1886, Arlington Dist., pneumonia, 1y6m, Benj. & Rose, Alexa. Co., Benj. Green, father, p.48.

GREEN, Julia, (f), F, 3 JUL 1873, Arlington Twp., consumption, 23y, Harrison Green, p.33.

GREEN, Lucy, (f), F, 7 DEC 1887, Alexa. Co., old age, 80y, --, Culpeper, widow, Arth. Green, son, p.49.

GREEN, Marcus W., W, M, 24 MAY 1853, Alexa., cro. croup, 3y, J. & M. Green, Alexa., Mary Sincox, mother, p.2.

GREEN, Margt., W, F, FEB 1867, Alexa., diarrhea, 30y, unknown, Ireland, laborer, married, Hannah Mills, friend, p.22.

GREEN, Marshall, (f), M, APR 1893, Alexa. Co., consumption, 10y, Isaac & Mary, Alexa. Co., Isaac Green, father, p.56.

GREEN, Mary A., (f), F, 8 MAR 1892, Alexa. Co., consumption, 30y, --, Va., consort of Isaac Green, Isaac Green husband, p.54.

GREEN, Mary S., (f), F, 23 MAY 1895, Alexa. Co., consumption, 18y, Isaac & Mary, Alexa. Co., Sarah Schools, aunt, p.60.

GREEN, Richard, (f), M, NOV 1867, Alexa., --, 1y, Richd. & Kitty Green, Alexa., none, single, Richd. Green, father, p.22.

GREEN, Wm., (f), M, FEB 1892, Alexa. Co., killed, 48y, --, Va., laborer, consort of Susan Green, Susan Green, wife, p.54.

GREEN, [not named], (f), F, AUG 1877, Alexa. Co., --, 4d, Wm. & Fannie, Alexa. Co., Wm. Green, father, p.49.

GREENWOOD, Alice, W, F, 10 SEP 1856, Alexa., spine affection, 5y, J. & E. Greenwood, Alexa., Jane Jefferson, aunt, p.8.

GREENWOOD, Eliza, W, F, 30 JUL 1856, Alexa., consumption, 38y, Z. & A.M. Wade, Washn. D.C., consort of James Greenwood, Jane Jefferson, sister, p.8.

GREENWOOD, Grace, W, F, 15 MAR 1856, Alexa., measles, 3y, J. & E. Greenwood, Alexa., Jane Jefferson, aunt, p.8.

GREENWOOD, James, W, M, 13 MAR 1856, Alexa., pneumonia, 44y, -- Greenwood, Alexa., consort of Eliza Greenwood, Jane Jefferson, sister in law,

Alexandria (Arlington) County, Virginia Death Records, 1853-1896

GREER, Chauncey F., W, M, 27 JAN 1886, Arlington Dist., pneumonia, 58y, Wm. & Susan Greer, Wash. D.C., consort of Nancy Greer, Nancy Greer, wife, p.48.

GREGG, Caroline, W, F, 17 SEP 1853, Alexa., typhoid fever, 62y, S. & R. Solomon, England, consort of Joseph Gregg, J. Gregg, husband, p.4.

GREGORY, Marck Nelson, W, M, 17 MAR 1856, cholera infantum, 1y6m7d, Edward A. & E. Gregory, Edward A. Gregory, p.16.

GRETER, Eliza, W, F, DEC 1895, Alexa. Co., old age, 83y, --, Va., widow, H. Thomas, son in law, p.60.

GRIFFEN, John, (f), M, 8 JAN 1894, Alexa. Co., convulsions, 3m, John & Emily, Alexa. Co., John Griffin, father, p.58.

GRIFFIN, Ann R., W, F, 29 AUG 1858, Alexa., scarlet fever, 1y7m, Robt. & Jane Griffin, Alexa., Robt. Griffin.

GRIFFIN, George, --, 1 MAY 1889, Alexa. Co., killed, 20y, Jno. & Emily Griffin, Va., laborer, John Griffin, father, p.51.

GRIFFIN, Herbert, (f), M, 15 JUL 1892, Alexa. Co., consumption, 2y, John & Emily, Alexa. Co., John Griffin, father, p.54.

GRIFFIN, John, (f), M, 23 DEC 1880, Fairfax Co., fits, 4m, John & Emily Griffin, Fairfax Co., John Griffin, father, p.40.

GRIFFIN, John E., (f), M, 28 JAN 1881, near Slater's, congestive chill, 4y, John & Emily Griffin, Alexa. City, John Griffin, father, p.42.

GRIFFIN, Lotta, (f), F, 17 FEB 1883, Alexa. Co., --, 2y, John & Emily Griffin, Alexa. Co., Emily Griffin, mother, p.44.

GRIFFITH, Cathe., W, F, 4 FEB 1859, Alexa., unknown, 47, consort of Rev. Alfred Griffith, Rev. Alfred Griffith, husband.

GRIFFITH, M.S.V., W, F, 27 AUG 1855, Alexa., consumption, 2y6m, J. & E.

Griffin, Alexa., E. Griffin, mother, p.13.

GRIMES, J.R., W, M, 4 MAY 1859, Alexa., consumption, 35y, --, shoemaker, consort of Ellen Travis Grimes, Henry Brown, brother in law.

GRIMES, John F., W, M, 31 DEC 1858, Alexa., consumption, 35y6m, --, consort of Elener Grimes, Elener Grimes, wife.

GRIMES, Maria, (f), F, SEP 1886, Jefferson Dist., diphtheria, 8y, Charles & Alvira, Alexa. Co., Chas. Grimes, father, p.48.

GRIMES, Patrick, W, M, 20 MAY 1855, Alexa., unknown, 54y, A. & N. Grimes, Ireland, labor, S. Grimes, widow, p.13.

GRINDER, [not named], W, M, 23 OCT 1893, Alexa. Co., --, 1d, Richard C. & Della, Wash. D.C., Richard C. Grinder, father, p.56.

GRINNELL, Cornelius, W, M, 13 JUN 1853, Alexa., cholera, 50y, -- Grinnell, unknown, shoemaker, Mary E. Jeffries, daughter, p.3.

GROVE, Mary E., W, F, 7 OCT 1894, Alexa. Co., pneumonia, 43y7m, --, Va., housekeeper, consort of George Grove, Geo. Grove, husband, p.58.

GROVES, Eliza, W, F, 23 AUG 1895, Alexa. Co., congestion of brain, 38y, Wm. & Margt., Ireland, merchant, widow, Maggie Alexander, sister, p.60.

GUNNELL, M.W., W, F, 5 NOV 1856, Alexa., consumption, 4y, R.H. & A.E. Gunnell, Fairfax, M.C. Jackson, gra'mother, p.8.

GUTSHALL, Hezakiah, W, M, 3 MAR 1894, Alexa. Co., paralysis, 65y, --, Rockingham Co., --, Amanda Gutshall, daughter, p.58.

GUY, Benjamin F., W, M, 10 DEC 1856, pneumonia, 7y8m, James & Sarah Guy, Alexa., James Guy, head of family, p.17.

GUY, Mary E., W, F, 14 OCT 1853, Alexa., unknown, 8m, C.H. & H. Guy, Alexa., H. Guy, mother, p.3.

GUY, Minasoti, W, M, [no date] 1857.

GUY, [blank], (f), F, 4 AUG 1880, canal

Alexandria (Arlington) County, Virginia Death Records, 1853-1896

basin, cold, 4m, Anna Guy, Alexa. Co., Emiline Guy, grandmother, p.40.
GWIN, E.G., W, F, 26 OCT 1854, Alexa., croup, 6y, D.S. & F.J.T. Gwin, Madison Co., D.S. Gwin, father, p.9.
GWIN, S.M., W, F, 15 JUN 1854, Alexa., pneumonia, 4y, D.S. & F.J.T. Gwin, Madison Co., D.S. Gwin, father, p.9.
GWINN, George, W, M, 5 AUG 1859, Alexa., dysentery, D.S. & M. Gwinn, Alexa., W.S. Gwinn, father.
GWINN, George, W, M, 10 AUG 1858, Alexa., dysentery, 6y2m, D.S. & T.A. Gwinn, Alexa., D.S. Gwinn.

H

HACKETT, William, W, M, 12 DEC 1854, poor house, consumption, 55y, -- Hackett, Ireland, John Stephenson, keeper, p.10.
HACKLEY, Ella, (f), [F], AUG 1866, Alexa., summer complaint, 1y4m, Jas. & Martha Hackley, Orange Co., laborer, married, Martha Hackley, mother, p.20.
HACKLEY, Ella, (f), F, AUG 1867, Alexa., summer complaint, 1y4m, Jas. & Martha Hackley, Alexa., none, single, Jas. Hackley, father, p.23.
HAGAN, Elizabeth, W, F, 6 APR 1859, Alexa., old age, 78y, --, Dr. Maher, physician.
HAGER, John F., Jr., W, M, 3 FEB 1892, Alexa. Co., killed, 15y, John & Ophelia, Alexa. Co., John F. Hager, Sr., father, p.54.
HALL, Annie T., W, F, 17 NOV 1865, Alexa., fever, 16y, Andrew [sic] & Mary, Fairfax Co., cartman, Geo. H. Hall, father, p.19.
HALL, Bazil, W, M, 15 MAY 1888, Washington [Dist.], old age, 73y, --, Washington, D.C., farmer, consort of Frances A. Hall, Walter Hall, son.
HALL, Bazil, W, M, MAY 1890, Alexa. Co., --, 1m, E.C. & Hatie, Alexa. Co., E.C. Hall, father, p.52.
HALL, Catherine, (f), F, 23 SEP 1877, near Slaters, teething, 1y, Sarah & Cyrus Hall, near Slaters, Cyrus Hall, father, p.37.
HALL, Dianah, W, F, 26 FEB 1856, Alexa., water on brain, 20d, A.J. & N. Hall, Alexa., N. Hall, mother, p.8.
HALL, Frances A., W, F, 10 DEC 1888, Washington [Dist.], pneumonia, 53y, Robt. & Columbia Harrison, Washington, D.C., widow, Walter Hall, son.
HALL, Frances E., W, F, 2 AUG 1855, Alexa., consumption, 4y, T. & J.E. Hall, Alexa., J.E. Hall, mother, p.13.
HALL, Mrs. H.W., W, M, 15 FEB 1856, Alexa., gout, 70y7m, --, Md., consort of Myer J. Hall, J.W. Bryce, head of family, p.15.
HALL, Isaac, (f), M, 19 DEC 1875, Jefferson Mag. Dist., 10d, Cyras Hall, Alexa. Co., p.35.
HALL, John, W, M, 12 NOV 1890, Alexa. Co., hurt, 42y, Wm. & Anna, England, carpenter, consort of Emily Hall, Emily Hall, wife, p.52.
HALL, Joseph, (f), M, 8 NOV 1896, Alexa. Co., --, 1y8m8d, Wm. & Sarah, Alexa. Co., Sarah Hill [sic], mother, p.62.
HALL, Joseph, W, M, 7 NOV 1867, Alexa., --, 10d, Geo. W. & Martha A. Hall, Alexa., none, single, Martha A. Hall, mother, p.23.
HALL, M., W, M, JUL 1857, Alexa., drowned, 30y, --, N.Y., organist, Gazette.
HALL, M.A., W, F, 23 JUL 1856, Alexa., unknown, 1m, M. & A. Hall, Alexa., A. Hall, father, p.8.
HALL, Robert, W, M, 2 DEC 1853, Alexa., old age, 75y, J. & W. Hall, Alexa., merchant, Ann H. Hall, daughter, p.1.
HALL, Rozie, W, M, JUN 1889, Alexa. Co., --, 18d, E.C. & K.A. Hall, Va., Eli Hall, father, p.51.
HALL, Samuel, W, M, 3 JUL 1856, Alexa., consumption, 19y, Peter & Susan Hall, Alexa., shoemaker, Rebecca Lawson,

Alexandria (Arlington) County, Virginia Death Records, 1853-1896

cousin, p.8.

HALL, Selina, W, F, [no date] 1857.

HALL, Temp, W, M, 12 SEP 1855, Alexa., unknown, 33y, J. & M. Hall, Fairfax, shoemaker, consort of J.E. Hall, J.E. Hall, widow, p.13.

HALL, [blank], W, F, SEP 1866, Alexa., unknown, --, Geo. & Martha Hall, Alexa., single, Geo. Hall, father, p.21.

HALLOWELL, Thomas R., W, M, [3 APR] 1855, Alexa., croup, 10m, C.S. & A.R. Hallowell, Alexa., C.S. Hallowell, father, p.11.

HALLS, Isiah, (f), M, 15 DEC 1874, near poor house, spasms, 9d, Syrus & Sarah Halls, Caroline Co., laborer, married, Sarah Halls, head of family, p.34.

HAM, Annie, (f), F, 15 FEB 1879, Jefferson Dist., croup, 4m15d, --, Jefferson Dist., Mary Ham, mother, p.39.

HAMERSON, Abraham, (f), M, 24 MAY 1895, Alexa. Co., heart disease, 76y, --, Alexa. Co., labor, consort of Harriet Hamerson, H. Hamerson, wife, p.60.

HAMILL, Geo. Wash., W, M, 6 AUG 1858, Alexa., scarlet fever, 3y6m20d, Patr. & Bridget Hamill, Alexa., Susannah, Patrick Hamill.

HAMILL, Lucy Ann, W, F, 27 AUG 1858, Alexa., --, 6m, Patr. & Bridget Hamill, Patrick Hamill.

HAMILL, Margret E., W, F, 12 AUG 1858, Alexa., scarlet fever, 1y6m20d, Patr. & Bridget Hamill, Patrick Hamill.

HAMILTON, Amanda, W, F, 30 NOV 1853, Alexa., inflam. rheuma., 19y, -- Hamilton, Fairfax Co., E. Norris, employer, p.3.

HAMILTON, George, (f), M, 11 JAN 1867, Alexa., found dead natural cause, 52y, unknown, unknown, laborer, married, Jas. T. Walsh, T.A. Stoutenburg, cor., p.22.

HAMILTON, Jonas, (f), M, 4 AUG 1855, Alexa., consumption, 53y, P. & C. Hamilton, Fairfax, consort of Maria Hamilton, Milly Triplett, sister, p.12.

HAMILTON, Maria, (f), F, 1 AUG 1853, Alexa., consumption, 44y, -- Taylor, Alexa., washing, consort of Jonas Hamilton, J. Hamilton, husband, p.3.

HAMILTON, Willie H., W, M, 10 MAR 1853, scarlet fever, 4y10m, H.H. & M.S. Hamilton, Middleburg, M.S. Hamilton, mother, p.1.

HAMMELL, Arthur, W, M, 18 SEP 1855, Alexa., poison, 24y, P. & M. Hammell, Ireland, carpenter, M. Hammell, H. Hammell, brother, p.10.

HAMMELL, Arthur, W, M, 15 OCT 1855, Alexa., suicide [poison], 21y, R. & M. Hammell, Ireland, Mary Quirk, sister, p.13.

HAMMILL, Mary A., W, F, 15 JUL 1868, Alexa., summer complaint, 1m, P. & E. Hammill, Alexa., none, single, P. Hammill, father, p.25.

HAMMOND, Ann, W, F, [16] SEP 1866, Mt. Ida, near Alexa., unknown, 60y, unknown, Shepherdstown, married, E.J. Lloyd, friend, p.21.

HAMPSON, Joseph, W, M, 20 SEP 1854, poor house, unknown, 45y, -- Hampson, unknown, John Stephenson, keeper, p.9.

HANCOCK, James, W, M, 31 JUL 1853, alms house, dysentery, 55y, -- Hancock, unknown, laborer, John Stephenson, poor house keeper, p.5.

HANCOCK, Mary, W, F, 25 JAN 1866, Alexa., paralysis, 67y, John & Mary Hall, unknown, married, John B. Hancock, husband, p.20.

HANDERHAM, Mike, W, M, 3 OCT 1859, Alexa., bilious fever, 43y, --, Ireland, laborer, Dr. D.M. French, physician.

HANDY, Selernetta, (f), F, 10 AUG 1896, Alexa. Co., --, 8m, Thos. & Hannah, Alexa. Co., Hanah Handy, mother, p.62.

HANNESTY, John, W, M, 19 MAY 1855, Alexa., unknown, 35y, stranger, Alexa., C. Neale, coroner, p.14.

HANTZMAN, Ella, W, F, 3 OCT 1858, Alexa., scarlet fever, 8m, Robt. & Mary Hantzman, Robt. Hantzman.

Alexandria (Arlington) County, Virginia Death Records, 1853-1896

HANTZMAN, Ida, W, F, 1 AUG 1859, Alexa., whooping cough, 3y, W.H. & M. Hantzman, Alexa., M. Hantzman, mother.

HANTZMAN, Jas. Lee, W, M, 2 JUN 1867, --, congestion of brain, 1y, Mary J. & Wm. H. Hantzman, Alexa., none, single, Wm. Hantzman, father, p.23.

HANTZMON, James Lee, W, M, 3 JUL 1865, Alexa., brain disease, 1y, Willm. H. & Mary Jane, Baltimore, gas fitter, single, W.H. Hantzmon, father, p.19.

HANZNAN, Wm. H., W, M, 14 JUL 1856, Alexa., unknown, 7d, H.W. & M.F. Hanznan, Alexa., M.J. Hanznan, mother, p.8.

HARCUM, Robt. J., (f), M, 15 JUN 1876, Georgetown Road, typhus fever, 3y, Wm. & Harriet Harcum, Georgetown Road, Wm. Harcum, father, p.36.

HARDEN, L.B., W, M, 18 MAR 1858, Alexa. Co., consumption, 47y, --, Washington, clerk & farmer, consort of S. Hooe Harden, B. Hummer, overseer.

HARGROVE, John G., W, M, 28 NOV 1856, --, p.17.

HARLOW, John, W, M, 16 FEB 1867, Alexa., --, John & Rosa Harlow, Alexa., none, single, John Harlow, father, p.23.

HARLOW, Mary F., W, F, 19 AUG 1867, Alexa., --, 5d, Geo. H. & Sallie Harlow, Alexa., none, single, Sallie Harlow, mother, p.22.

HARPER, Norris, (f), M, MAY 1853, Alexa., pneumonia, 2y, T. & R. Harper, Alexa., R. Harper, mother, p.4.

HARPER, William, (f), M, MAY 1853, Alexa., pneumonia, 7m, T. & R. Harper, Alexa., R. Harper, mother, p.4.

HARRIS, Ben, (f), M, 4 DEC 1854, poor house, consumption, 45y, -- Harris, Alexa., John Stephenson, p.9.

HARRIS, Charlotte, (f), F, SEP 1866, Alexa., pleurisy, 50y, unknown, Madison Co., laborer, married, David Hyden, friend, p.21.

HARRIS, Della, (f), F, 20 APR 1896, Alexa. Co., --, 4m, Minor S. & Nancy, Alexa. Co., M.S. Jackson, father, p.62.

HARRIS, Emma, (f), F, 16 JUL 1866, Alexa., whooping cough, 9y, Thos. & Adeline Harris, Alexa., laborer, single, Adeline Harris, mother, p.21.

HARRIS, Fannie, (f), F, 28 JAN 1872, Arlington Dist., spasms, 4d, Farmer [sic] & Martha, Arlington, laborer, Sam'l. Harris, father, p.32.

HARRIS, George, W, M, 16 AUG 1858, Alexa., scarlet fever, 1y6m, Wm. & Mary Harris, Wm. Harris, father.

HARRIS, John, (f), M, 8 JAN 1873, Arlington Twp., croup, 8d, Farmer & Mary Harris, Arlington, p.33.

HARRIS, John, (f), M, NOV 1875, Arlington Mag. Dist., --, 7y, Farmer Harris, Alexa. Co., p.35.

HARRIS, Lucy, (f), F, 4 SEP 1877, canal basin, sore throat, 2y, Adline & Thos. Harris, near canal basin, Adline Harris, mother, p.37.

HARRIS, Maria, (f), F, 1 MAY 1876, Preston farm, 1d, -- & Millie Harris, Preston farm, Millie Harris, mother, p.36.

HARRIS, Rebecca J., (f), F, AUG 1867, Alexa., chills, 15m, Fanny & Henry Harris, Madison [Co.], none, single, Mary Bolden, friend, p.23.

HARRIS, Rosetta, (s), F, DEC 1855, Alexa., hectic fever, 35y, -- Harris, P. William, slave, C.L. Richards, master, p.10.

HARRIS, Samuel, (f), M, 29 JUN 1876, Freedmen's Village, mortification, 4m, Farmer & Martha, Freedmen's Village, Farmer Harris, father, p.36.

HARRIS, Samuel, (f), M, DEC 1875, Arlington Mag. Dist., --, 8y, Farmer Harris, Alexa. Co., p.35.

HARRIS, Solomon, (f), M, [no date] 1893, Alexa. Co., consumption, 40y, Austin & Lucy, King & Queen Co., consort of Jane Harris, Jane Harris, wife, p.56.

HARRIS, Thomas, (f), M, 4 AUG 1879, Jefferson Dist., sun struck, 50y, --,

Alexandria (Arlington) County, Virginia Death Records, 1853-1896

Culpeper, labor, consort of Adline Harris, Albert Montague, next door neighbor, p.39.

HARRIS, William, W, M, 20 SEP 1867, Alexa., summer complaint, 1y, Marg't. & Moses Harris, Washington, none, single, Marg't. Harris, mother, p.23.

HARRISON, Benj., W, M, NOV 1854, Alexa., intemperance, 47y, -- Harrison, Alexa., carpenter, consort of Lucy Harrison, L. Harrison, widow, p.9.

HARRISON, Jennie, W, F, 25 SEP 1896, Alexa. Co., heart disease, 24y, Lewis Shelhorn, N.J. or Pa., housekeeping, consort of Chas. E. Harrison, F.H. Harrison, father in law, and Chas. Harrison, husband, p.62 (2 entries same page).

HARRISON, Jennie, W, F, 18 JUL 1896, Alexa. Co., --, 1y, Chas. E. & Jennie, Alexa. Co., Chas. Harrison, father, p.62.

HARRISON, Peter A., W, M, 28 AUG 1881, chain bridge, --, 4y7m, Peter C. & Mary Harrison, Md., Peter C. Harrison, father, p.42.

HARRISON, Robert, W, M, 18 NOV 1873, Washington Twp., consumption, 65y, William Harrison, farmer, Dr. T.B.J. Frye, p.33.

HARRISON, Thos. S., W, M, 30 JUL 1859, Alexa., bowel complaint, 9m14d, G.W. & V.B. Harrison, Alexa., V.B. Harrison, mother.

HARROLD, David, (f), M, JUN 1893, Alexa. Co., old age, 90y, --, Thornton Hyatt, keeper of Poor House, p.56.

HART, A.O., W, M, 17 NOV 1856, Alexa., typhoid fever, 21y1m, --, Alexa., M.D., single, Wm. A. Hart, head of family, p.15.

HART, Conway, (f), M, 22 MAR 1889, Alexa. Co., consumption, 60y, --, Va., laborer, M. Hart, wife, p.51.

HART, Florence, (f), F, 16 JAN 1877, Washington, D.C., burnt to death, 17y, Mildred & Conway Hart, Va., housework, unmarried, Conway Hart, father, p.37.

HART, John B., W, M, 11 AUG 1853, Alexa., consumption, 52y, A. & E. Hart, Albemarle Co., merchant, W.A. Hart, son, p.1.

HART, Margret, F, 22 FEB 1880, near Ft. Craig, hemorrhage, 28y, Conway & Mildred Hart, Va., housework, single, Conway Hart, father, p.40.

HART, Michael, W, M, 18 NOV 1884, near Slater's, --, 46y, --, Ireland, clerk, consort of Bridget F. Hart, Fredk. W. Hart, nephew, p.45.

HART, Mildred (f), F, 11 FEB 1892, Alexa. Co., --, 54y, --, widow, Minnie Green, daughter, p.54.

HASKINS, John Henry, (f), M, 20 JUL 1866, Alexa., summer complaint, 1m14d, Chas. & Mary Haskins, Alexa., Mary Haskins, mother, p.21.

HASKINS, [blank], W, F, OCT 1866, thrush, 9d, Geo. & Candia Haskins, Alexa., single, Geo. Haskins, father, p.21.

HATCH, L.W., W, M, 6 NOV 1886, Jefferson Dist., suicide, 40y, Harvey & Harriet, N.Y., farming, consort of Catherine Hatch, W.H. Hatch, brother, p.48.

HAULS, Albermia, (f), M, 16 FEB 1892, Alexa. Co., grip, 1y4m, Cyrus & Sarah, Alexa. Co., Sarah Hauls, mother, p.54.

HAULS, Cyrus, Jr., (f), M, 21 JAN 1885, Alexa. Co., whopping cough, 7y, Cyrus & Sarah, Alexa. Co., Sarah Hauls, mother, p.47.

HAULS, Emily B., (f), F, 10 JAN 1885, Alexa. Co., brain fever, 5y, Cyrus & Sarah, Alexa. Co., Sarah Hauls, mother, p.47.

HAULS, George, Jr., (f), M, 20 JUN 1879, Jefferson Dist., --, 1y5m, George & Mildred Hauls, Alexa. City, Geo. Hauls, father, p.39.

HAULS, James E., (f), M, 19 FEB 1884, near Slater's, --, 2y8m, Cyrus & Sarah, Alexa. Co., Cyrus Hauls, father, p.45.

Alexandria (Arlington) County, Virginia Death Records, 1853-1896

HAULS, Lulla, (f), F, 26 MAY 1887, Alexa. Co., teething, 1y1m2d, Cyrus & Sarah, Alexa. Co., Cyrus Hauls, father, p.49.

HAULS, Maurice, (f), F, 17 SEP 1880, Poor House Lane, teething, 11m4d, George & Millie Hauls, Alexa. Co., George Hauls, father, p.40.

HAULS, Molly, (f), F, 3 APR 1893, Alexa. Co., grip, 19y, Cyrus & Sarah, Alexa. Co., single, Cyrus Hauls, father, p.56.

HAULS, Oliver, (f), M, 9 SEP 1890, Alexa. Co., pneumonia, 1y9m, Cyrus & Sarah, Alexa. Co., labor, Cyrus Hauls, father, p.52.

HAULS, Walker, (f), M, 19 JAN 1885, Alexa. Co., whooping cough, 2y, Cyrus & Sarah, Alexa. Co., Sarah Hauls, mother, p.47.

HAVENER, Lilly, W, F, 10 JAN 1877, Washington Dist., teething, 8m, Ma[r]tha & Wesley Heaverner [sic], Washn. Dist., Martha Haverner, mother, p.37.

HAVENER, Mason, W, M, 23 OCT 1886, Washington Dist., --, 1y9m, Wesley & Martha, Alexa. Co., Wesley Havener, father, p.48.

HAVENER, [blank], W, F, OCT 1896, Alexa. Co., --, 6m, Wesley & Martha, Alexa. Co., Wesley Havener, father, p.62.

HAWES, Isaac F., W, M, 8 AUG 1894, Alexa. Co., heart disease, 52y, Thos. & Annie, Va., laborer, consort of Mary Hawes, W.H. Hawes, cousin, p.58.

HAWKINS, Wm., (f), M, [no date] 1890, Alexa. Co., killed by cars, 53y, --, Md., H. Drummond, neighbor, p.52.

HAWKINS, [blank], (s), F, NOV 1855, Alexa., intermittent, 1m, T. & M. Haskins [sic], Alexa., A.H. Toulson, master, p.13.

HAYES, Alonzo R., W, M, 3 FEB 1884, near Ballston, stomach trouble, 4m, Alonzo G. & Mary, Alexa. Co., A.G. Hayes, father, p.45.

HAYES, Conn Washington, W, M, 11 FEB 1856, scarlet fever, 2y2m1d, Winfred & Ann Hayes, Winfred Hays, p.16.

HAYES, Etta M., W, F, 6 DEC 1895, Alexa. Co., consumption, 38y, --, housekeeping, consort of W. Douglass Hayes, W.D. Hayes, husband, p.60.

HAYES, James Nathaniel, W, M, 9 FEB 1856, scarlet fever, 21m16d, Winfred & Ann Hayes, Winfred Hays, p.16.

HAYES, Julia, W, F, JUL 1867, Alexa., summer complaint, 27d, Jere. & Johanna Hayes, Alexa., none, single, Johanna Hayes, mother, p.23.

HAYES, Mary C., W, F, JUL 1867, Alexa., summer complaint, 21d, Jere. & Johanna Hayes, Alexa., none, single, Johanna Hayes, mother, p.23.

HAYMAN, George, (f), M, MAR 1892, Alexa. Co., shot, 21y, John & Bettie, Va., laborer, single, Andrew Hayman, brother, p.54.

HAYNES, Mary, W, F, 5 OCT 1875, Jefferson Mag. Dist., summer sickness, 5m2d, Patrick Haynes, Alexa. Co., p.35.

HAYNIE, Eliza, W, F, MAY 1853, Alexa., brain fever, 14y, H. & W. Haynie, Northumberland Co., Va., H. Haynie, father, p.4.

HAYNIE, Jerome, W, M, JUL 1853, Alexa., dysentery, 11m, H. & W. Haynie, Northumberland Co., Va., H. Haynie, father, p.4.

HEARD, Alex., (f), M, FEB 1868, Alexa., unknown, 60y, unknown, Va., laborer, widower, Col. L.P. Lee, coroner, p.25.

HEILMAN, J.G., W, M, 26 MAY 1857, Alexa., --, Chr. Neal, coroner.

HEINBUCH, Rachel, W, F, 22 JAN 1894, Alexa. Co., --, 6d, J.C. & Mary E., Alexa. Co., J.C. Heinbuch, father, p.58.

HELMREN, A.W., W, F, 3 OCT 1895, Alexa. Co., consumption, 24y, H.H. & J.S., Wash. D.C., engraver, single, A.C. Ruebsam, brother in law, p.60.

HENDERSON, Emma, W, F, 7 JUN 1857, Alexa., teething, 1y, Euell & Julia, Alexa.

HENDERSON, John, W, M, AUG 1855, Alexa., unknown, 5m, J. & M.

Alexandria (Arlington) County, Virginia Death Records, 1853-1896

Henderson, Alexa., J. Henderson, father, p.11.

HENDERSON, Mary, W, F, 9 SEP 1859, Alexa., consumption, 22y, --, Alexa., Rose Harper, head of family.

HENDERSON, Parrie, (f), M, NOV 1867, Alexa., --, 6m, Geo. L. & Georgia Henderson, Alexa., none, married, Chloe A. Violett, friend, p.23.

HENDERSON, Rachel, (f), F, 28 SEP 1876, Washington, D.C., consumption, 20y, Allen & Nancy Henderson, Prince Geo. Co. Md., housework, Cornelius West, brother in law, p.36.

HENDERSON, Ruth, W, F, 5 JUL 1865, Alexa., fever, 1m, Georgianna & George, Alexa., bricklayer, single, Geo. Henderson, father, p.19.

HENRIETTA, Thos., W, M, 12 AUG 1859, Alexa., killed on railroad, 30y, --, Ireland, laborer, Dr. C.W. Chancellor, coroner.

HENRY, A.A., W, M, 7 JUN 1855, Alexa., water on the brain, 4m, R. & A. Henry, Alexa., R. Henry, father, p.11.

HENRY, Geo. A., (f), M, 5 FEB 1853, Alexa. Co., scarlet fever, 13y, G. & S. Henry, Fairfax, Guy Henry, father, p.5.

HENRY, Guy B., (f), M, 12 APR 1890, Alexa. Co., abscess, 35y, Guy & Sarah, Alexa. Co., labor, widower, Mary Scott, sister, p.52.

HENRY, Kate, (f), F, 1 MAY 1884, near Col. Pike, consumption, 26y, --, Orange Co., consort of Guy B. Henry, G.B. Henry, husband, p.45.

HENRY, Margaret E., W, F, 6 APR 1895, Alexa. Co., heart disease, 76y, --, widow, M.C. Mitchell, son, p.60.

HENSON, [not named], W, M, JUL 1893, Alexa. Co., cholera infantum, 6m, H.S. & Emma, Alexa. Co., H.S. Henson, father, p.56.

HEPBURN, Francis, W, F, 14 JUN 1858, Alexa., childbirth, 21y, --, Alexa., consort of James Hepburn, James Hepburn, husband.

HERBERT, Mrs., W, F, JUL 1867, Alexa., --, 25y, unknown stranger, Alexa., housekeeper, married, Lucy McIntosh, friend, p.23.

HERBERT, Sally, (s), F, SEP 1855, Alexa., child bed, 19y, slave, Fairfax, W.B. Scarce, owner, p.12.

HERRICK, Mary Catherine, W, F, 11 JUN 1865, Alexa., diphtheria, 2y3m, Wm. T. & Catherine, Tennessee, N.Y. and Alexa., saddler, single, Wm. T. Herrick, father, p.19.

HEWES, Deborah, W, F, 27 APR 1856, old age, 85y, --, Deborah Stabler, p.16.

HEWES, Thos., (f), M, 11 DEC 1868, Alexa., consumption, 2y1m2d, Wm. & A. Hewes, Alexa., none, single, Annie Hewes, mother, p.25.

HEWITT, Frank, W, M, NOV 1867, Alexa., --, 18y, Wm. & Jane Hewitt, Fauquier Co., laborer, single, Mary Armstrong, friend, p.23.

HEWITT, Margaret Boyd, W, F, 24 MAY 1854, Alexa., apoplexy, 56y, A.J. & S. Smith, Alexa., T.W. Hewitt, R.J. Smith, brother, p.9.

HEWS, David, (f), M, JUL 1855, Alexa., old age, 75y, D. & -- Hews, consort of Maria Hews, M. Hewes, widow, p.12.

HEYMES, Catharine, W, F, 16 DEC 1856, consumption, 39y, --, grocer, consort of John Heymes, housekeeper, p.17.

HEYMES, John, W, M, 15 OCT 1856, --, p.17.

HIGDEN, John L., W, M, 11 DEC 1855, Alexa., infla. of liver, 5y, J.H. & M.A. Higden, J.H. Higden, father, p.10.

HIGDON, J.H., W, M, 31 DEC 1859, Alexa., bilious diarrhea, 38y, --, tailor, consort of Mary Ann Higdon, J.W. Higdon, brother.

HIGDON, Julia, W, F, 18 JAN 1858, Alexa., overdose laudanum, 30y, consort of J.W. Higdon, J.W. Higdon, husband.

HIGDON, Rebecca, W, F, 16 FEB 1867, Alexa., pleurisy, 76y, Wm. & Hannah

Alexandria (Arlington) County, Virginia Death Records, 1853-1896

Reynolds, Alexa., housekeeper, married, Wm. E. Atwell, friend, p.23.
HILES, Isabella, W, F, [no date] 1858, Alexa., old age, 83y.
HILL, A.W., W, M, 25 OCT 1879, Arlington Dist., [ty]phoid fever, 14y, E.J. & Sarah R. Hill, Md., E.J. Hill, father, p.39.
HILL, Jabus, (f), M, 21 JUL 1879, Washington Dist., --, 1y3m22d, Chas. & Kate Hill, Washington Dist., Kate Hill, mother, p.39.
HILL, Kate, (f), F, SEP 1881, Sissonville, heart disease, 28y, --, consort of Charles Hill, Lucy Hill, mother in law, p.42.
HILL, Spencer, (f), M, [no date] 1881, Sissonville, --, 2y, Chas. & Kate Hill, Alexa. Co., Lucy Hill, grandmother, p.42.
HILL, W.E., W, M, OCT 1858, Alexa., cholera infantum, 9m, J.T. & E. Hill, J.T. Hill, father, p.10.
HILLERY, Alice, W, F, 19 JAN 1891, Alexa. Co., pneumonia, 24y6m, J.W. & Mary Hillery, Alexa., single, J.W. Hillery, father, p.53.
HILLERY, Irene, W, F, [no date] 1858, Alexa., diarrhea, 2y3m, Theodore & Verlinda Hillery, Theodore Hillery.
HILLERY, Theodore, W, M, [no date] 1858, Alexa., convulsions, 5y, Theodore & Verlinda Hillery, Theodore Hillery.
HINDELLS, G.L., W, M, 26 SEP 1868, Alexa., consumption, 20m, Wm. & M.C. Hindells, Alexa., none, single, M.A. Hindells, mother, p.25.
HINES, Benj., (f), M, 20 FEB 1896, Alexa. Co., killed, 28y, Benj. & Frances, Alexa. Co., labor, consort of Georgia Hines, Grant Hines, brother, p.62.
HINES, G., (f), M, DEC 1895, Alexa. Co., consumption, 17y, Benj. & Fanny, Alexa. Co., labor, single, Benj. Hines, father, p.60.
HINKIN, Geo. H., W, M, 2 FEB 1866, Alexa., lung disease, 2y9m, Geo. H. & Caroline Hinkin, Alexa., wagoner, married, Geo. H. Henkin, father, p.21.
HINMAN, Arrinetta, W, F, JUN 1853, Portsmouth, whooping cough, 3y, C.C. & F.H. Henman, Portsmouth, C.C. Henman, father, p.1.
HINSON, Thos. S., W, M, 22 OCT 1857, Alexa., croup, 26y.
HODGE, Ellen, (f), F, 7 OCT 1859, Alexa., paralysis, 40y, --, Alexa., cook, G.L. Stewart, head of family.
HODGES, A.P., W, M, 29 JUL 1858, Alexa., consumption, --, Richmond, John Hodges, father.
HODGES, Thomas, W, M, FEB 1853, Alexa., pneumonia, 30y, -- Hodges, Va., ship carpenter, M. Johns, tenant, p.3.
HODGSON, Anna J., W, F, 11 MAY 1892, Alexa. Co., congestion of lungs, 4d, T.A. & Lilly, Alexa. Co., T.A. Hodgson, father, p.54.
HOENSTINE, Fredrick, Sr., W, M, 26 SEP 1877, near Tacey's, old age, 77y, --, Germany, farmer, unmarried, Henry Abitz, son in law, p.37
HOEY, Thomas, W, M, 26 JUL 1856, debility, 75y, --, p.17.
HOFFMAN, Carol C., (f), F, 8 MAR 1895, Alexa. Co., --, E.C. & Henrietta, Alexa. Co., E.C. Hoffman, father, p.60.
HOGAN, Daniel, (f), M, 20 SEP 1886, Arlington Dist., old age, 76y, --, Md., consort of Eliza Hogan, Eliza Hogan, wife, p.48.
HOGAN, Eliza, (f), F, 21 JAN 1895, Alexa. Co., old age, 70y, --, Md., labor, widow, Edward Hogan, son, p.60.
HOGAN, Lizzie, (f), F, 15 FEB 1878, near F. Village, consumption, 24y, Dan'l. & Eliza Hogan, Md., housework, single, Daniel Hogan, father, p.38.
HOLLAND, Nathaniel, (f), M, 10 SEP 1879, Maryland Dist., bank fell on him, 60y, --, consort of Mary Holland, Albert Montague, next door neighbor, p.39.
HOLLAND, Wm., W, M, 7 SEP 1883, Alexa. Co., dropsy, 64y, --, England,

Alexandria (Arlington) County, Virginia Death Records, 1853-1896

consort of Mary Holland, Mary Holland, wife, p.44.

HOLLAND, [blank], (f), M, 5 SEP 1879, Fauquier Co., --, 7d, John & Louisa, Fauquier Co., John Holland, father, p.39.

HOLLINSBURY, John, W, M, 16 JUN 1856, cancer, 83y7m, --, J. Wesley Hollinsbury, head of family, pp. 15 & 16.

HOLMES, Burnette, (f), M, 28 JUL 1895, Alexa. Co., --, 52y, --, Va., consort of James Holmes, C. Holmes, son, p.60.

HOLMES, Cornelius B., (f), M, 18 OCT 1887, Alexa. Co., brain fever, 8m20d, Henry L. & Emma B., Alexa. Co., H.L. Holmes, father, p.49.

HOLMES, Isabella, (f), F, 12 MAR 1886, Arlington Dist., --, 17y, Ruffin & Margaret, Alexa. Co., single, Ruffin Holmes, father, p.48.

HOLMES, Maud, (f), F, 27 JUN 1895, Alexa. Co., --, 4m, H.L. & Emma B., Alexa. Co., H.L. Holmes, father, p.60.

HOLMES, Robt. W., (f), M, 25 JUN 1888, Arlington [Dist.], teething, 9m6d, H.L. & E.B. Holmes, Arlington [Dist.], H.L. Holmes, father.

HOLMES, Ruffin, (f), M, 25 NOV 1896, Alexa. Co., heart failure, 52y, --, King & Queen Co., labor, consort of Margaret Holmes, Margaret Holmes, wife, p.62.

HOLMES, Wm., (f), M, 5 JUL 1895, Alexa. Co., --, 50y, --, Caroline Co., labor, consort of Caroline Holmes, Caroline Homes, wife, p.60.

HOLMES, [blank], (f), M, 26 MAY 1880, Ft. Craig, --, 6d, H.L. & E.B. Holmes, Alexa. Co., H.L. Holmes, father, p.40.

HOLMES, [not named], --, 4 MAR 1889, Alexa. Co., --, H.L. & E.R. Holmes, Va., H.L. Holmes, father, p.51.

HOLMES, [not named], (f), F, 20 AUG 1894, Alexa. Co., --, 2d, Burnett & Jannie, Alexa. Co., Burnett Holmes, father, p.58.

HOMES, Alsey, (f), F, OCT 1875, Arlington Mag. Dist., old age, 80y, mother in law G. Custis, p.35.

HOMES, Mildred, (f), F, 6 APR 1875, Arlington Mag. Dist., --, wife of Joseph Homes, p.35.

HONESTY, Chas., (f), M, [no date] 1875, --, 55y, --, Dranesville, p.35.

HOOFF, John, W, M, 19 DEC 1859, Alexa., inflammation bowels, 58y, --, Alexa., cashier in bank, consort of Blincoe Hooff, Lewis Hooff, brother.

HOOFF, Lewis E., W, M, 10 DEC 1868, Alexa., consumption, 32y, Wm. Hooff, Alexa., printer, married, Wm. Murry, father, p.25.

HOOK, A.M., W, F, 20 MAY 1854, Alexa., pneumonia, 9m, W.H. & S.B. Hook, Alexa., S.B. Hook, mother.

HOOK, W.B., W, M, 16 MAY 1856, Alexa., pneumonia, 7y, W.H. & S.B. Hook, S.B. Hook, mother, p.8.

HOPKINS, Cath., (f), F, 3 AUG 1858, Alexa., summer complaint, 16y, Joseph & Martha Hopkins, Joseph Hopkins.

HOPKINS, Chas., W, M, 30 AUG 1857, Alexa., --, Chr. Neal, coroner.

HORNER, Louisa, W, F, 16 NOV 1886, Jefferson Dist., old age, 71y, Wm. T. & Frances, Alexa. Co., single, T.W. Swann, brother, p.48.

HORTIN, Ned., (f), M, 21 AUG 1868, Alexa., drowned, 40y, unknown, unknown, laborer, single, J. O'Neal, coroner, p.25.

HOSKINS, Thadeus, W, M, JUN 1853, Alexa., scarlet fever, 3y, J.O.C. & J.E. Hoskins, Alexa., J.O.C. Hoskins, father, p.5.

HOSLAR, Daniel, (f), M, 13 SEP 1888, Arlington [Dist.], killed, 40y, Lewis & Mary Hoslar, Va., labor, consort of Martha Hoslar, Martha Hoslar, wife.

HOUGH, W.S., W, M, 6 OCT 1857, drowned, 3y.

HOUGH, Willie, W, M, 6 AUG 1855, Alexa., accident, 4m, -- Hough, Alexa., C. Neale, coroner, p.14.

Alexandria (Arlington) County, Virginia Death Records, 1853-1896

HOUSE, David, W, M, 30 MAY 1854, Alexa., old age, 100y, -- House, Pa., white smith, Ann House, daughter in law, p.7.
HOWARD, Alexander, (f), M, 15 MAR 1880, Col. Pike, spasms, 42y, Thomas & Celia Howard, Alexa. Co., labor, consort of Rachel Howard, Rachel Howard, wife, p.40.
HOWARD, H.E.W., W, F, 15 MAR 1859, Alexa., consumption, 13y, David & Mary Howard, Stafford, David Howard, father.
HOWELL, Lillen Lucy, W, F, 3 FEB 1865, Alexa., fever, 1y2m, John & Mary, Alexa., hatter, single, John Howell, father, p.19.
HOWISON, Ann G., W, F, 1 APR 1858, Alexa., measles, 8m, A. & J. Howison, A. Howison.
HOWISON, Mary Ellen, W, F, 2 JUN 1858, Alexa., measles, 1y6m, A. & J. Howison, A. Howison.
HOXTON, Dr. William W., W, M, 24 AUG 1855, Alexa., consumption, 43y, S. & M. Hoxton, Alexa., physician, E.S. Hoxton, S.W. Griffith, aunt in law, p.12.
HOXTON, Eliza L., W, [c.MAR] 1854, Alexa., consumption, 37y, C. & -- Griffith, Alexa., consort of W.W. Hoxton, W.W. Hoxton, husband, p.9.
HOYDEN, Michael, W, --, 10 JUL 1856, cholera, 32y, Thos. Swann, p.16.
HUGHES, Lydia, W, F, [15 JUN] 1853, Alexa., typhoid fever, 61y, -- Smedley, Jefferson Co., C.C. Berry, nephew, p.3.
HUGHES, Maria, (f), F, 7 NOV 1853, alms house, consumption, 45y, --, unknown, John Stephenson, poor house keeper, p.5.
HULL, Fredk. W., W, M, 13 OCT 1884, Col. Pike, --, 24y, Truman P. & Eliza E., --, farmer, single, T.P. Hull, father, p.45.
HULL, Mary E., W, F, 26 JUL 1891, Alexa. Co., cholera infantum, 1y8m5d, W.S. & Mary J., Alexa., W.S. Hull, father, p.53.
HULL, Morton T., W, M, 9 JAN 1889, Alexa. Co., drowned, 18y, T.P. & E.E. Hull, Va., sailor, T.P. Hull, father, p.51.
HUMPHREYS, C.H., W, M, 6 MAR 1856, Alexa., unknown, 8d, J.D. & S.A. Humphreys, Alexa., S.A. Humphreys, mother, p.8.
HUMPHREYS, Eliza, (s) of J.B. Daingerfield, F, 25 DEC 1854, Alexa., unknown, 55y, slave, J.B. Daingerfield, master, p.6.
HUMPHRIES, Ana, W, F, 5 MAY 1859, Alexa., consumption on bowels, 2y, Jno. & Annie Humphries, Alexa., Dr. Maher, physician.
HUMPHRIES, Edwd., W, M, 13 JAN 1859, Alexa., scarlet fever, 1y8m, Wm. & Susan Humphries, Alexa., Wm. Humphries, father.
HUMPHRIES, Lin., W, M, 13 JAN 1859, Alexa., scarlet fever, 2y, Jno. & Virginia Humphries, Alexa., John Humphries, father.
HUNGERFORD, Thos., W, M, 14 MAR 1855, Alexa., unknown, 56y, stranger, C. Neale, coroner, p.14.
HUNTER, Bernard [Franklin], W, M, JUN 1853, Alexa., scarlet fever, 10m, J.H. & M. Hunter, Alexa., J.H. Hunter, father, p.2.
HUNTER, Charles Sidney, W, M, 4 SEP 1853, Alexa., unknown, 13m, J.T. & V. Hunter, Alexa., J.T. Hunter, father, p.5.
HUNTER, Fannie, (f), F, 28 JUL 1896, Alexa. Co., --, 60y, --, Jackson Hunter, husband, p.62.
HUNTER, Jos. A., W, M, 22 MAR 1867, pneumonia, 19y, Mary & J.H. Hunter, Alexa., none, single, Jas. H. Hunter, father, p.23.
HUNTER, Mary, (f), F, 22 JAN 1882, Washington, D.C., diphtheria, 13y7m, Saml. T. & Lucinda Hunter, Va., housework, single, Lucinda Hunter, mother, p.43.
HUNTINGTON, [blank], W, M, JUN 1853, Alexa., unknown, 3m, T. & E. Hunttington, Alexa., T. Hunttington,

Alexandria (Arlington) County, Virginia Death Records, 1853-1896

father, p.5.

HUNTON, H. Francis, W, F, 24 OCT 1854, Alexa., accidental, 23y, E. & E. Brent, Alexa., R.H. Hunton, Geo. W. Hunton, brother, p.6.

HUNTT, Anna, W, F, 25 AUG 1859, Alexa., summer complaint, 1y6m, Wm. & Helen Huntt, Alexa., Wm. Huntt, father.

HUTCHINS, Cassa, W, F, SEP 1854, Alexa., unknown, 1d, B.F. & S. Hutchins, Alexa., B.F. Hutchins, father, p.6.

HUTCHINSON, Leroy, W, M, 19 JUN 1887, Alexa. Co., --, 10d, Robt. S. & A.M., Alexa. Co., R.S. Hutchinson, father, p.49.

HUTCHINSON, M.A., W, F, 13 MAY 1853, Alexa., unknown, 9d, J. & M.A. Hutchinson, Alexa., M.A. Hutchinson, mother, p.2.

HUTCHINSON, Margaret, W, F, NOV 1855, Alexa., consumption, 28y, W. & S. Palmer, Va., Jas. Hutchinson, C. Hutchinson, sister, p.13.

HUTCHINSON, Reuben, W, M, 11 MAY 1853, Alexa., unknown, 5m, J. & M.A. Hutchinson, Alexa., M.A. Hutchinson, mother, p.2.

HUTCHINSON, Rodney, W, M, 28 SEP 1890, Alexa. Co., cholera infantum, 9m, E.P. & Sarah Hutchinson, Alexa. Co., Sarah Hutchinson, neighbor [sic], p.52.

HYATT, Thornton, (f), M, MAY 1896, Alexa. Co., old age, 70y, --, Va., single, E.D. Jones, neighbor, p.62.

HYDE, Margret, W, F, 22 OCT 1880, Washington Road, pneumonia, 72y, --, France, widow, George Hyde, son, p.40.

HYOTT, Alfred, (f), M, AUG 1875, Jefferson Mag. Dist., killed by cars, 19y, Thornton Hyott, laborer, p.35.

HYSON, Charles, (f), M, 25 NOV 1883, Alexa. Co., killed, 26y, Sam'l. & Louisa Hyson, Alexa. Co., labor, consort of Rosa Hyson, Hannah Handy, sister, p.44.

HYSON, John, (f), M, 11 SEP 1876, Washington District, sunstruck, 42y, Jas.

& Lila Hyson, Alexa. Co., laborer, Mary Hyson, wife, p.36.

HYSON, Louisa E., (f), F, 10 JUN 1877, Washington Dist., teething, 11m, Rose & Chas. Hyson, Washn. Dist., Chas. Hyson, father, p.37.

HYSON, Margaret, (f), F, JUL 1891, Alexa. Co., paralysis, 66y, Lewis & Luvenia, Alexa. Co., housework, widow, Charlotte Chinn, daughter, p.53.

HYSON, Mariah, (f), F, MAY 1873, Washington Twp., --, 16y, p.33.

HYSON, Saml., (f), M, 23 FEB 1853, Alexa. Co., typhoid fever, 45y, S. & M. Hyson, Alexa. Co., farmer, consort of Louisa Hyson, L. Hyson, widow, p.5.

HYSON, Spencer, (f), M, 5 AUG 1889, Alexa. Co., consumption, 74y, --, Va., laborer, consort of Sarah Hyson, Albert Hyson, son, p.51.

HYSON, Thornton, (f), M, 30 DEC 1882, Brown's Bend, cold, 59y, Spencer & Nellie Hyson, Va., labor, consort of Margret Hyson, Margret Hyson, wife, p.43.

I

IKER, Sophia, W, F, 31 DEC 1858, Alexa., consumption, 29y6m, --, pauper, consort of Albert Iker, A. Iker.

INGLAND, [blank], W, --, 29 SEP 1857, Alexa., --, 3y, Jas. N. Ingland, Fairfax Co., farmer.

INGRAM, Frances, W, F, 22 FEB 1896, Alexa. Co., old age, 55y, --, Alexa. Co., widow, Molly Ingraham, niece, p.62.

INNIS, Alexander, W, M, 9 DEC 1880, near Fairfax Seminary, hemorrhage, 53y, Cornelius & Elizabeth Ennis, N.Y., dairyman, consort of Virginia Innis, Virginia Innis, [mother], p.41.

INNIS, M. Lemoine, W, M, 25 SEP 1888, Jefferson [Dist.], hemorrhage, 24y, Alex. & Virginia Innis, La., divinity student,

Alexandria (Arlington) County, Virginia Death Records, 1853-1896

single, Virginia Innis, mother.
IRVING, Euell, (f), M, FEB 1893, Alexa. Co., --, 17d, -- & Helen Chase, Alexa. Co., John Chase, grandfather, p.56.
IRWIN, Bettie, W, F, 22 JAN 1858, Alexa., consumption, 26y, Joseph & Alfurna Broders, J. Broders.
IRWIN, James, W, M, [no date] 1856, Alexa., erysipelas, 56y, --, Md., W.H. Bro., head of family, p.15.

J

JACKSON, Andrew, (f), M, 29 JUN 1853, Alexa., croup, 4m, T. & H. Jackson, Alexa., H. Jackson, mother, p.3.
JACKSON, Ann L., (f), F, 5 FEB 1893, Alexa. Co., --, 3m, Hosea & Mary, Alexa. Co., Mary Jackson, mother, p.56.
JACKSON, Anna, W, F, 19 SEP 1867, Alexa., --, 38y, M. & Mariah Jackson, Washington, housekeeper, married, Dora E. Jackson, daughter, p.23.
JACKSON, Arthur, (f), M, 28 NOV 1881, Ft. Albany, --, 3y6m, Dallas & Harriet Jackson, Alexa. Co., Harriet Jackson, mother, p.42.
JACKSON, Bernard A., (f), M, 13 DEC 1893, Alexa. Co., --, 4m, Lewis & Charity, Alexa. Co., Lewis Jackson, father, p.56.
JACKSON, Chas., (f), M, AUG 1893, Alexa. Co., asthma, 76y, --, Va., widower, John Jackson, son, p.56.
JACKSON, Chas., (f), M, 25 DEC 1875, --, 6m, Jas. Jackson, Fairfax Co., p.35.
JACKSON, Chas. A., (f), M, 16 OCT 1891, Alexa. Co., burnt, 6m, Lewis & Charity, Wash. D.C., Charity Jackson, mother, p.53.
JACKSON, Daniel, (f), M, 26 OCT 1895, Alexa. Co., typhoid fever, 51y, --, Alexa. Co., labor, consort of Jane Jackson, Jane Jackson, wife, p.60.
JACKSON, Daniel, (f), M, 31 DEC 1888, Arlington [Dist.], cold, 10m, Daniel & Jane Jackson, Arlington [Dist.], Jane Jackson, mother.
JACKSON, Edith, (f), F, [no date] 1896, Alexa. Co., --, 60y, --, Lucinda Jackson, daughter, p.62.
JACKSON, Frederick, (f), M, JUN 1894, Alexa. Co., typhoid fever, 12y, Joseph & Hattie, Alexa. Co., Joseph Jackson, father, p.58.
JACKSON, Gabriel, (f), M, 19 APR 1893, Alexa. Co., heart disease, 60y, --, Caroline Co., consort of Nancy Jackson, Nancy Jackson, wife, p.56.
JACKSON, George, (f), M, 29 SEP 1881, Arlington farm, congestive chill, 38y, George & Rachel Jackson, Va., labor, consort of Maria Jackson, Maria Jackson, wife, p.42.
JACKSON, Henry, (f), M, MAR 1875, Jefferson Mag. Dist., --, 9m, Dalice Jackson, Alexa. Co., p.35.
JACKSON, Isiah, Jr., (f), M, 1 DEC 1895, Alexa. Co., consumption, --, -- & Georgianna, Alexa. Co., Georgianna Jackson, mother, p.60.
JACKSON, Isiah, Sr., (f), M, 28 NOV 1895, Alexa. Co., consumption, 29y, Robert & Alice, Alexa. Co., labor, consort of Georgianna Jackson, Georgianna Jackson, wife, p.60.
JACKSON, Jane, (f), F, 9 JUN 1888, Arlington [Dist.], --, 3y, Daniel & Jane Jackson, Arlington [Dist.], Jane Jackson, mother.
JACKSON, John, (f), M, 3 SEP 1889, Alexa. Co., asthma, 69y, --, Va., farmer, consort of Eliza Jackson, Francis Jackson, son, p.51.
JACKSON, John, (f), M, 5 MAR 1859, Alexa., teething, 19y, John & Lucy Jackson, Alexa., John Jackson, father.
JACKSON, Josiah, (f), M, [no date] 1886, Jefferson Dist., typhoid fever, 1y, Cyrus & Edith, Alexa. Co., Cyrus Jackson, father, p.48.

Alexandria (Arlington) County, Virginia Death Records, 1853-1896

JACKSON, Josias, (f), M, JAN 1885, Alexa. Co., --, 3y, --, Va., Winnie Easter, aunt, p.47.

JACKSON, Lawrence P., (f), M, 22 SEP 1893, Alexa. Co., --, 1m14d, Lewis & Charity, Alexa. Co., Lewis Jackson, father, p.56.

JACKSON, Lettie, (f), F, 24 FEB 1896, --, 4m, Minor S. & Nancy, Alexa. Co., M.S. Jackson, father, p.62.

JACKSON, Lettie, (f), F, 24 FEB 1895, Alexa. Co., --, 1m, Minor S. Jackson, Alexa. Co., Mary E. Jackson, mother, p.60.

JACKSON, Lila, (f), F, 6 JUN 1878, Pimmitt's Run, paralysis, 40y, --, Va., housework, consort of John Jackson, John Jackson, husband, p.38.

JACKSON, Lucinda, (f), F, 24 SEP 1876, near Canal basin, thrush, 1y, Fairfax & Annie Jackson, near canal basin, Fairfax Jackson, father, p.36.

JACKSON, Lucy, (f), F, 28 MAR 1866, Alexa., heart disease, 59y, unknown, Alexa., married, Henry Jackson, husband, p.21.

JACKSON, Lula, (f), F, 9 JUN 1884, Rosslyn, 3m4d, Daniel & Jane, Alexa. Co., Jane Jackson, mother, p.45.

JACKSON, Marietta, (f), F, NOV 1895, Alexa. Co., consumption, 2y6m, Julius & Lula, Alexa. Co., Julius Jackson, father, p.60.

JACKSON, Martha, (f), F, 10 AUG 1896, Alexa. Co., --, 42y, Edward & Ann, --, Emma Pollard, sister, p.62.

JACKSON, Martha, (f), F, 7 OCT 1894, Alexa. Co., heart Disease, 51y, Chas. & Caroline, Alexa. Co., housekeeper, consort of Moses Jackson, Moses Jackson, husband, p.58.

JACKSON, Rebecca, (f), F, AUG 1867, Alexa., summer complaint, 1y, Gabriel & Nancy Jackson, Alexa., none, single, Gabriel Jackson, father, p.23.

JACKSON, Richard, (f), M, 1 AUG 1891, Alexa. Co., dysentery, 3m, Hosea & Mary, Alexa., Mary Jackson, mother, p.53.

JACKSON, Robert, (f), [M], 30 JAN 1872, Washington Twp., --, 10y, Chas. Jackson, Washington Twp., laborer, p.32.

JACKSON, Rosa Ann, (f), F, AUG 1866, Alexa., dysentery, 9y, Moses & Maria Jackson, Alexa., laborer, single, Maria Jackson, mother, p.21.

JACKSON, Shadrach, (f), M, 9 SEP 1867, Alexa., congestive chills, --, Jno. & Sarah Jackson, Culpeper, laborer, married, Marg't. Jackson, widow, p.23.

JACKSON, Shedrick, (f), M, 20 DEC 1876, Leesburg Pike, thrush, 2m, Jas. & Kitty Jackson, Leesburg Pike, James Jackson, father, p.36.

JACKSON, Susan, (f), F, 27 MAY 1896, Alexa. Co., --, 60y, --, housework, widow, Hosea Jackson, stepson, p.62.

JACKSON, Thornton, (s) of Daniel Minor, M, JAN 1856, Alexa., pneumonia, 40y, J. & M. Jackson, Fairfax Co., slave, Harriet Jackson, H. Jackson, widow, p.8.

JACKSON, Virgi, (f), F, 28 AUG 1888, Arlington [Dist.], hemorrhage, 5y, Andrew & Fanny, Arlington [Dist.], Andrew Jackson, father.

JACKSON, Wm. H., (f), M, 24 SEP 1878, near F. Village, whooping cough, 1y27d, George & Maria Jackson, near F. Village, Geo. Jackson, father, p.38.

JACKSON, [blank], (f), M, AUG 1867, --, 1d, M. & J. Jackson, Alexa., none, single, Mary Jackson, mother, p.24.

JACKSON, [blank], (f), F, 21 MAR 1884, canal basin, --, 1d, Fairfax & Anna, Alexa. Co., Fairfax Jackson, father, p.45.

JACKSON, [blank], (f), M, 1 SEP 1882, canal basin, --, 1m14d, Fairfax & Ann Jackson, Alexa. Co., Fairfax Jackson, father, p.43.

JACOBS, Thomas, W, M, 2 APR 1855, Alexa., old age, 85y, -- Jacobs, Fairfax, tailor, consort of Ch. Jacobs, C. Jacobs,

Alexandria (Arlington) County, Virginia Death Records, 1853-1896

widow, p.12.

JACOBS, Wm. H., W, M, 6 SEP 1859, Alexa., unknown, 62y, --, J.B. Johnson, physician.

JACOBS, [blank], W, M, 10 SEP 1855, Alexa., unknown, 2d, A. & B.E. Jacobs, Alexa., A. Jacobs, father, p.11.

JAMES, Jesse, (f), M, 31 DEC 1888, Arlington [Dist.], --, 6m20d, Chas. & Agnes James, Arlington [Dist.], Agnes James, mother.

JAMES, Mary, (f), F, FEB 1886, Jefferson Dist., --, 43y, --, housekeeping, consort of Robt. James, Robt. James, husband, p.48.

JAMES, Mary E., (f), F, 24 MAY 1881, Rosslyn, childbirth, 23y, Flemming & Julia Taylor, Richmond, housekeeping, consort of Charles James, Flemming Taylor, father, p.42.

JAMES, [blank], (f), M, 14 JUN 1881, Rosslyn, --, 1m2d, Chas. & Mary E. James, Rosslyn, Flemming Taylor, grandfather, p.42.

JAMIESON, E.D., W, F, OCT 1854, Alexa., congestion of brain, 15d, A. & E.V. Jamieson, Alexa., A. Jamieson, father, p.7.

JAMIESON, John, W, M, 21 APR 1853, Alexa., paralysis, 74y, A. & J. Jamieson, Scotland, consort of M.C. Jamieson, M.C. Jamieson, widow, p.5.

JAMIESON, Penelope, W, F, 3 AUG 1854, Alexa., old age, 86y, W. & S. Triplett, Fairfax Co., Mar. Jamison, daughter, p.9.

JAVINS, Geo., W, W, M, 8 JUL 1857, Alexa., --, Thompson Javins, --, shoemaker.

JAVINS, Jas. R., W, M, 15 MAR 1854, Alexa., catarrh fever, 3y4m, J.A. & S.A. Javins, Fairfax Co., J.A. Javins, father, p.7.

JAVINS, Sabina, W, F, DEC 1853, Alexa., consumption, 39y, W. & E. Hutchinson, Va., -- Javins, R.E. Lawson, niece, p.3.

JEFFERSON, Charlotte, W, F, 10 SEP 1855, Alexa., consumption, 34y, W. & A.E. Trunnell, Fredk. Co. Md., consort of William Jefferson, M.E. Posey, daughter, p.12.

JEFFERSON, Ida Lee, W, F, 24 FEB 1867, Alexa., pneumonia, 2y8m24d, Col. & Susan Jefferson, Alexa., none, single, Susan Jefferson, mother, p.23.

JEFFERSON, Julia A., (f), F, 2 MAR 1894, Alexa. Co., --, 9m, George A. & Lucinda, Alexa. Co., Geo. A. Jefferson, father, p.58.

JEFFERSON, Nelson, (s), M, 5 NOV 1853, Alexa., consumption, 60y, slaves, P. William Co., carpenter, consort of Fanney, Elizabeth Adam, owner, p.4.

JEFFERSON, Susan Ann, (f), F, 10 AUG 1875, Jefferson Mag. Dist., summer sickness, 2y, Henry Jefferson, Alexa. Co., p.35.

JEFFERSON, Thomas, (f), M, 13 SEP 1882, F. Vill[age], malaria fever, 7y1d, H.A. & Lucy Jefferson, Va., Lucy Jefferson, mother, p.43.

JEFFERSON, [blank], W, M, 5 OCT 1857, fits, 7d, Saml. & Louisa, farmer.

JENKINS, Catherine, W, F, 1 MAR 1859, Alexa., bursting blood vessel, 31y, --, Alexa., consort of B.H. Jenkins, B.H. Jenkins, husband.

JENKINS, Elizabeth, W, F, 17 JUL 1859, Alexa., childbirth, 17y, --, Md., consort of Nicholas Jenkins, Nicholas Jenkins, husband.

JENKINS, Walter, (f), M, [no date] 1890, Alexa. Co., --, 2y, Wm. & Mary J., Alexa. Co., M.J. Jenkins, mother, p.52.

JENNINGS, Roberta, W, F, 28 MAR 1858, Alexa., pneumonia, 6y, John & Julia Ann Jennings, John Jennings.

JETT, James Thomas, W, F, 14 JUL 1866, Alexa., whooping cough, 11y10m, John & Sarah F. Jett, Alexa., carpenter, single, John J. Jett, father, p.20.

JEWETT, Joseph, W, M, 10 FEB 1859, Alexa., colic, 55y, --, Alexa., clerk, J.D. Corse, employer.

JOHNSON, Anna, (f), F, OCT 1894, Alexa.

Alexandria (Arlington) County, Virginia Death Records, 1853-1896

Co., --, 3y, Oscar & Anna, Alexa. Co., Anna Johnson, mother, p.58.

JOHNSON, Annie, (f), F, 4 NOV 1881, Georgetown Road, consumption, 30y, Tibbett & Harriet Allen, Md., housekeeping, consort of George Johnson, George Johnson, husband, p.42.

JOHNSON, Annie Julia, W, F, 7 OCT 1859, Alexa., whooping cough, 5m, J.T. & C.M. Johnson, Alexa., John T. Johnson, father.

JOHNSON, Chas., (f), M, 17 JUL 1891, Nauck, old age, 72y, --, Va., consort of Susan Johnson, Mary A. Lee, daughter, p.53.

JOHNSON, Cornelius, (f), M, 6 AUG 1877, Freedmen's Village, teething, 1y, Sinna & C.F. Johnson, Freedmen's Village, Sinna Johnson, mother, p.37.

JOHNSON, Ellen, W, M, 1 APR 1855, Alexa., croup, 10m, Tho. & M. Johnson, Alexa., Tho. Johnson, father, p.11.

JOHNSON, Ferdean, (f), M, 28 APR 1882, F. Vill[age], small pox, 7y4m, F.W. & Maggie Johnson, Alexa. Co., F.W. Johnson, father, p.43.

JOHNSON, Frances, (f), F, JUL 1894, Alexa. Co., fits, 65y, --, Va., --, Margaret Holmes, daughter in law, p.58.

JOHNSON, Frank W., (f), M, 21 APR 1882, F. Vill[age], small pox, 1y2m2d, F.W. & Maggie Johnson, Alexa. Co., F.W. Johnson, father, p.43.

JOHNSON, Henry, (f), M, 23 OCT 1876, Washington, D.C., rheumatism, 30y, Joshua & Maria Johnson, Prince Geo. Co. Md., laborer, husband of Patsey Johnson, Patsey Johnson, wife, p.36.

JOHNSON, Henson, (f), M, 16 AUG 1880, Georgetown Road, consumption, 21y, George & Mary Johnson, Md., labor, single, Geo. Johnson, brother, p.41.

JOHNSON, John, (f), M, JUL 1881, Poor House Lane, killed on R.R., 70y, --, widower, Jane Burrell, next door neighbor, p.42.

JOHNSON, John, W, M, APR 1855, Alexa., unknown, 2y, J.F. & E. Johnson, J.F. Johnson, father, p.11.

JOHNSON, Leticia, W, F, 17 JUN 1853, Alexa., cholera, 42y, P. & -- McLaughlin, Alexa., consort of Wm. Johnson, W. Johnson, husband, p.1.

JOHNSON, Martha, (f), F, 29 MAR 1880, F. Village, teething, 1y1m, F.W. & Margret Johnson, Alexa. Co., F.W. Johnson, father, p.41.

JOHNSON, Mary, (f), F, 13 AUG 1885, Alexa. Co., --, 30y, --, Va., consort of Geo. Johnson, Mary Slaughter, friend, p.47.

JOHNSON, Mary Jane, (f), [F], 12 FEB 1866, Alexa., consumption, 26y, Sarah & Wm. Cooper, Alexa., married, Richd. H. Lancaster, father in law, p.21.

JOHNSON, Omer Doggett, W, M, JAN 1866, Alexa., information of the brain, 7m, Lydia & J.B. Johnson, Alexa., physician, single, Dr. J.B. Johnson, father, p.21.

JOHNSON, Peter A., (f), M, 21 JAN 1893, Alexa. Co., kidney trouble, 70y, --, Fairfax Co., labor, consort of Ann Johnson, Ann Johnson, wife, p.56.

JOHNSON, Robert (f), M, AUG 1868, Alexa., teething, 2y2m, Wm. & E. Johnson, Alexa., none, single, Martha Brooks, aunt, p.25.

JOHNSON, Samuel, (f), M, 25 AUG 1876, near Brickyard, from a fall, 2m, Henry & Patsey Johnson, Alexa. Co., Patsey Johnson, mother, p.36.

JOHNSON, Secelia, (f), F, 20 OCT 1875, Jefferson Mag. Dist., summer sickness, 13m, C.F. Johnson, Alexa. Co., p.35.

JOHNSON, Susan, (f), F, 24 JUL 1891, --, old age, 68y, Ralph & Harriett, Va., widow, Mary Lee, daughter, p.53.

JOHNSON, Sydney, W, M, NOV 1857.

JOHNSON, W., W, M, 17 AUG 1857, Alexa., --, 3m, Jacob & Sarah.

JOHNSON, [blank], (f), F, 5 OCT 1866,

Alexandria (Arlington) County, Virginia Death Records, 1853-1896

Alexa., unknown, 2d, Mathew & Lucinda Johnson, Alexa., L.W. Brooks, friend, p.21.

JOHNSON, [blank], (f), --, 1 SEP 1880, Woodward's yard, --, 1m15d, Lizzie Johnson, Alexa. Co., Maria Johnson, grandmother, p.41.

JOHNSON, [blank], (s) of W. Keen's est., F, NOV 1856, Alexa., unknown, 4d, S. Johnston, Alexa., J. Guisendaffer, hirer, p.8.

JOHNSTON, Ellen R., W, F, 2 OCT 1884, Col. Pike, --, 3d, W.C. & A.F. Johnston, Alexa. Co., W.C. Johnston, father, p.45.

JOHNSTON, Frank, W, M, 8 JUN 1865, Alexa., summer complaint, 1y, J.F. & Clara, Va., mer., J.F. Johnston, father, p.19.

JOHNSTON, Frank, W, M, OCT 1892, Alexa. Co., --, 7m, W.H. & Mary J., Wash. D.C., Wm. H. Johnston, father, p.54.

JOHNSTON, H.H.M., W, M, 3 NOV 1854, Alexa., croup, 2y6m, J.M. & R.J. Johnston, Alexa., J.M. Johnston, father, p.7.

JOHNSTON, Hannah, (s) of W. Keen's est., F, NOV 1856, Alexa., old age, 70y, Fairfax, slave, J. Guisendaffer, hirer, p.8.

JOHNSTON, J.D., W, M, 23 FEB 1856, Alexa., croup, 4y, J.R. & E. Johnston, Alexa., Elizabeth Johnston, mother, p.8.

JOHNSTON, John M., W, M, 15 OCT 1877, Columbia Pike, teething, 1y, M.G. & R.W. Johnston, Alexa. City, R.W. Johnston, father, p.37.

JOHNSTON, Mary A., W, F, 15 MAR 1876, Columbia Pike, old age, 70y, R. & Eliza Windsor, Fairfax Co., widow, John R. Johnston, son, p.36.

JOHNSTON, Robt. Y., W, M, 4 NOV 1894, Wash. D.C., consumption, 2y27d, B.B. & Elizabeth, Wash. D.C., laborer, B.B. Johnston, father, p.58.

JOICE, Chas., W, M, 19 JUL 1858, Alexa., scarlet fever, 3y9m, Chas. & Atha Joice, A. Joice.

JONES, Annie, (f), F, 12 OCT 1886, Jefferson Dist., --, 2y, Isaac & Maria, Alexa. Co., Isaac Jones, father, p.48.

JONES, Annie, W, F, 3 JUL 1877, near Rosslyn, teething, 2y, Mary & Joseph Jones, Georgetown D.C., Joseph Jones, father, p.37.

JONES, Bartley, (f), M, 13 JUN 1853, alms house, pneumonia, 23y, -- Jones, Alexa., laborer, John Stephenson, poor house keeper, p.5.

JONES, Cellia, (f), F, 10 JUL 1876, near Slaters, cancer, 45y, Martin & Millie Bailey, Caroline Co., housework, consort of Daniel Jones, Daniel Jones, husband, p.36.

JONES, Chs. E., W, M, 24 MAY 1853, Alexa., scarlet fever, 1y, W. & L. Jones, Prince Wm. Co., Lidea A. Jones, mother, p.4.

JONES, Ednor C., (f), F, 5 SEP 1878, Sissonville, teething, 1y1m, Washn. & Sarah Jones, Sissonville, Sarah Jones, mother, p.38.

JONES, Edward Z., W, M, 26 NOV 1866, Alexa., consumption, 55y, Edward Jones, Charles Co. Md., mason, married, Edwd. H. Jones, son, p.21.

JONES, Eliasha, (f), M, 19 MAR 1878, Four Mile Run, croup, 6m, Edward & Sarah Jones, Four Mile Run, Edward Jones, father, p.38.

JONES, Errisee, (f), F, 1 JUL 1879, Jefferson Dist., cholera, 4m, Wm. H. & Sarah E. Jones, Alexa. City, Wm. H. Jones, father, p.39.

JONES, Estella, (f), F, 15 JUL 1879, Jefferson Dist., teething, 5m, Dan'l. & Mary Jones, Jefferson Dist., Mary Jones, mother, p.39.

JONES, Ezekiel, W, M, 23 DEC 1858, Alexa., doctors, 30y, --, fisherman, E. Jones.

JONES, Frances, W, F, AUG 1853, Alexa., unknown, 10m, J.& M. Jones, Alexa.,

Alexandria (Arlington) County, Virginia Death Records, 1853-1896

John Jones, father, p.1.
JONES, Francis, (f), F, 13 MAR 1866, Alexa., heart disease, 13y, Julia Jones, Middleburg, single, Alex. Jones, friend, p.21.
JONES, Frederick, (f), M, 3 APR 1876, near Slaters, strangled, 1y, --, Nancy Jones, mother, p.36.
JONES, Gertrude, (f), F, 13 APR 1887, Alexa. Co., consumption, 3y, Edward & Selvey, Alexa. Co., Edward Jones, father, p.49.
JONES, Ida, (f), F, 30 APR 1878, near Slater's, --, 2y3m, Henderson & Nancy Jones, near Slater's, Henderson Jones, father, p.38.
JONES, John, (f), M, 30 MAR 1896, N.Y., pneumonia, 22y, Edward & Silvey, --, single, E.D. Jones, father, p.62.
JONES, John C., (f), M, 1 APR 1895, N.Y., pneumonia, 23y, Edward & Sidney, Alexa. Co., labor, single, Edward Jones, father, p.60.
JONES, John H., (f), M, 27 APR 1894, Alexa. Co., pneumonia, 59y, --, Alexa. Co., laborer, consort of Mary C. Jones, Lizzie Jones, daughter, p.58.
JONES, Julia, W, F, 14 SEP 1858, Alexa., consumption, --, John & Sarah, John Jones.
JONES, Ladoo, (f), M, 4 DEC 1855, Alexa., consumption, 2y, W. & E. Jones, Alexa., Phil Hamilton, uncle, p.12.
JONES, Lena, (f), F, 25 JUL 1878, near Slater's, --, 1y, Henderson & Nancy Jones, near Slater's, Henderson Jones, father, p.38.
JONES, Levi, (f), M, 22 JUL 1886, Arlington Dist., old age, 86y, --, Fairfax Co., consort of Ann Jones, Ann Jones, wife, p.48.
JONES, Lila, (f), F, SEP 1886, Georgetown, D.C., hemorrhage, 25y, Henry & Jennie, Alexa. Co., single, Martha Jones, stepmother, p.48.
JONES, Lizzie, (f), F, 7 MAR 1879, Arlington Dist., --, 20y, Levi & Ann Jones, Alexa. Co., housework, single, Levi Jones, father, p.39.
JONES, Lucy, (f), F, 26 FEB 1879, Arlington Dist., diphtheria, 7y, Harrison & Julia Jones, Alexa. Co., Harrison Jones, father, p.39.
JONES, Lucy, (f), [F], 28 JAN 1866, Alexa., old age, 86y, unknown, Va., married, Gilbert Jones, son, p.21.
JONES, Mary, (f), F, 9 FEB 1878, Rosslyn, whooping cough, 8m, Harrison & Julia Jones, Rosslyn, Julia Jones, mother, p.38.
JONES, Mary, (f), F, DEC 1866, Alexa., unknown, 2d, Albert & Mary Jones, Alexa., laborer, married, Albert Jones, husband, p.20.
JONES, Mary C., (f), F, 27 APR 1894, Alexa. Co., pneumonia, 57y, Chas. & Francis Coats, Alexa. Co., laborer, consort of John H. Jones, Lizzie Jones, daughter, p.58.
JONES, Mary E., (f), F, 23 APR 1876, Washington District, pneumonia, 11m, Washn. & Sarah Jones, Washn. District, Sarah Jones, mother, p.36.
JONES, Mary J., (f), F, 7 AUG 1895, Alexa. Co., consumption, 29y, Wm. & Mary, Alexa. Co., single, Mary Jones, mother, p.60.
JONES, Moses, (f), M, MAR 1885, Alexa. Co., --, 18y, Henry & Jennie Jones, Alexa. Co., housework, single, Henry Jones, father, p.47.
JONES, Moses, (f), M, MAR 1886, Georgetown D.C., consumption, 20y, Henry & Jennie, Alexa. Co., single, Martha Jones, stepmother, p.48.
JONES, Peter, W, M, MAY 1853, Alexa., cholera morbus, 32y, J. & S. Jones, Prince Wm. Co., Harriet Jones, Lidea A. Jones, sister in law, p.4.
JONES, Sarah, W, F, 1 SEP 1856, Alexa., unknown, 1d, W.C. & A. Jones, Alexa., A. Jones, mother, p.8.
JONES, Teresa, (f), F, 20 OCT 1881, Four

Alexandria (Arlington) County, Virginia Death Records, 1853-1896

Mile Run, thrush, 5m, Ed & Silvey Jones, Alexa. Co., Silvey Jones, mother, p.42.

JONES, William, (f), M, 2 NOV 1893, Alexa. Co., typhoid fever, 20y, Isaac & Maria, Alexa. Co., labor, single, Isaac Jones, father, p.56.

JONES, Wm. L., W, M, 19 JUN 1877, near Rosslyn, --, 3m, Mary & Joseph Jones, near Rosslyn, Joseph Jones, father, p.37.

JONES, [blank], (f), F, 14 JAN 1876, Addison farm, 7d, Wm. & Mary Jones, Alexa. Co., Mary Jones, mother, p.36.

JONES, [blank], (f), F, 1 FEB 1882, F. Vill[age], small pox, --, Dallas & Elcey Jones, Alexa. Co., Elcey Jones, mother, p.43.

JONES, [blank], (f), M, 24 DEC 1876, Four Mile Run, 7d, Edward & Silvey Jones, Four Mile Run, Silvey Jones, mother, p.36.

JONES, [not named], (f), F, 28 DEC 1894, Alexa. Co., --, 20d, Chas. & Mary, Alexa. Co., Mary Carter [sic], mother, p.58.

JONES, [not named], (f), F, SEP 1891, Alexa. Co., --, 2d, Lemuel & Martha Jones, Alexa. Co., L. Jones, father, p.53.

JORDON, Clara, (f), F, 10 JAN 1866, Alexa., choleic, 3y, Thos. & Mary Jordon, Md., laborer, single, Thos. Jordon, father, p.20.

JORDON, Reuben, (f), M, 11 APR 1868, Alexa., old age, 100y4m, unknown, unknown, laborer, married, Moses Jordon, son, p.25.

JOURDAN, John H., (f), M, 8 FEB 1883, Alexa. Co., --, 3y6m, Robert & Josephine Jourdan, Alexa. Co., Robt. Jourdan, father, p.44.

JOURDAN, Mary E., (f), F, 7 DEC 1884, F. Vill[age], --, 10y4m, Robert & Josephine, Alexa. Co., Robt. Jourdan, father, p.45.

K

KEENAN, John, W, M, 24 JUN 1858, Alexa., consumption, 50y, --, Dr. Meagher, physician.

KEENE, J.W., W, M, 16 NOV 1855, Alexa., accident, 23y, M. & M. Keene, P. William Co., bricklayer, consort of Ann Keene, A. Keene, widow, p.12.

KEITH, Christian, W, M, 17 NOV 1855, Alexa., bilious, 45y, unknown, Germany, A. Kitchen, landlord, p.12.

KEITH, Margaret, W, F, 29 FEB 1859, Alexa., old age, 87y, --, Alexa., Thos. R. Keith, brother.

KEITH, Wm., W, M, JAN 1858, Alexa., old age, 80y, --, merchant.

KELL, John, W, M, 9 SEP 1853, Alexa., intemperance, 45y, J. & N. Kell, Alexa., coppersmith, consort of C. Kell, C. Kell, widow, p.5.

KELLY, Catharine, W, F, 3 JAN 1867, Alexa., pneumonia, 70y, Wm. & Mary Casey, Mitchell's Town, housekeeper, married, Mary Sullivan, daughter, p.23.

KELLY, Catherine, W, F, APR 1858, Alexa., fits, 5y, Patr. & Catherine Kelly, P. Kelly.

KELLY, Henry, (f), M, MAY 1893, Alexa. Co., --, 4m, Ephraim & Sarah, Alexa. Co., Ephraim Kelly, father, p.56.

KELLY, Mary, W, M, 31 SEP 1866, Alexa., whooping cough, 9m12d, John & Catharine Kelly, Alexa., merchant, single, John Kelly, father, p.20.

KELLY, Oscar, W, M, 21 MAR 1868, Alexa., fits, 1 hr., Jas. & M. Kelley, Alexa., none, single, M. Kelley, mother, p.25.

KENNERLY, P., W, M, JUL 1855, Alexa., Culpeper, bilious fever, 30y, -- Kennerly, Ireland, labor, Eliza Kennerly, E. Kennerly, widow, p.13.

KENNIE, Millie, (f), F, APR 1889, Alexa. Co., --, W.H. & Nellie Kennie, Va., W.H. Kennie, father, p.51.

Alexandria (Arlington) County, Virginia Death Records, 1853-1896

KENNIE, Nellie, (f), F, JUN 1887, Alexa. Co., --, 2m, William H. & Nellie, Alexa. Co., Wm. H. Kennie, father, p.49.

KERBY, Sally Shakes, W, F, [no date] 1857, Alexa., teething, 1y8m, Dr. John & Mary Kerby, Alexa., --, Mary Kerby, mother.

KERRIGAN, John, W, M, 17 JUL 1859, Alexa., drowned, 33y, --, laborer, Jacob Kerper, friend.

KESTERSON, Amos, W, M, JUN 1853, Alexa., scarlet fever, 11y, J. & D. Kesterson, Baltimore, J. Kesterson, father, p.2.

KESTERSON, Ann, W, F, JUN 1853, Alexa., scarlet fever, 6y, J. & D. Kesterson, Norfolk, J. Kesterson, father, p.2.

KEYS, Jane Fielder, W, F, 12 AUG 1858, Alexa., scarlet fever, 14m6d, John & Esther Keys, John Keys, father.

KEYS, Virginia, W, F, 25 AUG 1856, Alexa., cholera infantum, --, Francis & E. Keys, F. Keys, head of family, p.15.

KEYS, W.E., W, M, 1 AUG 1855, Alexa., unknown, 3m, J.A. & E. Keys, J.A. Keys, father, p.10.

KIDWELL, Catharine, W, F, APR 1854, Alexa., scarlet fever, 3y, P. & H. Kidwell, Fairfax Co., J.A. Javins, uncle, p.7.

KIDWELL, Charles, W, M, 16 AUG 1856, Alexa., cholera infantum, 7m7d, --, M. Eldridge, head of family, p.15.

KIDWELL, Clarence, W, M, 18 JAN 1894, Alexa. Co., --, 2m27d, Alfred & Ella, Alexa. Co., Ella Kidwell, mother, p.58.

KIDWELL, Jenny, W, F, 16 DEC 1894, Alexa. Co., typhoid fever, 26y, James & Elizabeth, Alexa. Co., housekeeping, consort of J.W. Kidwell, J.W. Kidwell, husband, p.58.

KIDWELL, Laura Jane, W, F, 18 MAR 1856, Alexa., consumption, 27y2m3d, --, Alfred Kidwell, head of family, p.15.

KIDWELL, Presley, W, M, AUG 1855, Alexa., unknown, 55y, -- Kidwell, Va., H.

Kidwell, Geo. Kidwell, son, p.11.

KIDWELL, Saml., W, M, 13 AUG 1853, Alexa., unknown, 3d, A. & L. Kidwell, Alexa., A. Kidwell, father, p.1.

KINCHELOE, Farell, W, M, 1 NOV 1856, bilious colic, 50y, p.17.

KING, Harrison, (f), M, 16 OCT 1895, Alexa. Co., killed, 54y, Alex. & Lucy, Alexa. Co., labor, consort of Sarah King, S. King, wife, p.60.

KING, Julia, (f), F, 7 AUG 1895, Alexa. Co., pneumonia, 19y4m, Henry & Elizabeth, Alexa. Co., housework, single, Elizth. King, mother, p.61.

KING, Wm., W, M, 18 AUG 1859, Alexa., murdered, 30y, --, sailor, Dr. C.W. Chancellor, coroner.

KING, [blank], W, M, AUG 1855, Alexa., unknown, 1m, S.H. & M.E. King, M.E. King, mother, p.13.

KING, [blank], W, F, JUL 1855, Alexa., unknown, 15d, S.H. & M.E. King, M.E. King, mother, p.13.

KINZEY, Zenas, W, M, 26 SEP 1858, Alexa., affection of heart, 78y, --, laborer.

KITCHER, William, W, M, 19 FEB 1867, Alexa., pneumonia, 2m6d, Gotlieb & Mary Kitcher, Alexa., butcher, single, Mary Kitcher, mother, p.23.

KNIGHT, Ellen Rebecca, W, F, 5 NOV 1865, Alexa., measles, 1y7m, Anna & Ferdinand, Leesburg, cooper, Ferdinand Knight, father, p.19.

KNIGHT, John, W, M, 19 MAR 1856, Alexa., consumption, 36y, J. & E. Knight, Alexa., waterman, A. Travers, sister, p.8.

KNORR, Agnes, W, F, 2 JUL 1854, Alexa., cholera infantum, 1y, S. & M. Knorr, Philadelphia, M. Knorr, mother, p.7.

KNOTT, Mary, W, F, 18 DEC 1853, alms house, intemperance, 65y, -- Knott, unknown, John Stephenson, poor house keeper, p.5.

KNOXVILLE, John T., W, M, 24 AUG 1891, Alexa. Co., Bright's disease, 62y, --, Stafford Co., widower, Kate Knoxville,

Alexandria (Arlington) County, Virginia Death Records, 1853-1896

daughter, p.53.
KOON, Eleanor M., W, F, 4 MAR 1895, Alexa. Co., pneumonia, 70y, --, Alexa. Co., widow, E.H. Purcell, son in law, p.61.

L

LACEY, Ida Jane, W, F, 7 NOV 1859, Alexa., bowel complaint, 11y, W.B. & Mary J. Lacey, Alexa., W.B. Lacey, father.
LACY, Susie V., W, F, 4 DEC 1895, Alexa. Co., --, 43, Calbert & Jane, Alexa. Co., housekeeping, consort of Henry L. Lacy, Effie Kidwell, daughter in law, p.61.
LAFFARTY, John, W, M, 12 SEP 1855, Alexa., spasms, 2m, C. & S. Laffarty, Ireland, S. Laffarty, mother, p.13.
LALLY, Barbara, W, F, APR 1866, Alexa., unknown, 19y, Matthew Lally, Ireland, servant, single, John Lally, uncle, p.21.
LAMBERT, J.L., W, M, 10 JAN 1855, Alexa., unknown, 50y, stranger, C. Neale, coroner, p.14.
LANE, F.W., W, M, 6 FEB 1854, Alexa., scalded, 2y11m, F.W. & M.A. Lane, Alexa., F.W. Lane, father, p.7.
LANEGAN, James, W, M, 9 MAY 1866, Alexa., unknown, 9d, Pat & Margaret Lanigan, Ireland, single, Margaret Lanigan, mother, p.21.
LANGDON, Mary, W, F, 2 DEC 1856, Alexa., old age, 80y, --, Alexa., p.17.
LANNON, William, (f), M, 31 DEC 1885, Alexa. Co., heart disease, 40y, --, labor, single, James Smith, next door neighbor, p.47.
LAPHIN, Peter, W, M, 31 JAN 1853, Alexa., consumption, 34y, P. & E. Laphin, Ireland, clerk, John Laphin, brother, p.1.
LATHROP, C.H., W, F, 3 NOV 1854, Alexa., dysentery, 1y, J.H. & M. Lathrop, Alexa., J.H. Lathrop, father, p.9.

LATNEY, Lewis, (f), M, 17 JUL 1879, Jefferson Dist., shot, 50y, --, Essex Co., labor, consort of Mary Latney, Mary Latney, wife, p.39.
LAUGHLIN, Mary, W, F, 23 AUG 1893, Alexa. Co., --, 6d, James & Martha, Alexa. Co., Martha Laughlin, mother, p.56.
LAUNON, Annie B., (f), F, 20 AUG 1876, near brickyard, information on bowls, 3y, Wm. & Harriet Launon, Washington, D.C., Wm. Launon, father, p.36.
LAURENCE, David, W, M, MAR 1853, Alexa., consumption, 50y, J. & M. Laurence, Ireland, consort of Mar: Laurence, M. Laurence, widow, p.5.
LAURENCE, Edward, W, F, 5 FEB 1867, Alexa., rheumatism, 17y, Eliz'h. & Henry Laurence, Alexa., none, single, Frs. Ann Laurence, sister, p.23.
LAURENCE, Eliz'h., W, F, 6 OCT 1867, Alexa., consumption, 46y, L. & J. Hall, St. Mary's Co. Md., housekeeper, married, Frs. Ann Laurence, daughter, p.23.
LEACH, Mary, W, F, SEP 1853, Alexa., dropsy, 80y, -- Leach, unknown, consort of Saml. Leach, C. Sutton, daughter in law, p.5.
LEADBEATER, Henry, W, M, MAY 1854, Alexa., diseased brain, 1y10m, J. & M.P. Leadbeater, Alexa., J. Leadbeater, father, p.7.
LEE, Dorsy, (f), F, 12 NOV 1896, Alexa. Co., --, 10m, -- & Alice, Alexa. Co., Nellie Lee, grandmother, p.62.
LEE, Emma J., (f), F, 10 NOV 1878, H.S. Johnston's yard, whooping cough, 1m, Dennis & Rachel Lee, H.S. Johnston's yard, Dennis Lee, father, p.38.
LEE, Joseph B., W, M, 17 SEP 1854, Fairfax Co., consumption, 32y, -- Lee, N. York, bar keeper, H. O'Neale, landlady, p.7.
LEE, Phillipa, W, F, 23 DEC 1853, Alexa., convulsions, 7y, C.F. & A.E. Lee,

Alexandria (Arlington) County, Virginia Death Records, 1853-1896

Alexa., C.F. Lee, father, p.1.
LEE, Rachel, (f), F, 20 AUG 1879, Jefferson Dist., --, 22y, Washington & Rachel Watkins, Md., housekeeping, consort of Dennis Lee, Richard Watkins, mother [sic], p.39.
LEE, Robert, (f), M, AUG 1867, Alexa., --, 12y, Chas. & -- Lee, Alexa., laborer, single, Frank Gaskin, friend, p.23.
LEE, Susan, W, F, 2 SEP 1856, disease of heart, 16y, --, Alexa., p.17.
LEE, W.G., W, M, JUN 1854, Alexa., unknown, 3d, C.F. & A. Lee, C.F. Lee, father, p.6.
LEE, William, (f), M, SEP 1888, Jefferson [Dist.], --, 40y, --, labor, consort of Nellie Lee, Nellie Lee, wife.
LEE, Wm. Ludwell, W, M, 10 MAY 1858, Alexa., heart disease, 20y, C.F. Lee, C.F. Lee, father.
LEE, [blank], W, --, 20 DEC 1895, Alexa. Co., --, 7m, Wm. & Ellen, Alexa. Co., Wm. Lee, father, p.61.
LEEDS, Anna W., W, F, 20 SEP 1854, Alexa., unknown, 4d, S. & M. Leeds, Alexa., Saml. Leeds, father, p.7.
LEEDS, [blank], W, M, 9 DEC 1892, Alexa. Co., --, 3d, Chas. T. & Mary V., Alexa. Co., M.V. Leeds, mother, p.54.
LEEPER, Mary, W, F, MAR 1854, Alexa., unknown, 2d, O. & H. Leeper, Alexa., O. Leeper, father, p.7.
LEMON, Ella S., W, F, 2 AUG 1856, cholera infantum, 10m, Jas. & Isabella Lemon, Jos. Lemmon, head of family, p.15.
LENNON, M.E., W, F, 16 MAR 1855, Portsmouth, measles, 1y5m, J.G. & J.R. Lennon, Alexa., J.G. Lennon, father, p.10.
LEWIS, Anna, (f), F, AUG 1891, Alexa. Co., --, 15d, Jesse & Amanda, Alexa. Co., Amanda Lewis, mother, p.53.
LEWIS, Benj. F., (f), M, 4 JUL 1884, near Geo. Reed's, --, 17y2m, Jesse & Amanda, Alexa. Co., Jesse Lewis, father, p.45.

LEWIS, Betsey, (f), F, JUN 1893, Alexa. Co., heart disease, 64y, --, Caroline Co., widow, Andrew Lewis, son, p.56.
LEWIS, Catherine, (f), F, 24 JUL 1892, Alexa. Co., consumption, 50y, --, consort of Daniel Lewis, Daniel Lewis, husband, p.54.
LEWIS, Edwin, W, M, 15 NOV 1859, Alexa., pneumonia, 6m, --, Md., Dr. D.M. French, physician.
LEWIS, Elizabeth, (f), F, 16 FEB 1880, F. Village, --, 6y1m15d, Richard & Bettie Lewis, Alexa. Co., Bettie Lewis, mother, p.41.
LEWIS, Ellen, (f), F, 29 NOV 1893, Alexa. Co., hemorrhage, 55y, --, Va., housework, consort of Jerry Lewis, W.A. Walker, son in law, p.56.
LEWIS, George, (f), M, 1 AUG 1873, Arlington Twp., teething, 1y, Richd. & Betsy Lewis, Arlington, p.33.
LEWIS, Gertie V., (f), F, 23 SEP 1882, Hall's Hill, --, Horace & Lucy Lewis, Alexa. Co., Horace Lewis, father, p.43.
LEWIS, John, (f), M, AUG 1891, Alexa. Co., --, 25d, Jesse & Amanda, Alexa. Co., Amanda Lewis, mother, p.53.
LEWIS, John, (f), M, 18 SEP 1874, Arlington, whooping cough, 5m, --, Arlington, none, p.34.
LEWIS, John H., (f), M, 26 JUL 1879, Arlington Dist., measles, 1y9m, Richard & Betsey Lewis, Arlington Dist., Richard Lewis, father, p.39.
LEWIS, Lucy A., (f), F, 10 MAY 1892, Alexa. Co., grip, 40y, Henry & Martha Honesty, Alexa. Co., consort of Horace Lewis, Horace Lewis, husband, p.54.
LEWIS, Mary, (f), F, 20 SEP 1884, Hall's Hill, --, 17y, Daniel & Catherine, Alexa. Co., Daniel Lewis, father, p.45.
LEWIS, Nelson, (f), M, 25 OCT 1894, Alexa. Co., --, 5m, Wm. & Cornelia, Alexa. Co., Wm. Lewis, father, p.59.
LEWIS, Nelson E., (f), M, 16 MAR 1885, Alexa. Co., teething, 2y, Dan'l. &

Alexandria (Arlington) County, Virginia Death Records, 1853-1896

Catherine Lewis, Alexa. Co., Daniel Lewis, father, p.47.
LEWIS, S.A., W, M, MAR 1855, Alexa., intemperance, 28y, W. & S. Lewis, Alexa., shoemaker, consort of E.M. Lewis, E.M. Lewis, widow, p.13.
LEWIS, Wm., (f), M, 5 JUN 1894, Alexa. Co., --, 15y, Richard & Bettie, Alexa. Co., Martha Pollard, sister, p.58.
LEWIS, [blank], (f), M, 12 FEB 1876, Washington Dist., 4d, Daniel & Catherine Lewis, Alexa. Co., Catherine Lewis, mother, p.36.
LEWIS, [blank], (f), F, 20 JUN 1883, Alexa. Co., --, 3d, Horace & Lucy Lewis, Alexa. Co., Horace Lewis, father, p.44.
LEWIS, [blank], (f), F, 18 JUN 1883, Alexa. Co., --, 1m, Horace & Lucy Lewis, Alexa. Co., Horace Lewis, father, p.44.
LEYCOCK, Martha, W, F, 21 JUL 1853, Alexa., unknown, 5d, E. & N. Leycock, Alexa., N. Leycock, mother, p.2.
LINDSEY, W., W, M, JUL 1854, Alexa., spasms, 2m, J. & Julia Lindsey, Alexa., Jas. Lindsey, father, p.9.
LINTLAR, John, W, M, 26 MAR 1892, Alexa. Co., consumption, 62y, --, Germany, farmer, consort of Caroline Lintlar, Caroline Lintlar, wife, p.54.
LIPSCOMB, Nelson, (f), M, 10 MAR 1875, Alexa. Co., dyspepsia, 45y, consort of Sally Lipscomb, p.35.
LIPSCOMB, Sarah, (f), F, 14 FEB 1895, Alexa. Co., --, 56y, --, Va., widow, Joe Lipscomb, son, p.61.
LIVINGSTON, James, W, M, 7 NOV 1859, Alexa., convulsions, 7d, --, Dr. D.M. French, physician.
LLOYD, George Francis, W, M, [1] OCT 1866, Alexa., consumption, 38y, John & Ann H. Lloyd, Alexa., merchant, married, E.J. Lloyd, brother, p.21.
LLOYD, Harriet Mason, W, F, MAY 1854, Alexa. Co., old age, 72y, A. & -- Lloyd, Pr. William, consort of Edwd. Lloyd, Henry Lloyd, son, p.10.
LOLEGER, John, W, M, 18 MAY 1886, Arlington Dist., cancer, 63y, --, Germany, farming, consort of Emma Loleger, Emma Loleger, wife, p.48.
LOMASON, Benj. P., W, M, 8 NOV 1892, Alexa. Co., heart failure, 64y, --, Pa., farmer, consort of Emma P. Lomason, E.P. Lomason, wife, p.54.
LOMAX, Henry, (f), M, 2 APR 1880, F. Village, consumption, 58y, --, Westmoreland Co., widower, Wm. H. Lomax, son, p.41.
LOMAX, [blank], (f), F, 30 OCT 1867, Alexa., --, H. & L.A. Lomax, Alexa., none, single, Lucy A. Lomax, mother, p.24.
LOVEJOY, Dean Isaac, W, M, 6 MAR 1859, Alexa., old age, 77y, --, Conn., cotton spinner, J.B. Lovejoy, son.
LOVELACE, Jas. M., W, M, [no date] 1853, Alexa., cramp, 3m, W. & M. Lovelace, Alexa., M. Lovelace, mother, p.5.
LOVELACE, William, W, [M], 27 APR 1856, fell in well & drowned, 2y, Wm. & Mary Lovelace, William Lovelace, p.16.
LOWE, Jane P., W, F, 29 JUN 1859, Alexa., consumption, 24y, J.F.M. Lowe, --, J.F.M. Lowe, father.
LUCAS, Edmonia, W, F, 26 OCT 1867, Alexa., consumption, 30y, Cath. & Beverly Petty, Fairfax, housekeeper, married, Mary E. Patty, friend, p.23.
LUCAS, Thomas, (f), M, AUG 1866, Alexa., summer complaint, 3y, Julian Lucas, Fairfax, single, Silas Jones, uncle, p.21.
LUCAS, William, W, M, 3 JUL 1855, poor house, unknown, 12y, W. & -- Lucas, Md., J. Stephenson, keeper poor house, p.14.
LUDEWIG, Frederick, W, M, 27 APR 1855, Alexa., spasms, 1m, R. & L. Ludewig, Va., R. Ludewig, father, p.10.
LUMPKINS, Delila, (f), F, 18 OCT 1866, Alexa., unknown, 2y0m9d, Cath. & Augustus Lumpkins, Alexa., single, Augustus Lumpkins, father, p.21.

Alexandria (Arlington) County, Virginia Death Records, 1853-1896

LUMPKINS, John, (f), M, 9 OCT 1880, Four Mile Run, [tirlic?], 65y, --, single, Isaac Green, overseer of poor, p.41.

LYNCH, A.V., W, F, NOV 1855, Alexa., unknown, 2m, J. & M.M. Lynch, Alexa., M.M. Lynch, mother, p.12.

LYNCH, John, W, M, 21 SEP 1855, poor house, intemperance, 45y, -- Lynch, Ireland, J. Stephenson, keeper poor house, p.14.

LYNCH, [blank], W, F, 15 AUG 1857, Alexa., congestion of brain, 28y, --, Ireland, consort of Patrick Lynch.

M

MACE, [blank], W, M, JUN 1853, Alexa., unknown, 3d, W. & E. Mace, Alexa., W. Mace, father, p.2.

MACOY, Rotia, (f), M, NOV 1868, Alexa., unknown, 2m, R. & S. Macoy, Alexa., none, single, S. Macoy, mother, p.25.

MADELLA, Susan, (f), F, 15 FEB 1857, Alexa., --, Chr. Neal, coroner.

MADISON, Austin, W, M, 8 JAN 1855, Alexa., pleurisy, 54y, Alexa., laborer, W. & A. Madison, Caroline Co., consort of Elizabeth Maddison, E. Maddison, widow, p.11, and pp. 15 & 16 with date 8 JAN 1856, cause: chronic disease, consumption, Mary Madison, daughter.

MADISON, Ostin, W, M, 8 JAN 1858, Alexa., consumption, 67y, --, Mary Madison.

MAGUON, Hannah, (f), F, DEC 1853, Alexa., old age, 100y, -- Warner, unknown, consort of John Maguon, Emily Williams, daughter, p.3.

MAHONEY, Dennis, W, M, OCT 1867, Alexa., bowel complaint, 40y, --, Alexa., laborer, married, Cath. Sullivan, wife, p.23.

MAHONEY, W., W, M, 11 DEC 1855, poor house, whiskey, 35y, -- Mahoney, Ireland, J. Stephenson, keeper poor house, p.14.

MAJOR, Elizabeth B., W, F, 4 AUG 1856, --, 44y, --, Alexa., consort of J.J. Major, J.J. Major, head of family, p.17.

MAJOR, [blank], W, F, JUN 1854, Alexa., consumption, 6m, J.J. & E.B. Major, J.J. Major, father, p.6.

MALONEY, Daniel, W, M, 22 JUL 1854, poor house, sun struck, 40y, -- Maloney, Ireland, John Stephenson, keeper, p.9.

MALOSIER, Tho., W, M, 9 MAR 1855, Alexa., unknown, 54y, stranger, C. Neale, coroner, p.14.

MALOY, Ann, W, F, JUL 1853, Alexa., cholera, 23y, -- Maloy, Ireland, C. Donnelly, friend, p.5.

MANDEVILLE, Mary, W, F, 14 JAN 1858, Alexa., consumption, 50y, --, Mary Mandeville.

MANKIN, Ann E., W, F, 22 SEP 1853, Alexa., dropsy, 7y, M.M. & E.A. Mankin, Petersburg, M.M. Mankin, father, p.5.

MANKIN, D.M., W, F, 30 DEC 1868, Alexa., pneumonia, 83y, unknown, England, none, married, W. Mankin, husband, p.25.

MANKIN, E.G., W, F, JUL 1854, Alexa., pneumonia, 10m, W.E. & W.V. Mankin, W.E. Mankin, father, p.7.

MANKIN, James, W, M, 29 DEC 1855, Alexa., consumption, 55y, C. & -- Mankin, consort of Frances Mankin, C. Brengle, son in law, p.11.

MANKIN, James W., W, M, 7 OCT 1858, Alexa., --, 5y8m, M. & E.A. Mankin, M. Mankin.

MANKIN, William E., W, M, 2 JUN 1856, Alexa., consumption, 30y4m, --, watchman, W. Mankin, head of family, p.15.

MANNCROFT, Eliz'h., W, F, 12 FEB 1867, Alexa., female complaint, 45y, --, Germany, housekeeper, married, Chris Manncroft, husband, p.23.

MANSFIELD, Edward, W, --, 1 DEC 1858, Alexa., suddenly, 60y, --, coroner.

Alexandria (Arlington) County, Virginia Death Records, 1853-1896

MANSFIELD, Edwin, M, 6 JUN 1856, --, 6y, Freeman Mansfield, Freeman Mansfield, p.16.

MANSFIELD, Eugene, (f), M, OCT 1867, Alexa., fever, 1y9m, J. & M. Mansfield, Alexa., none, single, Malvina Mansfield, mother, p.23.

MANSFIELD, John H., (f), M, 12 SEP 1878, near Sissonville, measles, 6m, John & Rose Mansfield, Sissonville, John Mansfield, father, p.38.

MANSFIELD, Margaret, W, F, JUN 1857, Alexa., disease of heart, 36y, --, Ireland, consort of Freeman Mansfield, P.G. Henderson.

MANSFIELD, Mary Lewis, W, F, 22 FEB 1856, Alexa., --, 2y6m, Freeman Mansfield, Alexa., Freeman Mansfield, head of family, p.16.

MANSFIELD, Willis, (f), M, 16 JUL 1881, Sissonville, --, 1m28d, John & Rose Mansfield, Sissonville, John Mansfield, father, p.42.

MANTLEY, Frank, (f), M, 19 OCT 1881, Arlington farm, --, 37y, --, Va., labor, single, J.N. Temeton, Overseer [of the] Poor, p.42.

MARBURY, F.A., W, M, 11 DEC 1859, Alexa., consumption, 38y, --, Alexa., merchant, W.H. Marbury, brother.

MARBURY, Mary E., W, F, OCT 1858, Alexa., scarlet fever, 6y, Wm. H. & E. Marbury, Wm. H. Marbury.

MARBURY, Montgy., W, M, 5 OCT 1854, Alexa., consumption, 21y, F.F. & E.C. Marbury, F.A. Marbury, father, p.6.

MARBURY, Wm. H., W, M, OCT 1858, Alexa., scarlet fever, 9m, Wm. H. & E. Marbury, Wm. H. Marbury.

MARCEY, Charles, W, M, [no date] 1873, Washington Twp., brain fever, 1y, William Marcey, father, Dr. T.B.J. Frye, p.33.

MARCEY, Earl, W, M, FEB 1894, Alexa. Co., --, 1y14d, Jas. F. & Rose, Alexa. Co., J.F. Marcey, father, p.59.

MARCEY, Emma, W, F, 31 OCT 1873, Arlington Twp., consumption, 15y, --, Arlington, p.33.

MARCEY, James, W, M, NOV 1881, Old Mill Road, old age, 76y, John & Catherine Marcey, Va., widower, Sam'l. Marcey, son, p.42.

MARCEY, Lewis, W, M, 24 MAR 1890, Alexa. Co., old age, 78y, --, Alexa. Co., widower, Wm. Marcey, neighbor [sic], p.52.

MARCEY, Mamie, W, F, 13 SEP 1892, Alexa. Co., diphtheria, 4y, Robt. L. & Frances, Alexa. Co., Frances Marcey, mother, p.54.

MARCEY, Mary, W, F, 21 JUN 1873, Arlington Twp., consumption, 75y, p.33.

MARCEY, Oscar, W, M, 1 SEP 1892, Alexa. Co., diphtheria, 8m, Robt. L. & Frances, Alexa. Co., Frances Marcey, mother, p.54.

MARCEY, Robert O., W, M, 13 SEP 1892, Alexa. Co., diphtheria, 7y, Robt. L. & Frances, Alexa. Co., Frances Marcey, mother, p.54.

MARCEY, Talbott L., W, M, 6 AUG 1892, Alexa. Co., diphtheria, 12y, Robt. L. & Frances, Alexa. Co., Frances Marcey, mother, p.54.

MARCEY, Wm., W, M, 30 JUN 1893, Alexa. Co., suicide, 57y, James & Mary, Alexa. Co., farmer, consort of Bashoby Marcey, Wm. Marcey, son, p.56.

MARCEY, [blank], W, F, OCT 1885, Alexa. Co., --, John & Eva Marcey, Alexa. Co., John H. Marcey, father, p.47.

MARCHER, Grace, W, F, 27 JUL 1896, Alexa. Co., consumption, 21y, --, consort of John E. Marcher, John Marcher, father in law, p.62.

MARCHER, James, W, M, 26 OCT 1881, Washington Road, old age, 82, James & Elizth. Marcher, England, consort of Temperance Marcher, T. Marcher, wife, p.42.

MARKLEY, Chas., W, M, 14 JUL 1856,

Alexandria (Arlington) County, Virginia Death Records, 1853-1896

Alexa., dysentery, 8y, W.H. & H. Markley, Alexa., W.H. Markley, father, p.8.

MARKLEY, James, W, M, 21 JUL 1856, Alexa., dysentery, 1y6m, W.H. & H. Markley, Alexa., W.H. Markley, father, p.8.

MARON, Pat:, W, M, 24 MAY 1853, alms house, cholera, 40y, -- Maron, Ireland, laborer, John Stephenson, poor house keeper, p.5.

MARSTERS, Edith, W, F, OCT 1858, Alexa., scarlet fever, 6y, John & H. Marsters, Wm. H. Marbury.

MARTIN, Ada, W, F, 20 OCT 1866, Alexa., heart disease, 13y, Henry S. & Clarissa Martin, Alexa., single, Henry S. Martin, father, p.20.

MARTIN, Ida, W, F, 4 FEB 1859, Alexa., pneumonia, 2y9m, J. & J. Martin, Georgetown, John Martin, father.

MARTIN, James, (f), M, 15 DEC 1866, Alexa., scrofula, 18y, Lucinda Martin, Fauquier, laborer, single, Chas. Bow, friend, p.20.

MARTIN, John, W, M, 11 SEP 1858, Alexa., consumption, 40y.

MARTIN, L. Ann, (f), F, 28 JUL 1868, Alexa., fever, 3y, G. & E. Martin, Alexa., none, single, E. Martin, mother, p.25.

MARTIN, May, W, F, 20 NOV 1856, Alexa., consort of John Martin, John Martin, head of family, p.15.

MARTIN, Michael, W, M, 20 AUG 1853, Alexa., bilious fever, 39y, J. & M. Martin, Ireland, E. Martin, widow, p.5.

MASSEY, W.D., W, M, 16 APR 1855, Alexa., membra. croup, 4y6m, W.D. & C. Massey, Alexa., W.D. Massey, father, p.10.

MASTERSON, F.A., W, M, 25 MAR 1853, Alexa., pneumonia, 32y, S. & M.A. Masterson, Alexa., M.A. Masterson, mother, p.3.

MASTIN, Mary E., W, [F], 22 NOV 1856, suddenly, 45y, consort of John Mastin, J. Mastin, p.17.

MAXWELL, Kate, W, F, 23 DEC 1853, Alexa., croup, 2y, W. & S. Maxwell, Alexa., W. Maxwell, father, p.3.

MAYALL, John, W, M, 25 MAY 1855, poor house, old age, 80y, -- Mayall, Va., J. Stephenson, keeper poor house, p.14.

MAYO, Richard, (f), M, 8 JUN 1896, Alexa. Co., --, 5m, Jacob & Sarah, Alexa. Co., Sarah Mayo, mother, p.62.

McBURNEY, Eliza, W, F, 28 JAN 1854, Alexa., unknown, 12d, G. & N. McBurney, Alexa., Geo. McBurney, father, p.7.

McBURNEY, R.J., W, M, 11 DEC 1855, Alexa., unknown, 4m, G. & N. McBurney, Alexa., G. McBurney, father, p.11.

McCAFFERTY, Ella, W, F, 24 AUG 1854, Pa., brain fever, 4y, W. & S. McCafferty, Pa., W. McCafferty, father, p.6.

McCANN, Ann, W, F, 6 OCT 1859, Alexa., convulsions, 5y, Pat. & Jane McCann, Alexa., Pat. McCann, father.

McCANN, Frank, W, M, 11 MAY 1855, Alexa., accident, 8y, -- McCann, Ireland, Jane McSherry, friend, p.13.

McCARTY, Margaret E., W, F, 13 JUN 1858, Alexa., infanticide, 4d, John & Mary McCarty.

McCARTY, Mary J., W, F, 1 OCT 1867, Alexa., teething, 10m, F. & M. McCarty, Europe, none, single, Mary McCarty, mother, p.23.

McCARTY, [blank], W, F, 16 NOV 1857, Alexa., apoplexy, 30y, --, consort of F. McCarty.

McCLANAHAN, Wm., W, [M], 28 OCT 1857, Alexa., chronic dysentery, 56y, --, Alexa., S.J. Weadon.

McCLURE, James, W, M, 26 JUL 1856, teething, 2y7m, Wm. & Ann McClure, Wm. McClure, head of family, p.17.

McCORMICK, Catharine, W, F, 15 SEP 1856, Alexa., old age, 80y, S.J.

Alexandria (Arlington) County, Virginia Death Records, 1853-1896

McCormick, son, p.15.

McCORMICK, Eliza, W, F, 25 DEC 1858, Alexa., burned to death, 6y1d, Wm. & M. McCormick, Wm. McCormick.

McCORMICK, S.J., W, F, 29 MAY 1853, Alexa., cholera, 2y, W. & M. McCormick, Va., M. McCormick, mother, p.4.

McCORMICK, S.J., W, M, 25 MAY 1859, Alexa., bilious diarrhea, 33y, --, Alexa., auctioneer, consort of Maria McCormick, Maria McCormick, wife.

McCRACKEN, James, W, M, 19 MAY 1865, Alexa., inflammation, 55y, Nancy & James, Ireland, laborer, married, Jane McCracken, wife, p.19.

McCUEN, William, W, M, 24 DEC 1867, Alexa., consumption, 30y, J. & S. McCuen, Pr. Wm. Co., laborer, single, Silina McCuen, mother, p.23.

McCUIN, Alice, W, F, 20 AUG 1856, Alexa., --, Robt. & Mary Jane McCuin, R. McCuin, head of family, p.15.

McCULOUGH, Geo., (f), M, 28 JUL 1872, Alexa., sun stroke, 27y, unknown, Md., laborer, married, Thornton Heyron, friend, p.32.

McDERMOTT, Wm., W, M, 25 JUL 1855, Alexa., teething, 9m, P. & M. McDermott, Alexa., labor, M. McDermott, mother, p.13.

McDEVITT, John, W, M, NOV 1856, Alexa., drowned, 22y, -- McDevitt, Ireland, laborer, Ann McDevitt, A. McDevitt, widow, p.8.

McDONALD, C., W, F, DEC 1855, Alexa., unknown, 7d, P. & B. McDonald, Washington, B. McDonald, mother, p.13.

McDONALD, Michael, W, M, 8 JUN 1853, Alexa., cholera, 40y, J. & E. McDonald, Ireland, laborer, Mary McDonald, widow, p.3.

McDONOUGH, Mike, W, M, NOV 1855, Alexa., unknown, 3m, M. & B. McDonnough, M. McDonough, father, p.13.

McELHINING, J.J., W, M, 4 AUG 1895, Alexa. Co., old age, 81y, Robt. & Nocissa, Pa., consort of Ellen McElhining, R.J. McElhining, son, p.61.

McGEE, Geo. W., (f), M, 15 MAY 1887, Alexa. Co., consumption, 1y8m, Peter & Rebecca, Alexa. Co., Peter McGee, father, p.49.

McGEE, Georgana, (f), [F], DEC 1887, Alexa. Co., consumption, 1y4m, Peter & Rebecca, Alexa. Co., Peter McGee, father, p.49.

McGENITON, James, W, M, 27 NOV 1856, teething, 1y, Jas. & Eliza McGeniton, Alexa., Jas. McGeniton, p.16.

McGRAW, A., W, F, 1 OCT 1868, Alexa., unknown, 77y, -- Waters, Chas. Co. Md., storekeeper, widow, Julia McGraw, daughter, p.25.

McKENCHER, Mrs., W, F, 25 JAN 1875, Jefferson Mag. Dist., pneumonia, 45y, Alexa. McKencher, p.35.

McKENZIE, James, W, M, 10 NOV 1859, Alexa., chronic, 58y, --, Alexa., clerk, Lewis McKenzie, brother.

McKENZIE, Margt., W, F, 5 FEB 1859, Alexa., old age, 80y, --, Alexa., consort of Capt. Jas. McKenzie, Lewis McKenzie, son.

McKEOWN, Willie, W, M, 23 SEP 1866, Alexa., consumption, 20y, Robt. & Agnes McKeown, Ireland, laborer, single, Robt. McKeown, father, p.20.

McKNIGHT, Ferdinand, W, M, 17 NOV 1855, Alexa., whooping cough, 1y2m, F. & E. McKnight, Alexa., F. McKnight, father, p.12.

McKNIGHT, [Capt.] Charles, W, M, 11 MAR 1853, Alexa., old age, 79y, W. & -- McKnight, Baltimore, merchant, W.H. McKnight, nephew, p.2.

McLAY, Judith, W, F, 7 OCT 1859, Alexa., burnt to death, 20y, --, Ireland, consort of J. McLay, J. McLay, husband.

McLEAN, Mattie T., W, F, 19 OCT 1858, Alexa., consumption, 27y, consort of Wm.

Alexandria (Arlington) County, Virginia Death Records, 1853-1896

H. McLean, Wm. H. McLean.

McMAHON, J.A., W, M, 22 SEP 1857, Alexa., cholera infantum, 2y1m16d, Mary McMahon, servant.

McMAHON, John Alexander, W, M, 22 SEP 1857, Alexa., infantile convulsing, 2y1m22d, Dennis & Mary McMahon, Alexa., Dr. Stabler.

McMAHON, John, W, M, 9 FEB 1858, Alexa., consumption, 45y, --, laborer, Wm. McCormick.

McMULLIN, Thos., W, [M], 6 JUN 1857, Alexa., --, 28y.

McNAIR, Henry S., W, M, 13 AUG 1888, Washington [Dist.], malaria, 1y9m, Joseph & Alice, Alexa. Co., --, Alice McNair, mother.

McNAIR, Jos. M., W, M, 3 AUG 1895, Alexa. Co., --, 17d, Jos. E. & Alice A., Alexa. Co., J.E. McNair, father, p.61.

McNAIR, Wm. H., W, M, 30 JUL 1895, Alexa. Co., --, 14d, Jos. E. & Alice A., Alexa. Co., J.E. McNair, father, p.61.

McNEALE, W.R., W, M, 30 OCT 1855, Alexa., consumption, 30y, -- & C. McNeale, Md., carpenter, J.E. McNeale, M. Wheat, sister, p.13.

McQUEEN, Charles, W, M, 5 MAR 1873, Arlington Twp., teething, 9m, J.S. McQueen, Arlington, p.33.

McQUINN, Elizabeth, W, F, 5 JUL 1875, Alexa. Co., --, 3m, Mc. Quinn G.S., Alexa. Co., p.35.

McQUINN, Mary, W, F, 9 SEP 1875, Alexa. Co., enlargement of heart, 35y, wife of -- McQuinn, p.35.

McSWEENY, Mary, W, F, 5 NOV 1857, Alexa., consumption, 30y, --, Alexa., D.McSweeny, father.

MEADE, Capt. Theos., W, M, 13 DEC 1859, Alexa., consumption, 69y, --, Robert Meade, son.

MEADE, Franklin E., W, M, 27 JUN 1853, Alexa., unknown, 5m, W. & M.E. Meade, Alexa., Mary E. Meade, grandmother, p.4.

MEADE, Hiram, W, M, 4 JAN 1859, Alexa., scarlet fever, 3y6m, Robert & Rose Meade, Alexa., Rosa Meade, mother.

MERCHANT, Isabella, W, F, 9 AUG 1865, Alexa., chronic dysentery, 40y, Robt. & Isabella, Md., painter, married, Robt. Merchant, husband, p.19.

MERRITT, Joseph B., W, M, JUL 1896, Alexa. Co., --, 2m13d, John E. & Josephine, Alexa. Co., John E. Merritt, father, p.62.

METCALF, Dwight, W, M, 14 SEP 1857, Alexa., old age, 80y, --, A.G. Newton.

MEYNEBURG, Simon, W, M, 31 JAN 1856, pulmonary disease, 32y, --, Germany, merchant, A. Meyneburg, p.16.

MIDDLETON, Laura, (f), F, 26 APR 1888, Jefferson [Dist.], --, 45y, --, Sam'l. Steward, neighbor.

MIFFLETON, George Baley, W, M, [3] JUN 1853, Alexa., scarlet fever, 4y, H. & A. Miffleton, Alexa., H. Miffleton, father, p.2.

MILES, Cossuth, (s), M, JUN 1855, --, 6m, -- Sarah Ann, Alexa. Co., slave, T.W Swann, master, p.14.

MILES, James S., (f), M, 5 OCT 1893, Alexa. Co., --, 18d, Jas. S. & Mary, Alexa. Co., Mary Miles, mother, p.56.

MILES, Julia, (f), F, 29 MAR 1886, Washington Dist., cancer, 60y, --, Richmond Co., housekeeping, consort of Elias Willis, Elias Wiles [note 3 spellings], husband, p.48.

MILES, William T., W, M, 27 MAY 1856, brain fever, 31y, --, Charles Co. Md., farmer, May Miles, head of family, p.16.

MILLAN, Thomas, W, M, 17 JUL 1858, Alexa., scarlet fever, 11m3d, H.M. & Salina Millan, H.F. Millan, father.

MILLER, Harriet, (f), F, APR 1894, Alexa. Co., tumors, 56y, --, Va., widow, Richard Norris, son, p.59.

MILLER, Harriet, W, F, 3 JUL 1858, Alexa., --, 4m3d, Wm. & Rebecca Miller, W. Miller.

Alexandria (Arlington) County, Virginia Death Records, 1853-1896

MILLER, James H., W, M, 26 SEP 1856, Alexa., brain fever, 1y2m, F. & C. Miller, B. Hallowell, gra'father, p.8.

MILLER, Julia, (f), F, 4 SEP 1868, Alexa., brain fever, 6m, Y. & M. Miller, Alexa., none, single, M. Miller, mother, p.25.

MILLER, Mike, W, M, 6 APR 1854, Alexa., unknown, 3d, W.D. & C.V. Miller, Alexa., W.D. Miller, father, p.9.

MILLER, Mike, W, M, 2 APR 1854, Alexa., unknown, 1d, W.D. & C.V. Miller, Alexa., W.D. Miller, father, p.9.

MILLER, Wm. Thos., W, M, 10 DEC 1867, consumption, 4y4m, J.R. & Cath. Miller, Fairfax, none, single, Cath. Miller, mother, p.23.

MILLS, Catharine Virginia, W, [F], 30 AUG 1858, Alexa., scarlet fever, 5y6m, John & Mary Mills, Alexa., John Mills, father.

MILLS, Julia A., W, F, 29 JUN 1853, Alexa., brain fever, 6y, W.J. & S.J. Mills, Alexa., W.J. Mills, father, p.2.

MILLS, Margret, (f), F, 15 AUG 1878, near Pelham's, measles, 5y, Elias & Julia Mills, near Pelham's, Louisa Wilson, sister, p.38.

MILLS, Maria S., W, F, 1 SEP 1858, Alexa., --, 2y, Wm. J. & Sarah J. Mills, Wm. J. Mills.

MILLS, Martha, W, F, 9 DEC 1876, near Balston, consumption, 87y, A. & Mary Harden, Alexa. Co., John A. Mills, son, p.36.

MILLS, Milton M., W, M, 15 JUL 1856, bowel complaint, 12y6m, William & Sarah Jane, p.17.

MINCAS, Wm., W, M, 7 JUL 1859, Alexa., diseased, 60y, --, pauper, Jno. Stephenson, keeper poor house.

MINES, Benj., (f), M, 24 SEP 1894, Alexa. Co., --, 5y, Washn. & Sallie, Alexa. Co., Washn. Mines, father, p.59.

MINOR, John, (f), M, APR 1892, Wash. D.C., Bright's disease, 70y, --, Alexa. Co., laborer, consort of Mary Minor, Mary Minor, wife, p.54.

MINOR, John R., W, M, 4 DEC 1895, Alexa. Co., old age, 80y, --, Alexa. Co., widow, J.A. Trageser, tenant, p.61.

MINOR, John W., W, M, 1 NOV 1887, Alexa. Co., --, 1y, F.C. & Roberta L., Alexa. Co., F.C. Minor, father, p.49.

MINOR, Susan, (f), F, MAY 1880, Georgetown Road, heart disease, 50y, consort of John Minor, John Minor, husband, p.41.

MINOR, Virginia, (f), F, 25 AUG 1879, Jefferson Dist., teething, 1y6m, Thos. & Henretta Minor, Jefferson Dist., Henretta Minor, mother, p.39.

MINOR, Walker, (f), M, 11 AUG 1875, Jefferson Mag. Dist., consumption, 19y, Thos. Minor, Alexa. Co., p.35.

MINOR, Wm. J., W, M, 15 MAR 1880, near Saegmuller's, Bright's disease, 65y, Wm. & Catherine Minor, Alexa. Co., single, J.R. Minor, cousin, p.41.

MITCHELL, Grandeson, (s), M, JUL 1855, Alexa., brain affection, 40y, slave, Fauquier, labor, consort of Lucinda Mitchell, S. Noland, mistress, p.13.

MITCHELL, Mary, (f), F, 14 APR 1888, Washington [Dist.], tumor, 38y, Thornton & Margret Hyson, Alexa. Co., consort of John B. Mitchell, J.B. Mitchell, husband.

MONROE, Clara V., W, F, 4 SEP 1859, Alexa., unknown, 3y, J.H. & Elizth. Monroe, --, J.H. Monroe, father.

MONROE, Elizabeth Lafayette, W, F, 18 APR 1854, Alexa., pneumonia, 29y, J.H. & E. Brodus, Alexa., consort of H.L. Monroe, H.L. Monroe, husband, p.6.

MONROE, Emma V., W, F, 10 JUL 1854, Alexa., unknown, 3m, H.L. & E.L. Monroe, Alexa., H.L. Monroe, father, p.6.

MONROE, Ida E., W, F, 27 JUN 1859, Alexa., teething, 7m, H.L. & Ida E. Monroe, Alexa., H.L. Monroe, father.

MONROE, Sliter, W, M, 25 MAY 1853, Fairfax Co., Cramp, 32y, D.& E. Monroe, Alexa., cooper, C.L. Adams,

Alexandria (Arlington) County, Virginia Death Records, 1853-1896

brother in law, p.1.

MONROE, Wells, (f), M, 15 MAR 1880, G.R. Adam's farm, catarrh, 48y, --, single, F.J. Adams, employer, p.41.

MONTAENE, Albert, (f), M, FEB 1893, Alexa. Co., --, 2d, David & Maggie, Alexa. Co., Maggie Montaene, mother, p.57.

MONTAGUE, Albert, (f), M, JUN 1888, Jefferson [Dist.], --, 40y, Lewis & Lucinda, Lucinda Montague, mother.

MONTAGUE, George (f), M, APR 1888, Arlington [Dist.], catarrh of stomach, 60y, --, consort of Mary Montague, Mary Montague, wife.

MONTAGUE, Georgeanna, (f), F, 17 FEB 1882, near F. Vill[age], --, 18y12d, George & Mary Montague, Essex Co., housework, single, George Montague, father, p.43.

MONTAGUE, Lewis, (f), M, 10 JUN 1876, near canal basin, 9m, Albert & Louisa Montague, nr. canal basin, Albert Montague, father, p.36.

MONTAGUE, Lewis, (f), M, MAY 1888, Jefferson [Dist.], --, 75y, --, consort of Lucinda Montague, Lucinda Montague, wife.

MONTAGUE, [blank], (f), M, NOV 1881, Arlington farm, --, 1m, Georgana Montague, Arlington farm, Mary Montague, grandmother, p.42.

MOOD, Jacob, (f), M, 20 SEP 1872, Arlington Dist., old age, 85y, --, Md., laborer, married, Jacob Foster, father, p.32.

MOODY, Annie, W, F, SEP 1888, Washington [Dist.], --, 2m15d, Wm. Moody, Washington [Dist.], Wm. Moody, father.

MOONEY, Lucy A., (f), F, 4 OCT 1894, Alexa. Co., dropsy, 49y, --, Va., consort of Chas. Mooney, Sarah Mayo, daughter, p.59.

MOONEY, Robert, (f), M, 14 SEP 1877, near Robt. Butcher's shop, teething, 1y, Lucy & Chas. Mooney, near Robt. Butcher's shop, Lucy Mooney, Lucy Mooney, mother, p.37.

MOONEY, Robt., (f), M, 8 SEP 1879, Washington Dist., brain fever, 1y, Chas. & Lucy Mooney, Washington Dist., Lucy Mooney, mother, p.39.

MOONEY, Rosena, (f), F, 28 MAY 1893, Alexa. Co., childbirth, 25y4m, Henry & Elizabeth, Alexa. Co., consort of Richard Mooney, Richard Mooney, husband, p.57.

MOONEY, Rosena, (f), F, 1 JUL 1893, Alexa. Co., 2m, Richard & Rosena, Alexa. Co., Richard Mooney, father, p.57.

MOORE, Ann, W, F, FEB 1854, Alexa., brain fever, 11m, W.S. & A. Moore, Alexa., W.S. Moore, father, p.7.

MOORE, Isabella, W, F, OCT 1857, Alexa., choreic, 5m, John & Ann Moore, saddler.

MOORE, John, W, M, 10 JUL 1858, Alexa., --, 8m, John & Ann Moore, John Moore.

MOORE, Joseph C., W, M, 8 JUN 1867, Alexa., cancer, 71y, S. & P. Moore, Alexa., sea captain, married, Mary M. Moore, wife, p.23.

MOORE, Martha, (f), F, 4 APR 1888, Arlington [Dist.], pneumonia, 22y6m19d, --, housework, single, Jane Jackson, friend.

MOORE, Sarah O., W, F, 15 JUN 1867, consumption, --, N. & A. Dunham, Washington, N.Y., farmer, married, A. Moore, husband, p.23.

MOORE, Wm. S, (f), M, 8 AUG 1868, Alexa., fever, 4y8m, Ann & T. Moore, Alexa., none, single, Ann Moore, mother, p.25.

MORAN, Charlotte, W, F, 28 NOV 1868, Alexa., dyspepsia, 51y, Jas. & M. Frances, Dublin, Ireland, none, married, A. Moran, husband, p.25.

MORAN, Pat., W, M, JUL 1854, Alexa. Co., severe beating, 9y, Jos. & Margt. Moore, Ireland, Joseph Moore, father, p.6.

MORAN, S. Ann, W, F, 11 DEC 1853, Alexa., scarlet fever, 2y9m, A. & C.

Alexandria (Arlington) County, Virginia Death Records, 1853-1896

Moran, Alexa., A. Moran, father, p.1.
MORGAN, Anna, (f), F, 9 JUL 1878, Freedmen's Village, --, 28y, --, Ky., housework, consort of Joseph Morgan, Joseph Morgan, husband, p.38.
MORGAN, Catharine, W, F, 11 MAY 1854, Alexa., cancer, 55y, -- Padgett, Md., milliner, -- Padgett, W.C. Richards, son in law, p.6.
MORGAN, Clem, (f), M, 12 AUG 1878, Freedmen's Village, --, 6m, Joseph & Anna Morgan, Freedmen's Village, Joseph Morgan, father, p.38.
MORGAN, Joseph, (f), M, 15 MAY 1894, Alexa. Co., pneumonia, 56y, Daniel & Patsy, Va., laborer, widower, Nancy Johnson, daughter, p.59.
MORGAN, Lavinia, (f), F, 7 OCT 1867, Alexa., teething, 6m, Dan'l. & Mary E. Morgan, Alexa., none, single, Mary E. Morgan, mother, p.23.
MORGAN, Patsey, (f), F, 24 OCT 1883, Alexa. Co., consumption, 16y, Joseph & Ann Morgan, Alexa. Co., single, Joseph Morgan, father, p.44.
MORGAN, Virginia, (f), F, 5 FEB 1880, F. Village, --, 28y, --, single, W.H. Lomax, overseer of poor, p.41.
MORGAN, William, (f), M, 10 DEC 1879, Arlington Dist., --, 4y, Joseph & Ann Morgan, Arlington Dist., Joseph Morgan, father, p.39.
MORRIS, Elizabeth, (f), F, 10 NOV 1873, Arlington Twp., consumption, 25y, p.33.
MORRISON, [blank], (f), F, 14 OCT 1876, near Offords, 7d, Isom & Fannie Morrison, nr. Offords, Isem Morrison, father, p.36.
MORRISSEY, Ellen, W, F, AUG 1853, Alexa., ague & fever, 6m, Tho. & B. Morrissey, Alexa., B. Morrissey, mother, p.3.
MORROW, William, W, M, 7 DEC 1854, Alexa., diabetes, 60y, Ireland, Morrow, O. Fairfax, physician, p.10.
MORTIMORE, Chas. G., (f), M, 4 MAY 1859, Alexa., unknown, 1y, Mary Mortimore, Mary Mortimore, mother.
MORTIMORE, Louise, W, F, 25 AUG 1890, Alexa. Co., cancer, 58y, Caleb & A.C. Cleveland, Alexa. Co., housework, consort of Geo. H. Mortimore, G.H. Mortimore, husband, p.52.
MORTIMORE, [blank], W, M, 16 FEB 1874, Arlington, fever, 14d, --, Arlington, none, p.34.
MORTIMORE, [blank], W, M, 9 FEB 1874, Arlington, fever, 7d, --, Arlington, none, p.34.
MORTIMORE, [blank], W, F, 29 MAR 1872, Arlington Dist., birth, Geo. H. & Louisa, Arlington, wheelwright, Geo. H. Mortimore, father, p.32.
MOWBRAY, Ann W., W, F, 29 DEC 1877, Columbia Pike, consumption, 33y, --, consort of Geo. B. Mowbray, Geo. B. Mowbray, husband, p.37.
MOWBRAY, Wm., W, M, 4 JUL 1878, Roche's Springs, consumption, 7m, Geo. B. & Maria Mowbray, Roche's Springs, Geo. B. Mowbray, father, p.38.
MUIR, John, Jr., W, M, 30 JAN 1859, Alexa., cholera morbus, 28y, --, Alexa., engineer, consort of Lucretia Muir, John Muir, Sr., father.
MUIR, Lydia, W, F, 30 APR 1853, Alexa., child bed, 41y, N. & N. Robinson, Prince Wm. Co., consort of John Muir, J. Muir, husband, p.1.
MUIR, Nannie, W, F, 20 JUN 1854, Alexa., measles, 1y, J. & L. Muir, Alexa., J. Muir, father, p.9.
MULLEN, Joseph, W, M, 27 DEC 1853, alms house, consumption, 22y, -- Mullen, Alexa., cooper, John Stephenson, poor house keeper, p.5.
MULLEN, [blank], W, F, 30 AUG 1859, Alexa., unknown, 20d, Ann Mullen, Alexa. jail, --, J.R. Cole, jailer.
MULLONY, [blank], W, F, 17 AUG 1857, Alexa., cholera infantum, 1y, --, Alexa.
MUNSON, Hattie E., W, F, 16 JUN 1872,

Alexandria (Arlington) County, Virginia Death Records, 1853-1896

Arlington Dist., gastric fever, 27y, unknown, New York, farmer, consort of Ira F. Munson, Ira F. Munson, husband, p.32.

MURDOCK, Margret V., W, F, 10 APR 1892, Alexa. Co., --, 50y, Jas. & Mary, --, widow, W.P. Bosswell, friend, p.54.

MURPHY, Catherine, W, F, OCT 1853, Alexa., chills & fevers, --, Ireland, Ellen Murphy, daughter, p.3.

MURPHY, Mrs., W, F, NOV 1858, Alexa., murdered, 30y, consort of Pat. Murphy.

MURPHY, Tho., W, M, 13 DEC 1855, Alexa., unknown, 30y, -- Murphy, Ireland, C. Neale, coroner, p.14.

MURPHY, Thomas, W, M, OCT 1853, Alexa., unknown, 3y, Thos. & E. Murphy, Ireland, Ellen Murphy, mother, p.3.

MURRAY, Amelia, (f), F, 24 DEC 1867, Alexa., --, 55y, A. & -- Holmes, Alexa., housekeeper, married, Fanny Emerson, daughter, p.23.

MURRAY, Millie, (f), F, 28 MAR 1866, Alexa., rush of blood, 40y, Lizzie & Obert Slaughter, Orange Co., married, Lawrence Murray, husband, p.20.

MURRAY, Robt., W, M, 4 AUG 1859, Alexa., convulsions, 52y, --, Dr. D.M. French, physician.

MURRIAN, Harvey, W, M, 6 APR 1859, overlaid, --, Jas. & Mary Murrian, Jas. Murrian, father.

MURRY, Elizabeth, W, F, [no date] 1857, Alexa., 6m, Alexander & Martha Murry, Alexa.

MURRY, John H., (f), M, 3 JUN 1889, Alexa. Co., teething, 2y3m, J.H. & Margaret Alice, Va., J.H. Murry, father, p.51.

MURRY, Virginia, W, F, 14 FEB 1856, Alexa., cholera infantum, 11m, William & Elizabeth Murray, Alexa., William Murry, head of family, p.15.

N

NALLS, Ann E., W, F, NOV 1854, Alexa., unknown, 4y, W.B. & S.A. Nalls, W.B. Nalls, father.

NALLS, J.J., W, M, NOV 1854, Alexa., unknown, 2y, W.B. & S.A. Nalls, W.B. Nalls, father, p.6.

NALLS, J.W., W, M, 3 NOV 1859, Alexa., born & died, --, J.W. & Mary Nalls, Alexa., James W. Nalls, father.

NALLS, W, M, 2 JUL 1857, Alexa., --, miller.

NALLS, William M., W, M, 2 DEC 1856, Alexa., chronic, 65y, --, Prince William, T. Nalls, head of family, p.17.

NEALE, Mary E., W, F, 5 JUL 1855, Alexa., cong. of brain, 21y, S. & M. Colan, Stafford Co., C.W. Neale, C.W. Neale, husband, p.11.

NELSON, Chas., (f), M, 18 NOV 1896, Alexa. Co., --, 9m, Chas. & Mary, Va., Mary Nelson, mother, p.62.

NELSON, Fannie, W, F, 23 DEC 1855, Alexa., pneumonia, 2y6m, G.W. & E. Nelson, G.W. Nelson, father, p.11.

NELSON, George, (f), M, 22 JAN 1868, Alexa., hemorrhage, 60y, Jno. & C. Nelson, Alexa., drayman, married, Reb. Diggs, friend, p.25.

NELSON, John, (f), M, 20 NOV 1856, Alexa., heart disease, 65y, -- Nelson, unknown, drayman, consort of Patsey, Nelson, Celia Nelson, daughter, p.8.

NELSON, John, (f), M, 7 JUN 1858, Alexa., heart disease sudden, 50y, Judge Neale, coroner.

NELSON, William, (f), M, MAR 1868, Alexa., consumption, unknown, J. & V. Nelson, Alexa., none, single, Reb. Diggs, friend, p.25.

NELSON, Wm., (f), M, SEP 1894, Alexa. Co., cramps, 2y, Henry & Anna, Alexa. Co., Geo. Roland, grandfather, p.59.

NELSON, [blank], (f), M, 1 NOV 1857, Alexa., injuries before birth, 3d.

Alexandria (Arlington) County, Virginia Death Records, 1853-1896

NELSON, [blank], (f), --, 30 JAN 1858, Alexa., scarlet fever, 4y, Charlotte Nelson, C. Nelson.

NESMITH, A.S., W, F, 18 AUG 1877, near N.H., consumption, 41y, Mary & Geo. W. Nesmith, N.H., consort of Mary Nesmith, Mary Nesmith, wife, p.37.

NESMITH, Geo. M., W, M, 21 JUL 1872, Arlington Dist., cholera infantum, 7m10d, Arthur A. & Mary, Arlington, gentleman, parents, father, p.32.

NEWMAN, C.R., W, M, 25 AUG 1855, Alexa., consumption, 62y, R. & R. Newman, N.J., bricklayer, Eliza Newman, W.R. Newman, son, p.11.

NEWMAN, R., W, M, 24 FEB 1855, Alexa., catarrh fever, 8m, W.R. & M. Newman, Alexa., W.R. Newman, father, p.11.

NEWSON, James, W, M, 27 JAN 1895, Alexa. Co., --, Randolph Birch, coroner, p.61.

NEWTON, A.H., W, F, 20 JUN 1858, Alexa., scarlet fever, 3m, A.G. & H. Newton, A.G. Newton.

NICHOLSON, Margaret, W, F, 30 OCT 1853, Alexa., consumption, 67y, J. & M. Hineman, Alexa., consort of H. Nicholson, J. Jones, daughter, p.4.

NICHOLSON, Mary, W, F, AUG 1853, Alexa., consumption, 75y, -- Hineman, Alexa., consort of Henry Nicholson, W. Sellick, son in law, p.2.

NICKENS, Martha, (f), F, 25 DEC 1855, Alexa., typhoid fever, 16y, J. & Lucy Nickens, Alexa., L. Nickens, mother, p.13.

NICKENS, Mary, (f), F, 5 SEP 1855, Alexa., bilious fever, 18y, J. & Lucy Nickens, Alexa., L. Nickens, mother, p.13.

NIGHTINGALE, James, W, M, 31 MAY 1854, Alexa., drowned, 11y, John & J. Nightingale, Alexa., J. Nightingale, mother, p.7.

NIGHTINGILL, [blank], W, --, 28 SEP 1857, Alexa., --, Jos. Nightingill, Alexa., sexton.

NOBLE, Alberta, (f), F, 16 APR 1877, near Ft. Scott, consumption, 16y, Eugenia & E.S. Noble, near Ft. Scott, house work, Edward Noble, Edward Noble, father, p.37.

NOBLE, Eliza, (f), F, 10 OCT 1878, Ft. Scott, cold, 1m6d, Louisa Noble, Ft. Scott, Edward Noble, grandfather, p.38.

NOBLE, Henry, (f), M, 6 MAR 1880, Md., killed by cars, 27y1m6d, Edward & Eugenie Noble, Loudoun Co., labor, single, Edward Noble, father, p.41.

NOBLE, Martha, (f), F, SEP 1892, Alexa. Co., consumption, 13y, Richard & Maria, Va., Maria Noble, mother, p.54.

NOKES, Henson, (f), M, 6 DEC 1859, Alexa., pneumonia, 2y, Henson & Jane Nokes, Alexa., Henson Nokes, father.

NOLAND, Jane E., W, [F], 4 JUL 1857, Alexa., consumption, 29y, --, Alexa.

NOLAND, Mary, W, F, 17 OCT 1857, Alexa., consumption, 6y4m, Theophilus & Mary, Alexa., Mary Noland, mother.

NOLAND, R.E., W, M, 23 OCT 1855, Alexa., chills, 6m, Theo. & V. Noland, Alexa., V. Noland, mother, p.12.

NOLAND, Theophilus, W, --, 16 DEC, 1857, Alexa., consumption, 27y, --, Alexa., painter.

NOLAND, Theophilus, W, M, 25 AUG 1857, Alexa., consumption, 35y, --, Alexa., painter, Mary Noland, wife.

NORMAN, Nannie, (f), F, [no date] 1867, Alexa., --, 3m, Wm. & M. Norman, Alexa., none, single, Sylvia Galor, grandmother, p.23.

NORRIS, Chas. A., (f), M, 10 SEP 1892, Alexa. Co., --, 5d, Richard & Alice, Va., Richard Norris, father, p.55.

NORRIS, Dora, (f), F, MAY 1887, Alexa. Co., typhoid fever, 14y, John & Dora, La., W.H. Butler, uncle, p.49.

NORRIS, Gracie, (f), F, 15 JUN 1881, H.A. Lockwood's farm, --, 5m, Ambrose &

Alexandria (Arlington) County, Virginia Death Records, 1853-1896

Emma Norris, H.A. Lockwood's farm, Ambrose Norris, father, p.42.
NORRIS, Hattie B.W., (f), F, DEC 1889, Alexa. Co., grip, 1y9d, Richard & Alice Norris, Va., Richard Norris, father, p.51.
NORRIS, Leon, (f), F, [no date] 1858, --, pauper, John Stephenson.
NORRIS, Sarah, (f), F, 6 SEP 1872, Arlington Dist., old age, 81y, unknown, Va., Wesley Norris, son, p.32.
NORRISS, John, W, M, 2 JAN 1858, Alexa., consumption, 49y, --, Alexa., tailor, consort of Emeline, E. Norriss.

O

O'BRIAN, Hannah E., W, F, SEP 1858, Alexa., congestive chill, 9y6m, John & H.A. O'Brian, John O'Brian.
O'BRIEN, Ann, W, F, SEP 1855, Alexa., dysentery, 1y6m, P. & A. O'Brien, Alexa., Alice O'Brien, mother, p.12.
O'BRIEN, Elizabeth, (f), F, 5 AUG 1854, poor house, Pox, 30y, -- O'Brien, Ireland, John Stephenson, keeper, p.9.
O'BRIEN, J.H., W, M, 25 MAR 1855, Alexa., croup, 2y, J. & H.A. O'Brien, Alexa., Margaret Allen, gra'mother, p.12.
O'BRIEN, Julia, W, F, 27 OCT 1895, Alexa. Co., --, 1y11, Dennis & Mary, Wash. D.C., Dennis O'Brien, father, p.61.
O'CONNELL, Maurice, W, M, OCT 1855, Alexa., unknown, 1d, J. & M. O'Connell, J. O'Connell, father, p.11.
O'HARON, John, W, M, 30 MAR 1856, consumption, 24y, Andrew & Lucy Smith, laborer, Patrick Heneburg, p.16.
O'LEARY, Elizabeth W., W, F, 8 SEP 1885, Alexa. Co., spasms, 4y, Joseph & Lucy A. O'Leary, Alexa. Co., Joseph O'Leary, father, p.47.
O'NEALE, Ferdinand, W, M, 9 MAY 1855, Alexa., all sorts, 67y, C. & -- O'Neale, Loudoun Co., consort of Jane O'Neale, T. O'Neale, son, p.12.

O'NEALE, Jane, W, F, 10 JUN 1854, Alexa., old age, 69y, A. & S. Orrison, Loudoun Co., consort of F. O'Neale, Tho. O'Neale, son, p.6.
O'NEIL, Michael, W, M, 9 SEP 1872, Arlington Dist., congestive chill, 62y, unknown, Ireland, laborer, married, Randolph Birch, friend, p.32.
O'SULIVAN, James, W, M, JUL 1855, Alexa., unknown, 7d, M. & M. O'Sulivan, M. O'Sulivan, father, p.10.
O'SULIVAN, L., W, F, 2 OCT 1853, Alexa., unknown, 1d, D. & M. O'Sulivan, Alexa., D. O'Sulivan, father, p.2.
OBERTON, Lucy, (f), F, 1 FEB 1886, Arlington Dist., consumption, 11y, Jerry & Charity, Alexa. Co., Jerry Oberton, father, p.48.
OFFORD, Edward, (f), M, 2 APR 1881, near brick barn, --, 1y3m, Chas. & Elizth. Offord, near brick barn, Charles Offord, father, p.42.
OLIVER, James, (f), M, 1 OCT 1880, Windsor's yard, consumption, 1y6m, Malinda Queen, Alexa. Co., Malinda Quinn [sic], mother, p.41.
OLIVER, Mamie, W, F, 4 MAR 1890, Alexa. Co., shot, 4y, J.E. & Mary, Md., J.E. Oliver, father, p.52.
OSGOOD, Lidea A., W, F, 14 SEP 1853, Alexa., spasms, 3m, M.R. & R.C. Osgood, Alexa., M.R. Osgood, father, p.2.
OSTRANDER, Sadie, W, F, [no date] 1891, Alexa. Co., --, 17y, P.V.L. & Charolett E.M., Alexa. Co., P.V.L. Ostrander, father, p.53.
OSWALD, George, W, M, 10 NOV 1893, Alexa. Co., croup, 1y14d, Leo & Annie, Alexa. Co., Leo Oswald, father, p.57.
OTKINS, Johnny, W, M, OCT 1896, Alexa. Co., --, 9m, --, Wash. D.C., Millie Igraham, niece, p.62.
OWENS, Isaac, (f), M, 15 OCT 1890, Alexa. Co., old age, 60y, --, Md., Laura Cox, keeper of poor house, p.52.

Alexandria (Arlington) County, Virginia Death Records, 1853-1896

P

PADGETT, Arthur, W, M, NOV 1855, Alexa., unknown, 4m, -- & G. Padgett, Alexa., J.G. Padgett, gra'father, p.11.

PADGETT, [blank], W, --, 1 OCT 1857, Alexa., --, Wm. Henry Padgett, Alexa., mechanic.

PAGE, Washington C., W, M, 4 JUL 1854, Alexa., heart disease, 53y, Chs. & Ann Page, Alexa., cash. F. Bank, consort of Eliza Page, H.B. Clagett, bro. in law, p.6.

PALMER, Florence, (f), F, DEC 1892, Alexa. Co., --, 9y, Jas. & Lucy, Va., Lucy Palmer, mother, p.55.

PALMER, Hanah L., (f), F, 25 SEP 1884, near F. Vill[age], teething, 10m, William & Sarah, Alexa. Co., Wm. Palmer, father, p.45.

PALMER, Wm. W., W, M, 31 OCT 1888, Arlington [Dist.], --, 67y, --, Va., bricklayer, consort of Mary E. Palmer, M.E. Palmer, wife.

PANELL, Jas. H., (f), M, 30 JAN 1893, Alexa. Co., --, 10d, -- & Ellen Chase, Alexa. Co., John Chase, grandfather, p.57.

PARIS, Geo., (f), M, 23 MAY 1853, alms house, unknown, 45y, -- Paris, Alexa., laborer, John Stephenson, poor house keeper, p.5.

PARKER, Charlotte, (f), F, OCT 1887, Alexa. Co., drowned, 50y, Chas. & Fitia, Alexa. Co., M. Johnson, neighbor, p.49.

PARKER, Chester, (f), M, SEP 1888, Jefferson [Dist.], --, 6y, Richard & Laura, Alexa. Co., Samuel Stewart, neighbor.

PARKER, Edward, (f), M, JUN 1889, Alexa. Co., --, 3m18d, Jno. & Marth[a] Parker, Va., Martha Parker, mother, p.51.

PARKER, Emma, (f), F, 29 MAR 1888, Washington [Dist.], --, 8m, --, Jane Parker, mother.

PARKER, Jas. C., (f), M, 10 JAN 1866, Alexa., dropsy, 3y6m, John & Martha Parker, Dinwiddie, laborer, single, Martha Parker, mother, p.20.

PARKER, Mary, (f), F, 7 JUL 1879, Jefferson Dist., heart disease, 48y, Samuel & Maria Jones, Caroline Co., housekeeping, consort of Richard Parker, Annie Bailey, daughter, p.39.

PARKER, Richards, (f), M, 7 NOV 1884, Alexa. City, killed, 40y, --, Alexa. Co., labor, consort of Laura Parker, Weston Green, friend, p.45.

PARKER, [blank], (f), F, 29 FEB 1866, Alexa., unknown, 1d, Chris & Jane Parker, Alexa., Chris Parker, father, p.21.

PARKS, Emma, (f), F, 10 FEB 1885, Alexa. Co., dropsy, 30y, --, Va., housekeeping, consort of James Parks, Jas. Parks, husband, p.47.

PARKS, John, (f), M, 25 AUG 1877, near brick barn, teething, 1y, Emma & Jas. Parks, near brick barn, Emma Parks, mother, p.37.

PARKS, Joseph, (f), M, OCT 1894, Alexa. Co., teething, 1y6m, Jon. & Rockyan, Alexa. Co., R. Parks, mother, p.59.

PARKS, Mary E., (f), F, 28 MAY 1873, Arlington Twp., fits, 5d, James Parks, Arlington, p.33.

PARKS, Perry, (f), M, 15 SEP 1881, near brick barn, --, 1m14d, Wm. H.F. & Mary Parks, near brick barn, Wm. H.F. Parks, father, p.43.

PARKS, Ruffin, (f), M, 5 OCT 1878, near brick barn, teething, 8m20d, James & Emma Parks, near brick barn, James Parks, father, p.38.

PARRISH, Charles, W, M, 21 AUG 1856, consumption, 31y, --, Conn., John Thompson, head of family, p.17.

PASCOE, Honora, W, F, AUG 1853, Alexa., old age, 89y, -- Lidycoat, England, consort of Chs. Pascoe, A.D. Harmon, son in law, p.3.

PASCOE, Phillippa, W, F, APR 1854, Alexa., old age, 70y, W. & -- Pascoe, England, A.D. Harman, nephew, p.6.

PATTERSON, Martha, (f), F, 14 OCT 1874,

Alexandria (Arlington) County, Virginia Death Records, 1853-1896

Arlington, cold, 1y6m, --, Alexa. Co., none, p.34.
PATTERSON, Mary, (f), F, 12 APR 1874, Arlington, paralyzed, 38y, --, Alexa. Co., cook, p.34.
PATTERSON, Michell, W, M, [no date] 1893, Alexa. Co., typhoid fever, 21y, --, J.T. Raub, employer, p.57.
PATTON, James A., W, M, 22 DEC 1855, Alexa., dropsy, 39y, -- & M. Patton, P. William, Eliza Swansbury, kept madam, p.11.
PATTON, John F., W, M, 9 SEP 1858, Alexa., unknown, 6y, L. & J.E. Patton, Alexa., L. Patton, Jr., father, p.10.
PATTON, Margaret, W, F, 25 JAN 1855, Alexa., accidental, 61y, H. & M. Reeves, P.W. Co., consort of L. Patton, Sen., L. Patton, Jr., son, p.10.
PATTON, [blank], W, M, 7 SEP 1857.
PAUL, Arthur, W, M, 9 JUL 1855, Alexa., whooping cough, 2y, J. & M.J. Paul, Washn. City, J. Paul, father, p.11.
PAULIE, William, W, M, AUG 1855, Alexa., dysentery, 1y6m, W. & E.J. Paulie, Culpeper, W. Paulie, father, p.11.
PAYNE, Annie E., W, F, 3 DEC 1881, near H.W. Febrey's, heart disease, 44y, Sam'l. & Ann Brick, Alexa. Co., housekeeping, consort of Theo. W. Payne, T.W. Payne, husband, p.43.
PAYNE, Chas. W., Sr., W, M, 24 OCT 1886, Washington Dist., --, 65y, --, Md., Mrs. Hager, neighbor, p.48.
PAYNE, Howard, W, M, 9 AUG 1877, Washn. Dist., teething, 1y, Margret & A.R. Payne, Washn. Dist., A.R. Payne, father, p.37.
PEACH, Samuel, W, M, 25 FEB 1858, Alexa., run over by cars, 66y, --, Alexa., consort of Rebecca Peach, S.G. Peach.
PEARCE, Allan, W, M, 24 NOV 1873, Arlington Twp., cancer in stomach, 62y, --, Arlington, p.33.
PEARSON, Willy M., W, M, 20 MAY 1895, Alexa. Co., rheumatism, 8y, J.T. & Mary A., Fauquier Co., J.T. Pearson, father, p.61.
PEERCE, Florence, (s), F, [no date] 1855, Alexa., --, 5m, A. & L.A. Peerce, Alexa. Co., slave, T.W. Swann, master, p.14.
PEERCE, Rosetta, (s), F, [no date] 1855, Alexa., --, 5m, A. & L.A. Peerce, Alexa. Co., slave, T.W. Swann, master, p.14.
PELHAM, Elizabeth, (f), M, 5 DEC 1881, near Wunder's, cold, 16y7m, Moses & Isabella Pelham, Washington, D.C., single, Moses Pelham, father, p.43.
PELHAM, Hattie, (f), F, 4 JUL 1895, Alexa. Co., consumption, 18y, Moses & Isabella, Alexa. Co., housework, Moses Pelham, father, p.61.
PELHAM, Isabella, (f), F, 17 FEB 1892, Alexa. Co., heart failure, 65y, John & Hannah Washington, Culpeper Co., housekeeper, consort of Moses Pelham, Moses Pelham, husband, p.55.
PELHAM, John, (f), M, 28 MAR 1896, Alexa. Co., consumption, 23y, Moses & Isabella, Alexa. Co., Moses Pelham, father, p.62.
PEMBERTON, Daniel, (f), M, 1 FEB 1874, Alexa. Road, spasms, 21d, Bird & Sarah Pemberton, Va., laborer, married, Sarah Pemberton, head of family, p.34.
PENDLETON, Edna, (f), F, 14 OCT 1867, Alexa., consumption, 24y, S. & Ann Pendleton, Caroline Co., laborer, single, Ann Pendleton, mother, p.23.
PENN, Charlotte P., W, F, 27 JAN 1854, Alexa., cholera infantum, 9m, W.L. & M.E. Penn, Alexa., W.L. Penn, father, p.6.
PENN, Elizabeth, W, F, 13 MAY 1858, Alexa., consumption, 41y28d, consort of M.L. Penn, M.L. Penn.
PENN, Fannie, W, F, 26 FEB 1856, Alexa., teething, 1y, Mark L. & Elizabeth Penn, Mark L. Penn, head of family, p.15.
PENN, James, W, M, 9 DEC 1880, Dr. King's farm, consumption, 38y, Wm. & Sarah Penn, England, farmer, consort of

Alexandria (Arlington) County, Virginia Death Records, 1853-1896

Emma Penn, Sallie Penn, daughter, p.41.
PENN, Leonidus, W, M, 26 SEP 1854, Alexa., small pox, 4y, W.L. & M.E. Penn, Alexa., W.L. Penn, father.
PENN, Wm., W, M, 2 JUL 1857, Alexa., --, -- Penn, Alexa., mechanic.
PERKINS, Wm. T., W, M, 3 OCT 1880, Hunter's farm, old age, 87y, --, consort of Louisa A. Perkins, Louisa A. Perkins, wife, p.41.
PERNELL, Lott, (f), M, 6 AUG 1879, Jefferson Dist., consumption, 60y, --, Md., labor, consort of Eliza Pernell, Eliza Pernill, wife, p.39.
PERRY, Emily Granville, W, F, 29 SEP 1854, Alexa., asthma, 22y, -- Granville, Conn., consort of James Perry, James Perry, husband, p.7.
PERRY, Maria A., (f), F, 9 JUN 1895, Alexa. Co., --, 56y, --, Va., housework, consort of Benj. Perry, Benj. Perry, husband, p.61.
PERRY, Samuel, (f), M, 19 OCT 1885, Alexa. Co., consumption, 22y, Ben & Maria Perry, Alexa. Co., labor, single, Maria Perry, mother, p.47.
PERRY, William W., W, M, 9 SEP 1853, Alexa., dropsy on the brain, 9m, J. & E. Perry, Alexa., collier, James Perry, father, p.3.
PETERS, Zachariah, (f), M, 18 SEP 1872, Arlington Dist., congestive chill, 35y, unknown, Va., laborer, Mary, Geo. Mortimore, undertaker, p.32.
PETITT, Eliza, W, F, AUG 1883, Alexa. Co., dropsy, 67y, Jas. & Betsey Tillett, Fairfax Co., widow, George Petitt, son, p.44.
PETITT, Richard, W, M, AUG 1891, Alexa. Co., fits, 36y, Joseph & Sophia, Fairfax Co., single, Jos. Petitt, father, p.53.
PETTIT, Francis, W, M, 10 MAR 1868, Dangerfield's farm, Alexa. Co., shot by a gun, 30y, Father M. Pettit, mother unknown, Va., laborer, single, T.J. Edelin, coroner, p.25.

PETTITT James, W, M, 20 MAR 1856, Alexa., scarlet fever, 8y, G. & E. Pettitt, Alexa., E. Pettitt, mother, p.8.
PETTITT, Thos., W, M, 2 MAR 1857, Alexa., --, 1y.
PETTY, [blank], W, --, 28 JUN 1857, Alexa., --, C.E. Petty, Alexa., hotel keeper.
PEVERELL, John, W, M, 20 AUG 1855, Alexa., cholera infantum, 10m, J. & M. Peverell, Alexa., J. Peverell, father, p.12.
PEVERILL, Annie, W, F, 6 JUL 1883, Alexa. Co., --, 6m, Thos. & Lizzie Peverill, Alexa. Co., Thomas Peverill, father, p.44.
PEVERILL, Benjamin, W, M, 22 NOV 1895, Alexa. Co., croup, 3y10m, Lewis P. Peverill, Alexa. Co., Lewis Peverill, father, p.61.
PEVERILL, George A., W, M, NOV 1858, Alexa., --, 1y11m, J.J. & Mary Peverill, John Craven.
PEVERILL, James, W, M, 25 JUN 1879, Jefferson Dist., --, 1y10m, James & Sarah Peverill, Jefferson Dist., James Peverill, father, p.39.
PEVERILL, Lizzie, W, F, 28 JAN 1896, Alexa. Co., pneumonia, 38y, James & Ann, Alexa., housekeeping, consort of Thos. Peverill, Thos. Peverill, husband, p.62.
PEYTON, John B., W, M, [no date] 1853, Alexa., unknown, 38y, F. & S. Peyton, Alexa., [married], L. Peyton, brother, p.5.
PEYTON, Lucien, W, M, 11 NOV 1853, Alexa., typhoid fever, 12y, L. & M. Peyton, Alexa., L. Peyton, father, p.5.
PEYTON, W.W., W, M, 28 APR 1855, poor house, consumption, 40y, -- Peyton, Ireland, labor, J. Stephenson, keeper poor house, p.14.
PEYTON, [not named], (f), M, 18 MAY 1894, Alexa. Co., --, 15d, Barney & Caroline, Alexa. Co., Barney Peyton, father, p.59.
PHILIPS, Richard, (f), M, 4 JUL 1872,

Alexandria (Arlington) County, Virginia Death Records, 1853-1896

Arlington Dist., intermittent fever, 4y, William & Chloe, Arlington, laborer, William Philips, father, p.32.
PHILLIPS, Emma J., W, F, 10 AUG 1853, Alexa., scarlet fever, 2y2m2d, J.G. & C. Phillips, Alexa., C. Phillips, mother, p.3.
PHILLIPS, Jas. E., (f), M, [no date] 1857, --, 1y4m, S.J. & S. Phillips.
PHILLIPS, John, W, M, 2 JUN 1856, consumption, 35y, --, Alexa., shoemaker, Geo. Phillips, head of family, p.16.
PHILLIPS, Mary, W, F, 5 JUN 1856, grief, 29y, --, Alexa., John Phillips, Geo. Phillips, head of family, p.16.
PHILLIPS, William, (f), M, 5 NOV 1877, Washn. Forest, consumption, 39y, --, Va., farmer, consort of Clara Phillips, Clara Phillips, wife, p.37.
PIERSON, Harriet, (f), F, 18 SEP 1879, Jefferson Dist., burnt by coal oil, 63y, Lucinda & Marcus Baker, Fairfax Co., housekeeping, consort of James Pierson, James Pierson, husband, p.39.
PILES, C.A., (s), M, 14 AUG 1857, Alexa., burned to death, 1y3m, --, J.H.D. Smoot.
PINES, Lizzie, (f), F, MAY 1893, Alexa. Co., --, 18y, --, Alexa. Co., single, Heneretta Washington, mother, p.57.
PINES, Lizzie, (f), F, JUN 1892, Alexa. Co., --, 18y, --, Alexa., single, Henrietta Washington, mother, p.55.
PINES, [not named], (f), M, MAY 1893, Alexa. Co., --, 10d, --, Alexa. Co., Henretta Washington, grandmother, p.57.
PINKNEY, Eliza, (f), F, 7 APR 1867, Alexa., whooping cough, 2y6m, Robt. & Rachel Pinkney, Alexa., none, single, Robt. Pinkney, father, p.23.
PINKNEY, Sophia, (f), F, 14 APR 1867, Alexa., whooping cough, 3m1d, Robt. & Rachel Pinkney, Alexa., none, single, Robt. Pinkney, father, p.23.
PINN, Dennis, (f), M, 15 MAR 1893, Alexa. Co., pneumonia, 70y, --, Alexa. Co., labor, consort of Mary Pinn, Mary Pinn, wife, p.57.

PINN, Leanna, (f), F, 22 OCT 1895, Alexa. Co., diphtheria, 12y, Sidney & Mary, Alexa. Co., Mary Pinn, mother, p.61.
PINN, Lizzie, (f), F, 26 MAY 1887, consumption, 16y, Chas. & Fitia, Alexa. Co., Seymore Roy, father, p.49.
PINN, Lucy A., (f), F, DEC 1892, Alexa. Co., spasm, 1y3m, Abraham & Maria, Alexa. Co., A. Pinn, father, p.55.
PINN, Sidney, Jr., (f), M, 15 OCT 1895, Alexa. Co., diphtheria, 5y, Sidney & Mary, Alexa. Co., labor, Mary Pinn, mother, p.61.
PINN, Titia, (f), F, 14 AUG 1895, Alexa. Co., consumption, 55y, --, widow, Sidney Pinn, son, p.61.
PINN, Winnie, (f), F, 10 JUN 1885, Alexa. Co., --, 24y, Chas. & Tictia Pinn, Va., housework, single, Fictia Pinn, mother, p.47.
PIPER, E.A., W, F, 10 FEB 1855, Alexa., old age, 65y, T. & -- Ramsey, Fairfax, Jackson Piper, Jas. E. Piper, son, p.13.
PITTS, Robert, W, M, 23 SEP 1853, Alexa., consumption, 57y, J. & P. Pitts, Caroline Co., Nancy Pitts, Mildred Pitts, daughter, p.4.
PLAIN, George, W, M, 17 NOV 1855, Alexa., accident, 37y, G. & J. Plain, Annapolis Md., painter, consort of C.A. Plain, C.A. Plain, widow, p.13.
PLEASANT, Thos., (f), M, 6 JUN 1896, Alexa. Co., dropsy, 70y, --, Va., shoemaker, consort of Courtney Pleasant, C. Pleasant, wife, p.62.
PLEASANTS, [blank], (s), DEC 1855, Alexa., unknown, 1d, -- & Martha Pleasants, Alexa., F.L. Smith, master, p.14.
PLUMMER, Daniel W., (f), M, 26 SEP 1881, near brick barn, --, 3y9m, Wm. & Sarah Plummer, near brick barn, Wm. Plummer, father, p.43.
PLUMMER, Edward A., (f), M, 18 JUN 1890, Alexa. Co., --, 3m12d, Wm. & Sarah, Alexa. Co., Sarah Plummer,

Alexandria (Arlington) County, Virginia Death Records, 1853-1896

mother, p.52.

PLUMMER, Elias, (f), M, 22 JAN 1876, near brick barn, consumption, 59y, Barna. & Sallie Plummer, Md., Wm. Plummer, son, p.36.

PLUMMER, Emma B., (f), F, 29 AUG 1891, Alexa. Co., --, 5m, John H. & Julia, Va., Julia Plummer, mother, p.53.

PLUMMER, Fannie R., (f), F, 14 MAY 1878, near brick barn, --, 3m, Wm. & Sarah Plummer, near brick barn, Wm. Plummer, father, p.38.

PLUMMER, Geo. W., (f), M, 25 DEC 1894, Alexa. Co., --, 3y, John H. & Julia, Alexa. Co., Julia Plummer, mother, p.59.

PLUMMER, Georgia S., (f), F, AUG 1895, Alexa. Co., --, 4m, J.W. & Eugenia, Alexa. Co., J.W. Plummer, father, p.61.

PLUMMER, Louisa, (f), F, 5 MAY 1885, Alexa. Co., pneumonia, 11m11d, J.H. & Julia Plummer, Alexa. Co., Julia Plummer, mother, p.47.

PLUMMER, R.R., W, M, 21 JUN 1858, Alexa., scarlet fever, 7m, B.T. & A.E. Plummer, B.T. Plummer.

PLUMMER, Walter, (f), M, 28 DEC 1888, Arlington [Dist.], --, 3y, J.H. & Julia Plummer, Alexa. Co., Julia Plummer, mother.

POLLARD, James H., (f), M, 25 AUG 1880, S.W. of cemetery, diphtheria, 2y, Jesse & Lizzie Pollard, Alexa. Co., Lizzie Pollard, mother, p.41.

POLLARD, John, (f), M, 3 NOV 1896, Alexa. Co., killed, 32y, Fleming & Julia, Va., labor, consort of Elizabeth Pollard, F. Pollard, father, p.62.

POLLARD, Junius, (f), M, MAY 1892, Alexa. Co., --, 25y, Fleming & Julia, Va., laborer, consort of Ellen Pollard, Ellen Pollard, wife, p.55.

POLLARD, Maud, (f), F, [no date] 1892, Alexa. Co., --, 3m, Junius & Ellen, Alexa. Co., Ellen Pollard, mother, p.55.

POLLARD, Rosa, (f), F, SEP 1893, Alexa. Co., --, 1m, --, Addie Pollard, Alexa. Co., Nellie Pollard, grandmother, p.57.

POLLARD, Rosa, (f), F, 16 NOV 1868, Alexa., fever, 10m, H. & Susan Pollard, Alexa., none, single, S. Pollard, mother, p.25.

POLLARD, Sallie, W, F, 26 JUL 1859, Alexa., worms, 4y, Henry & Marian Pollard, Alexa., Henry Pollard, father.

POLLARD, [not named], (f), F, OCT 1893, Alexa. Co., --, 1d, Jesse & Elizabeth, Alexa. Co., Jesse Pollard, father, p.57.

PORTER, Francis, (f), F, 2 APR 1866, Alexa., scarlet fever, 4y, Betsy & Fra. Porter, Madison Co., laborer, single, Fras. Porter, father, p.20.

PORTER, Watson B., W, M, 31 JUL 1865, Alexa., accidental burn, 4y7m, Louis H. & Phoebe, Westville N.J., clerk, single, Louis H. Porter, father, p.19.

POSEY, Ellen, W, F, 26 FEB 1856, Alexa., cholera infantum, Jas. K. & Mary E. Posey, [F. Keys], head of family, p.15.

POSEY, Infant, W, --, 2 OCT 1857, Alexa., croup, --, Jas. Posey, Alexa.

POTTER, Winnie, (f), F, NOV 1868, Alexa., old age, 80y1m9d, unknown, Va., none, married, Harriet Potter, daughter in law, p.25.

POTTERTON, Caroline L., W, F, 27 DEC 1890, Alexa. Co., cancer, 41y, Henry O. & Caroline Welch, housework, consort of Chas. Potterton, Chas. Potterton, husband, p.52.

POTTS, Joseph, W, M, JUL 1853, Alexa., cholera, 12y, unknown, Alexa., J.L. Smith, friend, p.1.

POWELL, H. Brook, W, M, 7 NOV 1854, Alexa., infla. of bowels, --, W.L. & A.M. Powell, Loudoun, consort of C. Powell, L.B. Taylor, bro. in law.

POWELL, Hasty, (f), F, MAY 1891, Wash. D.C., --, 24y, Andrew & Louise, N.C., housework, consort of Otta Powell, Andrew Norfleet, father, p.53.

POWELL, Dr. William L., W, M, 4 SEP 1853, Alexa., apoplexy, 56y, B. & C.

Alexandria (Arlington) County, Virginia Death Records, 1853-1896

Powell, Loudoun, physician, L.B. Taylor, son in law, p.5.
POWERS, Margaret, W, M, 17 OCT 1856, croup, 8d, James & Mary Powers, James Powers, head of family, p.15.
POWERS, Thomas, W, M, AUG 1858, Alexa., consumption, 57y, --, Mrs. Powers.
POWERS, Thomas, W, M, 15 JAN 1859, Alexa., consumption, 54y, --, Ireland, Philip Parks, friend.
PRELEP, Wm. H., W, M, 4 OCT 1879, Jefferson Dist., intimating fever, 2y9m, Wm. & Catherine Prelep, Washington D.C., Wm. Prelep, father, p.39.
PRESSMAN, Frances, W, --, 10 OCT 1857, Alexa., childbirth, 35y, Wm. & Mrs. Fowle, Alexa., consort of B.F. Pressman, Wm. Fowle.
PRETTYMAN, Henry, W, M, 5 AUG 1853, Alexa., chronic diarrhea, 5m, R.F. & M.V. Prettyman, Alexa., R.F. Prettyman, father, p.2.
PRETTYMAN, Priscilla, W, F, 9 AUG 1856, old age, 70y, --, consort of David Prettyman, R.F. Prettyman, head of family, p.17.
PRICE, Benj. H., W, M, 10 AUG 1868, Alexa., unknown, 14y, Benj. & Mary Price, Alexa., carpenter, single, B.F. Price, father, p.25.
PRICE, Clarence, W, F, SEP 1853, Alexa., dysentery, 2y, G.C. & M.P. Price, Essex Co., G.C. Price, father, p.2.
PRICE, Clay, W, M, 27 AUG 1858, Alexa., scarlet fever, 5y3m, C.S. & M.A. Price, C.S. Price.
PRICE, E.F., W, F, 1 NOV 1856, Alexa., unknown, 1y, J.T. & E. Price, J.T. Price, father, p.8.
PRICE, Frank, W, M, 6 MAY 1859, Alexa., whooping cough, 1y6m, B.F. & Mary Price, Alexa., B.F. Price, father.
PRICE, Ruth, W, F, 17 JAN 1894, Alexa. Co., typhoid fever, 9y, Chas. P. & Virginia, Alexa. Co., Chas. P. Price, father, p.59.
PRICE, Walter C., W, M, 25 JUL 1854, New Orleans, yellow fever, 17y, W.B. & Sarah Price, Alexa., seaman, W.B. Price, father, p.6.
PRICE, [blank], (f), M, 8 JUN 1878, near F. Vill[age], --, 1d, John & Caroline Price, near F. Vill[age], Caroline Price, mother, p.38.
PUTMAN, Walter, W, M, 10 NOV 1892, Alexa. Co., --, 1m27d, E.C. & Madie, Alexa. Co., Madie Putman, mother, p.55.
PYE, Henrietta, (f), F, 20 JUL 1866, Alexa., unknown, 3y6m, Eliza & Fred Pye, Md., laborer, Eliza Pye, mother, p.20.
PYE, James, (f), M, OCT 1867, Alexa., --, 2y, Eliza & Fred Pye, Alexa., none, single, Eliza Pye, mother, p.23.

Q

QUAINTANCE, Susan, (f), F, OCT 1868, Alexa., teething, 1y2m, Tim & Hester Quaintance, Alexa., none, single, H. Quaintance, mother, p.25.
QUANDER, Jerry, (f), M, FEB 1853, county jail, pneumonia, 50y, --, Fairfax Co., stealing, H.L. Monroe, jailor, p.1.
QUINN, Robert, W, M, 15 SEP 1883, Alexa. Co., teething, 2y, Matthew & Eliza Quinn, Alexa. Co., Matthew Quinn, father, p.44.

R

RADCLIFFE, John, W, M, 19 AUG 1858, Alexa., scarlet fever, 1y2m, John & Mary Radcliffe, John Radcliffe.
RAFFARTY, P., W, M, 9 DEC 1855, Alexa., unknown, 30y, -- Raffarty, Ireland, C. Neale, coroner, p.14.
RAFFARTY, Patrick, W, M, 12 DEC 1855, Alexa., pneumonia, 25y, M. & M. Raffarty, Ireland, labor, Cath. Murphy, sister, p.13.

Alexandria (Arlington) County, Virginia Death Records, 1853-1896

RANDELL, Scarlot, W, [F], 3 DEC 1853, alms house, intemperance, 65y, -- Randell, P. Wm. Co., John Stephenson, poor house keeper, p.5.

RANSOM, Alberta, (f), F, 17 APR 1882, near F. Vill[age], 6m, George & Axion Ransom, Alexa. Co., George Ransom, father, p.43.

RANSOM, Axion, (f), F, 29 OCT 1893, Alexa. Co., cancer, 50y, Roy & Diana, Alexa. Co., housekeeping, consort of Geo. Ransom, George Ransom, husband, p.57.

RANSOM, Bert, (f), F, MAR 1885, Alexa. Co., --, 2y, George & Arion, Alexa. Co., George Ransom, father, p.47.

RANSOM, David, (f), M, OCT 1882, near F. Vill[age], --, George & Axion Ransom, Alexa. Co., George Ransom, father, p.43.

RANSOM, Diana, (f), F, 23 JAN 1876, Freedmen's Village, swallowed a pin, 7y, Geo. & -- Ransom, Freedmen's Village, Geo. Ransom, father, p.36.

RANSOM, Ida, (f), F, 16 SEP 1887, Alexa. Co., 5m, Joseph & Eliza, Alexa. Co., Eliza Ransom, mother, p.49.

RANSOM, [blank], (f), F, 18 FEB 1879, Arlington Dist., --, 1d, Geo. & Arion Ransom, Arlington Dist., George Ransom, father, p.39.

RANSOME, Axion, (f), F, 29 OCT 1892, Alexa. Co., cancer, 45y, James & Dianna, Va., housekeeper, consort of Geo. Ransome, Geo. Ransome, husband, p.55.

RAPHEAL, John, W, M, 5 JUL 1856, --, 9m, Robert J. & Julia Ann, Robt. Raphiel, p.17.

RATCLIFF, Jemima, (f), F, AUG 1855, Alexa., consumption, 29y, -- & Ratliff, Westmoreland, Joseph Ratcliff, Elizabeth Evans, cousin, p.12.

RATCLIFFE, R.B., W, M, 27 JUN 1859, Alexa., general debility, 61y, --, Alexa., carpenter, consort of Mary E. Ratcliffe, Mary E. Ratcliffe, wife.

RAY, Joseph, W, M, 13 DEC 1853, Alexa., consumption, 30y, -- Ray, Pa., carpenter, Thos. O'Neale, hotel keeper, p.2.

REAMER, S.M., W, F, 13 NOV 1853, Augusta Co., pneumonia, 2y, D. & R.A. Reamer, Augusta Co., D. Reamer, father, p.5.

REARDON, Elizabeth P., W, F, 17 JUN 1856, paralytic, --, consort of J.R. Reardon, p.16.

REED, Clem, (f), M, 27 APR 1881, canal basin, old age, 80y, --, Va., consort of Millie Reed, Millie Reed, wife, p.43.

REED, John E., W, M, 19 AUG 1856, Alexa., teething, 1y27d, J.F. & Mary Ann Reed, J.T. Reed, head of family, p.15.

REED, Joseph, (f), F, 12 AUG 1877, Washn. Dist., teething, 1y, Margret & Patrick Reed, Washn. Dist., Margret Reed, mother, p.37.

REED, Millie, (f), F, 12 JUN 1889, Alexa. Co., old age, 90y, ---, Va., Samuel Stewart, neighbor, p.51.

REEL, Annie V., W, F, 1 MAY 1879, Jefferson Dist., consumption, 20y, James L. & Elizth. C. Reel, Alexa., housework, single, James L. Reel, father, p.39.

REESE, [blank], (f), M, 17 MAY 1867, Alexa., --, H. & M. Reese, Alexa., none, single, Jas. Breen, friend, p.24.

REEVE, Joseph, W, M, AUG 1853, Alexa., unknown, 3m, L.W. & N. Reeve, Alexa., F.E. Reeve, aunt, p.2.

REEVE, Nancy, W, F, MAY 1853, Alexa., suicide, 24y, L. & L. Massey, Alexa., S.W. Reeve, F.E. Reeve, sister, p.2.

REID, Carrie E., W, F, 4 JUL 1888, Washington [Dist.], --, 2y, Geo. W., Jr. & Mary E., Washington [Dist.], Geo. W. Reid, Jr., father.

REID, Geo. W., Jr., W, M, JUL 1889, Alexa. Co., --, 6m, Geo. W. & Mary Reid, Va., G.W. Reid, father, p.51.

REID, Mary A., W, F, 1 JAN 1895, Alexa. Co., old age, 70y, --, widow, Randolph Birch, coroner, p.61.

REID, [blank], W, F, 23 DEC 1894, Alexa. Co., exposure, 75y, --, Alexa. Co.,

Alexandria (Arlington) County, Virginia Death Records, 1853-1896

Luvenia Galaway, neighbor, p.59.
RENNOE, Reverdy, W, M, 5 JUL 1858, Alexa., scarlet fever, --, Rev. & Harriot Rennoe, Harriot Rennoe, mother.
REYNOLDS, Delia, W, F, OCT 1855, Alexa., lock jaw, 6d, J. & J. Reynolds, J. Reynolds, father, p.11.
REYNOLDS, Eva, W, F, 20 DEC 1884, near Carlin's Springs, --, 4m, James & Virginia, Alexa. Co., James Reynolds, father, p.45.
REYNOLDS, John, W, M, 23 SEP 1867, Alexa., consumption, 4m, J. & Ann Reynolds, Alexa., none, single, Ann Reynolds, mother, p.23.
REYNOLDS, Laura V., W, F, 25 SEP 1881, near Carlin's, typhoid fever, 15y1d, James & Virginia Reynolds, near Carlin's, single, James Reynolds, father, p.43.
RICHARDS, Catherine R., W, F, JUL 1854, Alexa., unknown, 61y, -- Carlin, Fairfax, consort of John Richards, W.C. Richards, son.
RICHARDS, Dora, (f), F, 28 JUN 1892, Alexa. Co., consumption, 7m, Willis & Mary, Alexa. Co., laborer, Willis Richards, father, p.55.
RICHARDS, John M., W, M, 8 JUL 1866, Alexa., summer complaint, 10d, Mary Ann & W.C. Richards, Alexa., single, W.C. Richards, father, p.20.
RICHARDS, Mary Ann, W, M, 20 JUN 1866, Alexa., rush of blood to brain, 43y, Catharine Morgan, Alexa., married, W.C. Richards, husband, p.20.
RICHARDS, Wm. Henry, W, M, 5 JUL 1857, Alexa., --, 1y4m, Caleb Richards, Alexa.
RICHARDS, [not named], (f), F, DEC 1891, Va., --, 2d, Jos. & Nellie Richards, Alexa. Co., Nellie Richards, mother, p.53.
RICHARDSON, Carrie, (f), F, 12 DEC 1882, near brick barn, consumption, 6y, Dandridge & Della Richardson, Alexa. Co., D. Richardson, father, p.44.
RICHARDSON, Chas., (f), M, DEC 1889, Alexa. Co., --, 2m, Chas. & Francis Richardson, Va., --, Chas. Richardson, father, p.51.
RICHARDSON, Dandridge, Jr., (f), M, 13 DEC 1882, near brick barn, pneumonia, 1y10m, Dandridge & Della Richardson, Alexa. Co., D. Richardson, father, p.44.
RICHARDSON, Frances, (f), F, DEC 1889, Alexa. Co., consumption, 20y, David & Charity Green, Va., consort of Chas. Richardson, Chas. Richardson, husband, p.51.
RICHARDSON, Franklin, W, M, (forgotten) 1865, Alexa., croup, 6m, Geo. & Elizabeth, Alexa., laborer, Geo. Richardson, father, p.19.
RICHARDSON, Mary J., (f), F, 15 AUG 1878, near Ft. Whipple, old age, 80y, --, Middlesex Co., widow, John Richardson, son, p.38.
RICHARDSON, Richard, (f), M, 5 MAY 1878, near Ft. Craig, worms, 5y, 10d, Jasper & Ann Rose Richardson, near Ft. Craig, Jasper Richardson, father, p.38.
RICHARDSON, [blank], (f), F, 18 JAN 1879, Arlington Dist., --, 10d, Jasper & Ann Richardson, Arlington Dist., Jasper Richardson, father, p.39.
RICHIE, Mildred, (f), F, 19 MAR 1892, Alexa. Co., --, 13y, Wm. & Lucy, Alexa. Co., Wm. Richie, father, p.55.
RICKETTS, Elizabeth, W, F, 10 JUL 1853, Alexa., old age, 87y, -- Barr, Cecil Co. Md., David Ricketts, dec., R.J.T. Wilson, son in law, p.1.
RIDGELY, David G., W, --, 12 AUG 1858, Alexa., catarrh, 8m, J.E. & Mary Ridgely, J.E. Ridgely.
RIDGEWAY, Leland, W, M, 5 JUN 1890, Alexa. Co., cholera infantum, 6m, J.W. & Ella H., D.C., E.H. Ridgeway, mother, p.52.
RIDGLEY, Chas. C., W, M, 2 FEB 1857, Alexa., --, Jonathan & Mary Ridgley, Alexa., merchant.
RISTEN, Ann R., W, F, 11 DEC 1853,

Alexandria (Arlington) County, Virginia Death Records, 1853-1896

Alexa., apoplexy, 3y10m, B. & O. Risten, Alexa., Octavia Risten, mother, p.4.
RISTEN, Elizabeth C., W, F, 1 FEB 1855, Alexa., unknown, 9m, J.S. & M.E. Risten, Alexa., J.S. Risten, father, p.10.
RISTEN, Octavia, W, F, 11 SEP 1855, Alexa., 28y, Th. & M.E. Meade, B. Risten, C. Cox, bro. in law, p.11.
RISTON, James W., W, M, 3 NOV 1858, Alexa., brain diseased, 1y13d, Jas. & M.E. Riston, Jas. Riston.
RISTON, John H., W, M, 14 DEC 1858, Alexa., pneumonia, 60y.
RITCHIE, Lucy, (f), F, 15 JUL 1881, near Ft. Barry, childbirth, 40y, James & Mary Parker, Fort Royal, housekeeping, Wm. Ritchie, Wm. Ritchie, husband, p.43.
RITCHIE, [blank], (f), M, 4 MAY 1876, Columbia Pike, 1d, Wm. & Lucy Ritchie, Columbia Pike, Lucy Ritchie, mother, p.36.
RITCHIE, [blank], (f), M, 20 JUL 1881, near Ft. Barry, --, 12d, Wm. & Lucy Ritchie, near Ft. Barry, Wm. Ritchie, father, p.43.
ROACH, Berty, W, F, 27 JUL 1878, near Prospect Mill farm, typhoid fever, 10y, J.C. & Rebecca Roach, Prospect Hill farm, Rebecca Roach, mother, p.38.
ROACH, John A., W, M, 17 NOV 1855, Alexa., accident, 32y, J. & V. Roach, Alexa., merchant, consort of Eugenia Roach, M.A. Roach, sister, p.13.
ROBBINSON, Peggie, (f), F, 2 JAN 1866, Alexa., old age, 69y, unknown, Alexa., widow, Matilda Dixon, daughter, p.20.
ROBBINS, Edwin, W, M, 3 AUG 1857, Alexa., bilious, 11m, Mary F. Robbins, M.F. Robbins.
ROBERTS, Annie, W, F, 10 SEP 1879, Jefferson Dist., tumor, 65y, --, England, housekeeping, widow, Edward Roberts, son, p.39.
ROBERTS, John, W, M, 1 JAN 1853, Alexa., old age, 87y, -- Roberts, Cecil Co. Md., consort of Nancy Roberts, Matilda Sayers, daughter, p.5.

ROBERTS, Mary A., W, F, 31 MAR 1868, in her house Alexa., alcoholic fit, 27y, unknown, Alexa., wife, married, T.J. Edelin, coroner, p.25.
ROBERTS, Reuben, W, M, 17 NOV 1855, Alexa., scre. de. liver & kid., 44y, E. & Ann Roberts, N.J., miller, consort of Hannah Roberts, H. Roberts, widow, p.10.
ROBERTS, Sarah, (f), F, 24 MAR 1888, Jefferson [Dist.], burnt, 1y5m, Edward & Sarah, Jefferson [Dist.], Sarah Roberts, mother.
ROBERTS, [blank], W, F, 16 JAN 1855, Alexa., unknown, 1d, J.J. & C.S. Roberts, J.J. Roberts, father, p.10.
ROBERTS, [blank], W, F, 16 JAN 1855, Alexa., unknown, 1d, J.J. & C.S. Roberts, J.J. Roberts, father, p.10.
ROBERTSON, Mary E., W, F, 29 SEP 1892, Alexa. Co., heart failure, 46y, John & Mary Slater, Alexa. Co., consort of John Robertson, John Robertson, husband, p.55.
ROBEY, Mary Jane, W, F, 7 SEP 1859, Alexa., typhoid fever, 34y, --, Alexa., John Robey, brother.
ROBINSON, Arthur A., W, M, 29 JAN 1859, Alexa., --, 9d, A.S. & Henrietta Robinson, Alexa., A.S. Robinson, father.
ROBINSON, Cornelia, (f), F, DEC 1887, Alexa. Co., --, 4m, Nimrod & Amelia, Alexa. Co., Amelia Robinson, mother, p.49.
ROBINSON, Henrietta H., W, F, 20 JAN 1859, Alexa., childbirth, 20y9d, --, Albemarle, consort of A.S. Robinson, A.S. Robinson, husband.
ROBINSON, James, W, M, 1 JUL 1859, Alexa., --, 1m, George & W.F. Robinson, Alexa., Geo. Robinson, father.
ROBINSON, John H., (f), M, 25 OCT 1876, Freedmen's Village, yellow [fever?], 17y, Martha A. Moore, Kent Co., labor, single, Martha A. Moore, mother, p.36.
ROBINSON, Melvina A., W, F, 21 AUG 1859, Alexa., --, 16d, R.W. & Susan Robinson, Alexa., R.W. Robinson, father.

Alexandria (Arlington) County, Virginia Death Records, 1853-1896

ROBINSON, Nimrod, (f), M, FEB 1893, Alexa. Co., heart disease, 50y, Tasco & Winnie, Alexa. Co., labor, consort of Amelia Robinson, Amelia Robinson, wife, p.57.

ROBINSON, Nimrod, Jr., (f), M, 28 DEC 1894, Alexa. Co., --, 4y, Nimrod & Amelia, Alexa. Co., Amelia Robinson, mother, p.59.

ROBINSON, Nimrod, Sr., (f), M, 17 FEB 1894, Alexa. Co., heart disease, 40y, Sanford & Winnie, Alexa. Co., laborer, consort of Amelia Robinson, Amelia Robinson, wife, p.59.

ROBINSON, S.E., W, F, JUN 1854, Alexa., unknown, 1y6m, G.H. & M.F. Robinson, Westd. Co., G.H. Robinson, father, p.6.

ROBINSON, Sarah, W, F, 14 MAR 1856, old age, 95y6m, --, John Waddy, p.16.

ROBINSON, Susan, W, F, 5 AUG 1859, Alexa., childbirth, 36y, --, Alexa., consort of R.W. Robinson, R.W. Robinson, husband.

ROBINSON, William, W, M, [no date] 1858, --, pauper, John Stephenson.

ROCHFORD, Bartholemew C., W, M, 20 JUL 1856, diarrhea, 1y3m, Richard & Pamillia, p.17.

ROCK, Margaret, W, F, MAY 1855, Alexa., paralysis, 67y, G. & B. Springle, unknown, consort of Richd. Rock, W.W. Rock, son, p.10.

RODGERS, Lucy Ellen, W, F, 12 APR 1855, Alexa., consumption, 26y, F. & L. Williams, Alexa., consort of W.H. Rodgers, W.H. Rodgers, husband, p.11.

ROE, Mary, W, M, 26 NOV 1856, Alexa., --, 1y5m, John T. & Mary Price, p.15.

ROGERS, Alvin P., W, M, 13 AUG 1878, Loudoun Co., cholera, 3m, J.S. & Margret Rogers, Loudoun Co., J.S. Rogers, father, p.38.

ROGERS, Eliza, W, F, 10 APR 1855, Alexa., consumption, 45y, -- & Winney Spence, Westmoreland Co., -- Spence, F.A. Fones, daughter, p.13.

ROLAND, Solomon, (f), M, 15 JUN 1887, Alexa. Co., 10m, -- & Mattie Roland, Alexa. Co., Ellen Roland, grandmother, p.49.

ROLAND, [not named], (f), M, NOV 1891, Alexa. Co., --, 1d, Geo. & Ellen Roland, Alexa. Co., Geo. Roland, father, p.53.

ROLING, James, W, M, 21 JUL 1856, Alexa., cholera infantum, 37y [sic], --, F. Keys, head of family, p.15.

ROLLS, Child, W, M, 13 OCT 1857, Alexa., cholera infantum, Andrew & Mrs. Rolls, Alexa.

ROLLS, Mary E., W, F, 26 OCT 1855, Alexa., burnt, 7y, F. & D. Rolls, Alexa., D. [Rolls], mother, p.12.

ROSE, Elizabeth, W, F, 12 JUN 1853, Alexa., nervous affection, 45y, -- Bean, Md., merchant, consort of Thos. Rose, W.R. Emmerson, son in law, p.2.

ROSE, Emma L., W, F, 11 AUG 1868, Alexa., summer complaint, 5m, Jas. & S. Rose, Alexa., none, single, Sarah Rose, mother, p.25.

ROSS, Cornelius, (f), M, 11 SEP 1855, Alexa., dysentery, 2y, J. & M.J. Ross, Alexa., M.J. Ross, mother, p.12.

ROSS, Fanny, (f), F, 14 SEP 1854, poor house, old age, 90y, -- Ross, unknown, John Stephenson, keeper, p.9.

ROSS, Mary, (f), F, 6 JAN 1859, Alexa., --, 19d, John & Elizth. Ross, Alexa., John Ross, father.

ROSS, Rich'd. M., W, M, 20 DEC 1868, Alexa., unknown, 8d, Jno. & M. Ross, Alexa., none, single, M. Ross, mother, p.25.

ROSS, [blank], W, M, 3 JUL 1857, Alexa., --, Mr. Ross, Alexa., planter.

ROSSIN, Jas., W, M, 24 AUG 1857, Alexa., dysentery, 3y, --, Alexa.

ROSSUS, Mary M., W, F, 16 DEC 1856, --, consort of T. Travis Rossus, --, friend, p.17.

ROTCHFORD, Margaret E., W, F, 17 DEC 1858, Alexa., scarlet fever, 3y, R. &

Alexandria (Arlington) County, Virginia Death Records, 1853-1896

Mary J. Rotchford, R. Rotchford.
ROTCHFORD, Phillip, W, M, 19 OCT 1878, at Spring Park, Bright's disease, 58y, Bartholomew & Josephine Rotchford, Alexa. City, farmer, consort of Mary Rotchford, Mary Rotchford, wife, p.38.
ROUSE, Augusta, W, F, 4 DEC 1853, Alexa., scarlet fever, 3y, Mary Leycock, Alexa., unmarried, M. Leycock, mother, p.4.
ROWE, Charles W., (f), M, 20 OCT 1876, Georgetown Road, teething, 8m, Wm. A. & Ellen Rowe, Georgetown Road, Wm. A. Rowe, father, p.36.
ROWE, Eva G., (f), F, MAY 1891, Alexa. Co., --, 9m, Geo. K. & Martha E., Alexa. Co., Geo. K. Rowe, father, p.53.
ROWE, Lucinda, (f), F, JUL 1865, Alexa., fever, 2y, R.H. & Cecelia, Alexa., laborer, single, R.H. Rowe, father, p.19.
ROWE, Lucinda, (f), F, JUN 1866, Alexa., summer complaint, 21d, Henry & Cecelia Rowe, Alexa., laborer, single, Henry Rowe, father, p.20.
ROWE, Robt. D., (f), M, 13 DEC 1895, Alexa. Co., typhoid fever, 23y, W.A. & Elen, Alexa. Co., labor, single, W.A. Rowe, father, p.61.
ROWE, [not named], (f), F, 4 AUG 1894, Alexa. Co., --, 4d, Geo. K. & M.E., Alexa. Co., M.E. Rowe, mother, p.59.
ROXBURY, Charles, W, M, OCT 1853, Alexa., croup, 16m, J. & E.M. Roxbury, Alexa., Jacob Roxbury, father, p.1.
ROY, John, (f), M, SEP 1894, Alexa. Co., brain fever, 2m, Smith & Kate, Alexa. Co., Smith Roy, father, p.59.
ROY, John, (f), M, 4 JUN 1892, Alexa. Co., --, 16d, Smith & Kate, Alexa. Co., Kate Roy, mother, p.55.
ROY, Joseph, (f), M, 15 SEP 1880, Glenco farm, diphtheria, 6y, Smith & Catherine Roy, Fairfax Co., Smith Roy, father, p.41.
ROY, Joseph, (f), M, 2 AUG 1887, Alexa. Co., consumption, 16y, Seymore & Amanda, Alexa. Co., Seymore Roy, father, p.49.
ROY, Margret, (f), F, 2 DEC 1880, F. Village, --, 4y1m2d, Seymour & Manda Roy, Alexa. Co., Manda Roy, mother, p.41.
ROY, Ninnie, (f), F, MAY 1894, Alexa. Co., --, 1y6m, Smith & Kate, Alexa. Co., Smith Roy, father, p.59.
ROY, Rebecca, (f), F, 11 SEP 1881, F. Village, --, 5m5d, Seymour & Manda Roy, F. Village, Seymour Roy, father, p.43.
RUDD, Kate, W, F, 17 NOV 1855, Alexa., whooping cough, 1y6m, C.D. & A.F.M. Rudd, Alexa., C.D. Rudd, father, p.14.
RUDD, Mary F., W, F, 7 JUL 1859, Alexa., --, 7y1m, R.H. & Elizth. Rudd., Alexa., R.H. Rudd, father.
RUNNER, Mrs. J.H., W, F, 30 OCT 1854, Alexa., typhoid fever, 30y, -- Jackson, J.H. Runner, O. Fairfax, physician, p.10.
RUSHFORD, Richd. T., W, M, 1 JAN 1859, Alexa., scarlet fever, 1y6m, Richd. & Henrietta Rushford, Alexa., Richard Rushford, father.
RUSK, [not named], (f), F, SEP 1894, Alexa. Co., --, 3d, Wm. & Louisa, Alexa. Co., Wm. Rusk, father, p.59.
RUSSEL, Mrs. Betsey, (f), F, [no date] 1875, Alexa. Co., old age, 70y, mother of Wm. Sorrow, p.35.
RUSSELL, Arthur, (f), M, JUN 1892, Alexa. Co., --, 8m, Chas. & Maria, Alexa. Co., Chas. Russell, father, p.55.
RUSSELL, Charlotte, (f), F, 22 NOV 1890, Alexa. Co., consumption, 21y, Chas. & Maria, Alexa. Co., housework, single, Chas. Russell, father, p.52.
RUSSELL, Clara, (f), F, 18 APR 1884, Rosslyn, consumption, 3y1m, Charles & Maria, Alexa. Co., Maria Russell, mother, p.45.
RUSSELL, James, (f), M, AUG 1890, Alexa. Co., cold, 8m, Chas. & Maria, Alexa. Co., Chas. Russell, father, p.52.
RUSSELL, Josephine, (f), F, 21 APR 1891, Alexa. Co., consumption, 4y, Chas. &

Alexandria (Arlington) County, Virginia Death Records, 1853-1896

Maria, Maria Russell, mother, p.53.
RUSSELL, Josephine, (f), F, MAY 1892, Alexa. Co., --, 4y, Chas. & Maria, Alexa. Co., Chas. Russell, father, p.55.
RYAN, Edward, W, M, 13 APR 1857, Alexa., consumption, 30y, --, Ireland, laborer.
RYAN, William, W, M, JUL 1853, Alexa., heat, 40y, P. & E. Ryan, Ireland, laborer, Mary Ryan, sister, p.5 [written as Bryan Williams].
RYE, Wm. H., W, M, 7 NOV 1859, Alexa., shot by brother in law, 25y, --, Alexa., Rebecca Penn, sister.

S

SAILS, Scott, (f), M, DEC 1888, Jefferson, old age, 84y, --, Va., Robt. Monroe, friend.
SAILS, Willie, (f), M, 16 JUN 1882, F. Vill[age], --, 18y, Philip & Frances Sails, Alexa. Co., labor, single, Bettie Lewis, aunt, p.44.
SALES, Nanny, (f), F, 22 AUG 1868, Alexa., unknown, 2y10m, W. & Cath. Sales, Alexa., none, single, C. Sales, mother, p.25.
SAMUEL, Alice, (f), F, 3 OCT 1877, near Alexa. City, dropsy, 10y, Julia Butcher, Va., Julia Butler [sic], mother, p.37.
SAMUEL, Sarah P., W, F, 8 JAN 1856, debility & fever, 69y, --, Julia Tatsapaugh, p.16.
SANDERS, Ellen, (f), F, NOV 1882, near F. Vill[age], old age, 74y, --, Md., widow, Susan Sanders, daughter, p.44.
SANDERS, Ellen, W, F, 29 OCT 1855, Alexa., consumption, 38y, T. & B. Moore, consort of A.H. Sanders, A.H. Sanders, husband, p.13.
SANDERS, John, (f), M, 17 MAR 1882, Pa., drowned, 23y, Susan Sanders, Md., labor, single, Susan Sanders, mother, p.44.
SANGSTER, Capt. Thos., W, M, 19 MAR 1859, Alexa., consumption, 79y, --, Fairfax Co., land and claim agent, Jno. H.L. Sangster, nephew.
SANGSTER, Edward [P.], W, M, 14 OCT 1855, Alexa., consumption, 19y, E. & M. Sangster, Fairfax, E. Sangster, father, p.14.
SASSOR, John, W, M, 11 SEP 1855, poor house, unknown, 35y, -- Sassor, Ireland, J. Stephenson, keeper poor house, p.14.
SAULS, William, W, M, [no date] 1858, --, pauper, John Stephenson.
SAVOY, Wm., (f), M, 6 AUG 1858, Alexa., consumption, 58y, --, consort of Polly Savoy, P.S.
SAXTON, Matilda, W, F, 22 OCT 1853, Alexa., scarlet fever, 10y, R. & A. Saxton, Md., Matilda Crismond, aunt, p.3.
SCARCE, Ara, W, F, DEC 1854, Alexa., rheumatism, 68y, -- Hardy, Md., consort of Resin Scarce, W.B. Scarce, son, p.6.
SCHAFER, Laura M., W, F, 28 JUN 1868, Alexa., burned, 26y, C. & S. Shafer, Alexa., none, single, C. Shafer, father, p.25.
SCHAFFER, E.N., W, F, 14 OCT 1855, Alexa., --, 2y4m, C. & S. Schaffer, Alexa., C. Shaffer, father, p.11.
SCHLEVOGT, Annie, W, F, 19 SEP 1896, Alexa., heart failure, 25y, Joseph & Augusta, Alexa., single, Andrew Schlevogt, brother, p.62.
SCHLEVOGT, G.F.J., W, M, 14 OCT 1876, Four Mile Run, fever, 60y, --, Germany, basket maker, Wm. A. Schlevogt, son, p.36.
SCOTT, Geo. Oscar, (f), M, 12 SEP 1875, Jefferson Mag. Dist., infl. bowel, 8m, Geo. Scott, Alexa. Co., p.35.
SCOTT, Tho., W, M, JUL 1856, Alexa., intemperance, 48y, -- Scott, Washn. D.C., ship carpenter, consort of S.A. Scott, S.A. Scott, widow, p.8.
SCOTT, W.H., W, M, 9 OCT 1853, Alexa., consumption, 25y, Tho. & P. Scott, D.C., blacksmith, Thos. Scott, father, p.3.

Alexandria (Arlington) County, Virginia Death Records, 1853-1896

SCROGGIN, George, (f), M, 13 FEB 1867, Alexa., lung disease, 2y, C. & M. Scroggin, --, none, married, Minta Scroggin, mother, p.23.

SEALS, Charles, (f), M, 10 AUG 1858, Alexa., scarlet fever, 10y, Chas. & Sarah Seals, Alexa., Chas. Seals.

SEALS, James, (f), --, 15 AUG 1858, Alexa., scarlet fever, 9m, Chas. & Sarah Seals, Alexa., Chas. Seals.

SEARS, James W., W, M, JUN 1853, Alexa., cholera, 63y, W.B. & -- Sears, Fairfax Co., consort of Rebecca Sears, D. Sears, son, p.2.

SEARS, [blank], W, M, MAY 1853, Alexa., unknown, 1d, D. & E. Sears, Alexa., D. Sears, father, p.2.

SEATON, Adolphus, (f), M, 19 MAR 1865, Alexa., typhoid fever, 40y, Geo. & Lucinda, Alexa., carpenter, single, John Seaton, brother, p.19.

SEATON, Ephraighm, (f), M, 20 NOV 1866, Alexa., congestive chill, 75y, unknown, Culpeper Co., laborer, widower, Elizth. Dowling, niece, p.20.

SEATON, Lucinda, (f), F, 15 MAR 1865, Alexa., typhoid fever, 65y, unknown, Alexa., widower, John Seaton, son, p.19.

SELF, Mary E., W, F, [no date] 1858, Alexa., --, 11m, J.H. & M. Self, Alexa., John Craven.

SEMES, John Oscar, W, M, 14 OCT 1856, congestive fever, 17y, W.W. Harper, friend, p.17.

SHACKLEFORD, Frances, W, F, 10 JUL 1855, Alexa., old age, 76y, -- Harding, Va., -- Shackleford, Julia Shackleford, daughter in law, p.12.

SHAW, Thos., (f), M, 26 JUN 1895, Alexa. Co., Bright's disease, --, Va., consort of Laural Shaw, Mrs. Daniels, neighbor, p.61.

SHAY, Dennis, W, M, 3 JUN 1866, Alexa., unknown, 6m, Danl. & Bridget Shay, Alexa., single, Danl. Shay, father, p.21.

SHEEHEY, Robert, W, M, 30 JAN 1858, Alexa., consumption, 30y, Edward & Ann Sheehey, James Sheehey.

SHELES, John, W, M, 6 SEP 1853, alms house, unknown, 35y, -- Sheles, Md., John Stephenson, poor house keeper, p.5.

SHELTON, Carrie, (f), F, 25 OCT 1880, near Sissonville, --, 7m, Horace & Rose Shelton, Alexa. Co., Anna Spriggs, aunt, p.41.

SHELTON, Horace, (f), M, 13 SEP 1888, Washington [Dist.], killed, 41y, --, Va., Frank Williams, friend.

SHELTON, Julia R., (f), F, 16 JUL 1884, Hall's Hill, --, 1y4m, Horace & Eliza J., Alexa. Co., Horace Shelton, father, p.45.

SHELTON, Matilda, (f), F, JAN 1893, Alexa. Co., consumption, 9m, Horace & Eliza, Alexa. Co., Roy Bolden, stepfather, p.57.

SHELTON, Minor, (f), M, 25 NOV 1868, Alexa., dropsy, 11m, Tom & Nancy Shelton, Alexa., none, single, N. Shelton, mother, p.25.

SHELTON, Rose, (f), F, 15 OCT 1880, near Sissonville, consumption, 21y3m, Moses & Isabella Pelham, Culpeper Co., consort of Horace Shelton, Anna Spriggs, sister, p.41.

SHELTON, Sandy, (s) of Dr. Mershett, M, 5 APR 1853, alms house, unknown, 22y, slaves, Prince Wm. Co., John Stephenson, poor house keeper, p.5.

SHEPPARD, Henry, (f), M, 23 DEC 1867, Alexa., --, 3m27d, T. & E. Sheppard, Alexa., none, single, Eliza Sheppard, mother, p.23.

SHERLEY, Katee, W, F, 15 JUL 1854, Alexa., pneumonia, 1y, C.B. & S.C. Sherley, Alexa., C.B. Sherley, father, p.6.

SHERMAN, Bradford, W, M, 23 JUN 1853, Alexa., unknown, 2y, S.H. & A. Sherman, Alexa., S.H. Sherman, father, p.3.

SHERMAN, Raymond, W, M, 27 DEC 1895, Wash. D.C., diphtheria, 7y7m, A.J. & Bell, Wash. D.C., A.J. Sherman, father,

Alexandria (Arlington) County, Virginia Death Records, 1853-1896

p.61.
SHERWOOD, Elizabeth, W, F, 11 JUL 1853, Alexa., consumption, 32y, G. & E. Brooks, Fairfax Co., consort of J.W. Sherwood, E. Parsons, mother, p.4.
SHERWOOD, John W., W, M, 16 JUN 1853, Alexa., consumption, 26y, L. & M. Sherwood, Alexa. Co., shoemaker, consort of E. Sherwood, E. Parsons, mother [sic], p.4.
SHERWOOD, Martha, W, F, SEP 1855, Alexa. Co., summer complaint, 3m, L. & E. Sherwood, Alexa. Co., Lewis Sherwood, father, p.14.
SHERWOOD, Mary Alice, W, F, NOV 1865, Alexa., fever, 2m15d, Ellen & James, Alexa., shoemaker, James Sherwood, father, p.19.
SHERWOOD, Mary E., W, F, 7 JUL 1853, Alexa., consumption, 15m, J.W. & E. Sherwood, Alexa., E. Parsons, grandmother, p.4.
SHESTER, [blank], (s), M, [no date] 1855, --, dysentery, 1y, -- & Mary Shester, Alexa. Co., labor, H. Daingerfield, master, p.14.
SHIN, Fondeline, W, F, 16 JUN 1856, child bearing, 21y, --, J. Robinson Shin, J.R.S., head of family, p.16.
SHIPMAN, Irving K., W, M, 27 APR 1891, Alexa. Co., spinal meningitis, 2y15d, W.C. & Rebecca, Alexa. Co., W.S. Shipman, father, p.53.
SHIRLEY, Bettie, W, M, [no date] 1853, Alexa., --, 9m, W.H. & Jane Shirley, Alexa., W.H. Shirley, father, p.1.
SHIVERS, Mary, W, F, 8 OCT 1859, Alexa., whooping cough, 1y, Pat. & Mary Shivers, Alexa., Patrick Shivers, father.
SHOEMAKER, Anna, W, F, 11 SEP 1877, Geotn. Road, old age, 60y, --, Germany, consort of T. Shoemaker, T. Shoemaker, husband, p.37.
SHREVE, John W., W, M, 25 OCT 1894, Alexa. Co., diabetes, 38y5m25d, Samuel & Elizabeth J., Va., farmer, consort of Laura J. Shreve, Laura J. Shreve, wife, p.59.
SHREVE, Lucy, (f), F, 1 APR 1884, near Brown's Bend, --, 17y, Samuel & Elizabeth, Fairfax Co., single, Samuel Shreve, father, p.45.
SHREVE, Lucy, W, F, 1 APR 1883, Alexa. Co., --, 18y, Samuel & Elizabeth Shreve, Alexa. Co., single, Samuel Shreve, father, p.44.
SHREVE, Nellie, W, F, 29 JUN 1877, near Ballston, teething, 4m, Rose & B.R. Shreve, near Ballston, B.R. Shreve, father, p.37.
SHUTT, Sarah E., W, F, 24 OCT 1853, Alexa., scarlet fever, 9m, W. & S.A. Shutt, Alexa., W. Shutt, father, p.3.
SIBERT, Robert, (f), M, [no date] 1891, W.Va., --, Mr. Sorrell, neighbor, p.53.
SIGGERS, Jennie Cooper, W, F, 1 AUG 1857, Alexa., swallowing pins, 7m3d, Geo. & M.E. Siggers, Alexa., bookbinder, G. Siggers, head of family.
SILK, Mary, W, F, 17 MAY 1856, Alexa., unknown, 1y7m, E. & M. Silk, Mary Silk, mother, p.8.
SIMMONS, [not named], (f), M, 26 JAN 1893, Alexa. Co., --, 1d, Geo. H. & Maria, Alexa. Co., G.H. Simmons, father, p.57.
SIMMS, Daniel E., W, M, 4 DEC 1890, Fairfax Co., --, 8m, David & Bessie, Fairfax Co., D. Simms, father, p.52.
SIMMS, James, (f), M, 29 SEP 1867, Alexa., bilious fever, 75y, --, Md., farmer, single, Sarah Simms, wife, p.23.
SIMMS, Robert, (f), M, 9 APR 1880, near F. Village, old age, 70y, --, Md., consort of Harriet Simms, Tibbett Allen, step son, p.41.
SIMMS, [blank], (f), M, 28 OCT 1872, Arlington Dist., stillborn, Thomas & Leahanna, Arlington, laborer, Thos. Simmes, father, p.32.
SIMPSON, Ann, (s), F, 10 SEP 1855, Alexa. Co., quinsy, 1y, -- & Rachael Simpson,

Alexandria (Arlington) County, Virginia Death Records, 1853-1896

Alexa. Co., slave, W. Miner, master, p.14.
SIMPSON, Cath., W, F, 27 AUG 1856, Alexa., unknown, 45y, S. & M. Beach, Fairfax, laborer, B. Simpson, M.A. Simpson, daughter, p.8.
SIMPSON, E.H., W, M, 9 AUG 1854, Alexa., teething, 1y, A.M. & M. Simpson, Alexa., A.M. Simpson, father, p.7.
SIMPSON, Isiaah, (f), M, 25 OCT 1873, Arlington Twp., consumption, 46y, p.33.
SIMPSON, M.A., W, F, 3 APR 1855, Alexa., pneumonia, 1m, P.W. & M.A. Simpson, P.W. Simpson, father, p.11.
SIMPSON, M.J., W, F, 21 APR 1855, Alexa., pneumonia, 20d, P.W. & M.A. Simpson, P.W. Simpson, father, p.11.
SIMPSON, Margaret E., W, F, 22 SEP 1853, Alexa., bilious [fever], 41y, -- Thompson, Alexa., Jas. W. Simpson, J.W. Simpson, husband, 1y.
SIMPSON, Matilda, W, F, 7 SEP 1867, Alexa., cancer, 52y, H. & M.A. Tyler, Alexa., housekeeper, married, Sarah Bayliss, friend, p.24.
SIMPSON, Wilmer, W, M, 22 JUL 1858, Alexa., chills, 2m6d, P.W. & M.A. Simpson, Alexa., P.W. Simpson.
SIMPSON, [blank], W, F, JAN 1854, Alexa., premature, 1d, J.W. & C. Simpson, Alexa., J.W. Simpson, father, p.7.
SINCLAIR, Mary Va., W, F, 15 MAY 1866, Alexa., diphtheria, 7y8m, Priscilla & Thos. Sinclair, Alexa., Thos. Sinclair, father, p.21.
SISSON, Chas. R., W, M, 11 MAR 1884, near Windsor's, brain fever, 1y3m, Eugene T. & Carrie R., Alexa. Co., E.T. Sisson, father, p.45.
SISSON, Eugene B., W, M, 18 AUG 1894, Alexa. Co., --, 19y, E.T. & Carry R., Alexa. Co., E.T. Sisson, father, p.59.
SISSON, Philip, W, M, 12 AUG 1895, Alexa. Co., --, 5m, E.T. & Carrie R., Alexa. Co., E.T. Sisson, father, p.61.
SKIDMORE, Jesse, W, M, 23 DEC 1854, Alexa., paralysis, 65y, Edwd. & -- Skidmore, Fairfax Co., carpenter/joiner, consort of Sarah Skidmore, A.F. Skidmore, son, pp 6&7.
SKIDMORE, John W., W, M, 16 DEC 1865, Alexa., drunkenness, 47y, Jesse & Sarah, Alexa., carpenter, married, Louis C. Skidmore, brother, p.19.
SKINKER, J.C. W, F, AUG 1855, Clarke Co., unknown, 2y6m, T.J. & A.E. Skinker, Clarke [Co.], T.J. Skinker, father, p.10.
SKINNER, Leonard, W, M, 25 AUG 1893, Alexa. Co., --, 13y, Geo. W. & Mary, Alexa. Co., Geo. W. Skinner, father, p.57.
SKINNER, Malinda, (f), F, 22 JUN 1880, F. Village, old age, 60y, --, Va., widow, Isaac Green, overseer of poor, p.41.
SKINNER, Nellie, W, F, 24 AUG 1893, Alexa. Co., diphtheria, 8y11m, Geo. W. & Mary, Alexa. Co., Geo. W. Skinner, father, p.57.
SKINNER, Sam'l., W, M, 5 OCT 1856, Alexa., consumption, 41y, T.L. & E. Skinner, Fairfax Co., carpenter, J.M. Skinner, sister, p.8.
SKINNER, [blank], W, F, 10 JUL 1872, Arlington Dist., cholera infantum, 6m, George & Mary, Arlington, farmer, --, p.32.
SLACK, James E., (f), M, 28 OCT 1880, Ft. Craig, --, 4y8m, Thos. A. & Mary Slack, Alexa. Co., Thos. A. Slack, father, p.41.
SLACK, Lilly, (f), F, 16 JUL 1885, Alexa. Co., --, 11y5m9d, Thos. A. & Mary Slack, Alexa. Co., Thos. A. Slack, father, p.47.
SLACK, [blank], (f), M, 29 NOV 1882, Ft. Craig, --, 6d, T.A. & Mary Slack, Alexa. Co., Mary Slack, mother, p.44.
SLACK, [blank], (f), M, 14 MAY 1879, Arlington Dist., --, 1d, Thos. A. & Mary Slack, Arlington Dist., Thos. A. Slack, father, p.40.
SLATER, Matilda, W, F, 3 AUG 1879,

Alexandria (Arlington) County, Virginia Death Records, 1853-1896

Jefferson Dist., --, 54y, George & Elizabeth Collin, Alexa., housekeeping, consort of John Slater, John W. Slater, wife [sic], p.39.

SLAUGHTER, Thos. E., (f), M, 30 JUN 1886, Washington, D.C., tumor, 45y, --, Va., labor, consort of Mary Slaughter, Mary Slaughter, wife, p.48.

SLAUGHTER, Willie, (f), M, 17 OCT 1878, F. Village, had a fall, 1y5m, T.E. & Mary Slaughter, F. Vill[age], T.E. Slaughter, father, p.38.

SMALL, Michael, W, M, 7 OCT 1856, Alexa., congestive fever, 22y, -- Small, Ireland, laborer, consort of Rosa Small, R. Small, widow, p.8.

SMITH, A. [Eustace], W, F, 25 JUL 1855, Alexa., unknown, 2y8m, R.M. & E. Smith, Fauqr. Co., R.M. Smith, father, p.10.

SMITH, A.S., W, M, 21 JUN 1853, Alexa., dysentery, 4m, W.M. & H.S. Smith, Alexa., W.M. Smith, father, p.1.

SMITH, Amelia, W, F, 20 APR 1855, Alexa., rheumatism, 20y, D. & S.J. Whitback, N. York, consort of A.L. Smith, A.L. Smith, husband, p.11.

SMITH, Anna, (f), F, 24 OCT 1896, Alexa., typhoid fever, 28y, John & Bettie, Alexa. Co., consort of John S. Smith, John S. Smith, husband, p.63.

SMITH, Anna, W, F, 23 JUN 1854, Culpeper, summer complaint, 5m, W.M. & H.B. Smith, Alexa., W.M. Smith, father, p.6.

SMITH, Annie, (f), F, NOV 1886, Washington Dist., cancer, 45y, --, Md., consort of Samuel Smith, Samuel Smith, husband, p.48.

SMITH, Elizabeth Johnston, W, F, 17 SEP 1854, Alexa., 57y, A.J. & S. Smith, Alexa., R.J. Smith, brother, p.9.

SMITH, Ellen B., W, F, 20 JUL 1859, Alexa., --, R.M. & Ellen H. Smith, Alexa., R.M. Smith, father.

SMITH, Fannie B., (f), F, 6 MAR 1882, F. Vill[age], --, 5y5m, Robt. & Nancy Smith, Alexa. Co., Robt. Smith, father, p.44.

SMITH, H.D., W, M, 12 AUG 1879, Arlington Dist., paralysis, 44y, Henry & Ellen Smith, N.Y., farming, consort of Luania E. Smith, Luania E. Smith, wife, p.40.

SMITH, Harriet A., (f), F, 2 FEB 1882, F. Vill[age], --, 5m4d, Robt. & Nancy Smith, Alexa. Co., Robt. Smith, father, p.44.

SMITH, Hugh, W, M, [no date] 1856, old age, 80y, merchant, Jas. P. Smith, p.16.

SMITH, Hugh, W, M, MAR 1853, Alexa., scarlet fever, 3y, J.P. & M. Smith, Alexa., J.P. Smith, father, p.1.

SMITH, Hugh, W, M, OCT 1856, Alexa., old age, 87y16m [sic], --, J.P. Smith, son, p.15.

SMITH, Isabella, W, F, 29 SEP 1853, in: brain, 48y, A. & S. Keeghtley, Liverpool, Engd., consort of H.C. Smith, H.C. Smith, husband, p.5.

SMITH, James, (f), M, 14 DEC 1888, Jefferson [Dist.], consumption, 33y, --, Va., labor, widower, Susan Turner, friend.

SMITH, Jane, (f), F, 25 FEB 1873, Arlington Twp., fits, 5m, Robert Smith, Arlington, p.33.

SMITH, Jesse F., W, M, 6 FEB 1853, Alexa., scrofula, 17y, J.F. & E. Smith, Baltimore, J.F. Smith, father, p.3.

SMITH, John, (f), M, 8 APR 1880, F. Village, old age, 80y, --, King George Co., consort of Sarah Smith, Sarah Smith, wife, p.41.

SMITH, Joseph, (f), M, 27 DEC 1866, Alexa., cold, 24y, Ned. & Elizabeth Smith, Alexa., laborer, married, Elizabeth Smith, mother, p.21.

SMITH, Joseph, (f), M, OCT 1853, Alexa., unknown, 3y, H. & L. Ashton, Alexa., L. Ashton, mother, p.4.

SMITH, Joseph, (f), M, OCT 1873, Washington Twp., old age, 84y, laborer, p.33.

SMITH, Laura, (f), F, 15 SEP 1867, Alexa.,

87

Alexandria (Arlington) County, Virginia Death Records, 1853-1896

teething, 10m, Wm. & Lucinda Smith, Alexa., none, single, Lucinda Smith, mother, p.23.

SMITH, M.W., W, M, 13 JUL 1855, Alexa., dysentery, 5m, A.L. & A. Smith, Alexa., A.L. Smith, father, p.11.

SMITH, Margaret, W, F, 3 JUN 1853, Alexa., consumption, 6m, J.L. & M. Smith, Alexa., J.L. Smith, father, p.1.

SMITH, Mary J., (f), F, [no date] 1885, Alexa. Co., consumption, 28y, --, housekeeping, consort of James Smith, James Smith, husband, p.47.

SMITH, Mary, W, F, 1 MAR 1865, Alexa., old age, 73y, John & Mary, Ireland, widower, Michael Smith, son, p.19.

SMITH, Mary, W, F, 11 JUL 1858, Alexa., rheumatism, 74y, --, consort of John T. Smith, Wm. Smith.

SMITH, Nancy, (f), F, 20 OCT 1876, Washington D.C., spasm, 18y, Sandy & Caroline Smith, Prince Geo. Co. Md., house work, single, Annie Johnson, cousin, p.36.

SMITH, Nelson, (f), M, NOV 1867, Alexa., --, 17y, Mary & Simon Kemp, Madison, laborer, single, Mary Kemp, mother, p.23.

SMITH, Samuel, (f), M, 1 MAY 1883, Alexa. Co., --, 3y, Richard & Maria Smith, Alexa. Co., Eliza Boyd, grandmother, p.44.

SMITH, Sarah, (f), F, 27 SEP 1892, Alexa. Co., old age, 80y, --, Alexa. Co., widow, Margret Walker, daughter, p.55.

SMITH, Selena, (f), F, 12 JUL 1883, Alexa. Co., --, 5m, Robert & Nancy Smith, Alexa. Co., Robt. E. Smith, father, p.44.

SMITH, Susan, (s), F, 9 DEC 1859, Alexa., --, 55y, --, Alexa., D.M. French, physician.

SMITH, Susanna, W, F, OCT 1867, Alexa., --, 7d, Wm. & M.A. Smith, Alexa., laborer, married, Mary A. Smith, mother, p.23.

SMITH, Virginia, (f), F, 27 JAN 1868, Alexa., unknown, 28y, Edw. & Eliza Smith, Front Royal, none, married, E. Smith, mother, p.25.

SMITH, W., W, M, 20 JUN 1855, Alexa., unknown, 30y, stranger, Alexa., C. Neale, coroner, p.14.

SMITH, William, (f), M, 17 NOV 1880, Addison's farm, consumption, 20y, R. & Susan Smith, Richmond Co., labor, single, James Smith, brother, p.41.

SMITH, William, (f), M, 19 JAN 1873, Arlington Twp., small pox, 38y, p.33.

SMITH, Wm. A., W, M, 4 AUG 1859, Alexa., cholera infantum, 1y, W.H. & M.J. Smith, Alexa., W.H. Smith, father.

SMITH, [blank], (f), F, 25 JUL 1883, Alexa. Co., --, 2d, Nathaniel & Martha Smith, Alexa. Co., Nathaniel Smith, father, p.44.

SMITH, [blank], W, M, 14 DEC 1856, Alexa., --, Andrew & Lucy, Alexa., Andrew Smith, head of family, p.15.

SMITH, [blank], W, M, 27 MAY 1855, Alexa., unknown, 36y, stranger, Alexa., C. Neale, coroner, p.14.

SMOOT, Charles C., W, M, 31 JUL 1867, Alexa., cancer, 69y, Chas. & Mary Smoot, Chas. Co. Md., merchant, widower, J.B. Smoot, son, p.24.

SMOOT, H.B., W, M, 25 NOV 1856, chronic disease, 52y, W. Jamieson, head of family, p.17.

SMOOT, Phebe C., W, F, 25 JUL 1867, Alexa., --, 60y, C. & R. Lowe, Alexa., housekeeper, married, Carrie Smoot, daughter, p.23.

SNOOTS, Willie, W, M, 13 OCT 1893, Alexa. Co., --, 1y4d, Silas & Amy, Alexa. Co., Amanda Petitt, grandmother, p.57.

SNOW, Joseph, (f), M, MAR 1883, Alexa. Co., pneumonia, 3y, Nicholas & Annie Snow, Alexa. Co., Nicholas Snow, father, p.44.

SNOW, Nicholas, Jr., (f), M, 4 SEP 1878, near F. Village, congestive chill, 12y, Nicholas & Anna Snow, Arlington farm, Nicholas Snow, father, p.38.

SNOW, Wm. H., (f), M, 15 NOV 1873,

Alexandria (Arlington) County, Virginia Death Records, 1853-1896

Arlington Twp., croup, 6m, Nicholas Snow, Arlington, p.33.
SNOWDEN, Anna, (f), F, FEB 1896, Alexa., consumption, 4y6m, Wm. & Martha, Alexa. Co., Geo. Roland, grandfather, p.63.
SNOWDEN, Earnest O., (f), M, 12 APR 1895, Alexa. Co., --, 2m, Shirley & Clar, Va., Shirley Snowden, father, p.61.
SNOWDEN, Sherley E., (f), M, JUL 1892, Alexa. Co., --, 1y2m, Sherley & Clara, Alexa. Co., Sherley Snowden, father, p.55.
SNUDEKER, Catherine, W, F, 7 JUN 1859, Alexa., --, 21y, --, Washington D.C., J.P. Cheeck, neighbor.
SNYDER, Margaret, W, F, NOV 1853, Alexa., old age, 79y, -- Dailey, Baltimore Md., consort of Bn. Snyder, G. Snyder, son, p.1.
SOLOMON, George, (f), M, 7 JAN 1866, Alexa., unknown, 5d, Wilson & Mary E. Solomon, Alexa., single, Wilson Solomon, father, p.21.
SOLOMON, Hanah, (f), F, JUL 1867, Alexa., --, W. & A. Solomon, Alexa., laborer, single, Alfo. Solomon, brother, p.24.
SONOMAN, J.F., W, M, 19 JUL 1854, Alexa., dysentery, 11m, O. & R. Sonoman, Baltimore, R. Sonoman, mother, p.9.
SORRELL, Willie, W, M, [31] MAY 1894, Alexa. Co., consumption, 20y6m, Robert A. & Mary E., Alexa., laborer, single, Mary E. Sorrell, mother, p.59.
SORRELL, [blank], W, M, 29 JUL 1890, Alexa. Co., --, 1d, R.A. & Mary E., Alexa. Co., R.A. Sorrell, father, p.52.
SORROW, George, (f), M, JAN 1875, Alexa. Co., summer sickness, 2y, Wm. Sorrow, Alexa. Co., p.35.
SOUTHARD, Henry, W, M, 13 SEP 1858, Alexa., consumption, 33y, --, consort of James Goodwin, neighbor.
SOUTHERN, Richard, W, M, 12 APR 1877, near Ballston, old age, 87y, --, England, farmer, B.R. Shreve, grandson, p.37.
SPEIDEN, Marian, W, M, 28 OCT 1866, Alexa., complication, 56y2m, C.F. & Marian Coote, England, widower, Edgar Speiden, son, p.21.
SPINKS, Saml., W, M, 20 FEB 1854, Alexa., pneumonia, 3m, A. & M.A. Spinks, Alexa., A. Spinks, father, p.6.
SPOTSWOOD, Eva, (f), F, 29 SEP 1892, Alexa. Co., teething, 1y6m, Richard & Ellen, Alexa. Co., Ellen Spotswood, mother, p.55.
SPOTSWOOD, [blank], (f), M, APR 1886, Jefferson Dist., --, 3d, Richard & Ellen, Alexa. Co., Ellen Spotswood, mother, p.48.
SPRAGUE, [blank], W, M, MAR 1855, unknown, 3d, J. & A.M. Sprague, --, J. Sprague, father.
SPRIGG, Anna, (f), F, MAY 1893, Alexa. Co., pneumonia, 8m, Robt. & Anna, Alexa. Co., Robert Spriggs, father, p.57.
SPRIGGS, Nathan, (f), M, 2 JUN 1876, near Ft. Whipple, tumor, 35y, --, Md., labor, Martha Spriggs, Dan'l Carrall, brother in law, p.36.
SPRIGGS, Nathaniel, (f), M, 15 OCT 1885, Alexa. Co., teething, --, Robt. & Anna, Robt. Spriggs, father, p.47.
STABLER, Mary, W, F, NOV 1853, Alexa., pneumonia, 70y, W. & S. Hartshorne, Va., consort of Edwd. Stabler, Deb: Stabler, stepmother, p.4.
STABLER, Rebecca, W, M, 13 OCT 1866, Alexa., chronic disease, 50y, Edwd. & Mary Stabler, Alexa., single, Edwd. H. Stabler, brother, p.20.
STABLER, Robinson, W, M, 11 APR 1855, Alexa., brain fever, 1y8m, R.H. & J.J. Stabler, Alexa., R.H. Stabler, father, p.10.
STALLINGS, Lavina, W, F, 2 MAR 1859, Alexa., --, 2y, Andrew & Louisa Stallings, Alexa., Andrew Stallings, father.
STANLY, Mary, W, F, 7 APR 1859, Alexa., fever, 2y5m21d, J.T. & Emily Stanley,

Alexandria (Arlington) County, Virginia Death Records, 1853-1896

Alexa., James T. Stanley, father.
STANTON, Mary, W, F, 27 AUG 1855, Alexa., unknown, 2y, E. & J. Stanton, Alexa., E. Stanton, father, p.13.
STANTON, W.H., W, M, MAY 1854, Alexa., croup, 3y, E. & J. Stanton, Alexa., E. Staunton [sic], father, p.7.
STEARNS, W.A., W, M, 6 DEC 1859, Alexa., croup, 5y, Jacob Stearns, --, Jacob Stearns, father.
STEAVES, Emma, W, F, 2 SEP 1878, East Falls Ch. Station, consumption, 6m, Morgan & Amanda Steaves, E. Falls Ch. Station, Morgan Steaves, father, p.38.
STEEL, Edwin Olonzo, W, M, 21 AUG 1865, Alexa., teething, 11m29d, Edwin T. & Georgianna, Fairfax Co., --, single, Edwin T. Steel, father, p.19.
STEEL, James Carter, W, M, 15 DEC 1866, Alexa., croup, 2y3m, J.C. & Catharine Steel, Fairfax, laborer, single, J.C. Steel, father, p.20.
STEELE, Thomas, W, M, 12 MAY 1859, Alexa., consumption, 79y, --, shoemaker, Thos. Steele, Jr., son.
STELLYARDS, Jacob, (f), M, 20 OCT 1868, Alexa., unknown, 13m, M. & R. Stellyards, Alexa., sucker, single, M. Stellyards, mother, p.25.
STEPHENS, J.B., W, M, SEP 1854, Alexa., consumption, 26y, H. & S. Stephens, Loudoun, stone cutter, H.S.W. Barker, cousin, p.7.
STEPNIE, Henry (f), M, DEC 1855, Alexa., burnt, 3y, J.W. & M. Stepnie, Alexa. Co., M. Stepnie, mother, p.13.
STEPNIE, W.H. (f), M, AUG 1855, Alexa., spasms, 9m, J.W. & M. Stepnie, Alexa. Co., M. Stepnie, mother, p.13.
STERN, [blank], W, M, 27 MAR 1873, Arlington Twp., croup, 2d, Voley & Lizzie Stern, Arlington, p.33.
STERNES, James, W, M, 4 JUL 1854, Alexa., dysentery, 8y, W. & S. Stearnes [sic], Alexa., S. Sternes, mother, p.7.
STERNES, Mary A., W, F, 22 DEC 1853, Alexa., scarlet fever, 3y, W. & S. Sternes, Alexa., W. Sternes, father, p.2.
STERNES, Sarah V., W, F, 24 DEC 1853, Alexa., scarlet fever, 5y, W. & S. Sternes, Alexa., W. Sternes, father, p.2.
STEVENS, [blank], W, M, AUG 1854, Middleburg, born dead, J.M. & S.A. Stevens, Middleburg, J.M. Stevens, father, p.6.
STEVES, Amanda, W, F, OCT 1889, Alexa. Co., erysipelas, 51y, --, Canada, consort of Morgan Steves, M. Steves, husband, p.51.
STEWARD, Anna, (f), F, MAR 1893, Alexa. Co., old age, 88y, --, Va., widow, Joseph Gardner, nephew, p.57.
STEWARD, Harrison, (f), M, 23 JUN 1880, canal basin, --, 8d, Sam'l. & Ada Steward, Alexa. Co., Ada Steward, mother, p.41.
STEWARD, Robert, (f), M, AUG 1888, Jefferson [Dist.], --, 7d, Andrew & Ada, Jefferson [Dist.], Ada Steward, mother.
STEWARD, Rozier, (f), M, 11 DEC 1882, canal basin, --, 11m, Andrew & Ada Steward, Alexa. Co., Ada Steward, mother, p.44.
STEWARD, Samuel, (f), M, 30 JUL 1877, canal basin, bilious fever, 8y, Louisa & Sam'l. Steward, canal basin, Sam'l. Steward, father, p.37.
STEWART, Henry, (f), M, MAR 1867, Alexa., consumption, 19y, Jos. & Mary Stuart, Culpeper Co., laborer, single, Mary Stuart, mother, p.23.
STEWART, Joseph, (f), M, 13 APR 1881, canal basin, --, 1d, Sam'l. & Louisa Stewart, canal basin, Sam'l. Stewart, father, p.43.
STEWART, Matthew, (f), M, 25 SEP 1879, Jefferson Dist., old age, 94y, --, Va., consort of Annie Stewart, Annie Stewart, wife, p.40.
STEWART, Melvina, (f), F, 1 APR 1878, canal basin, cold, 6y1m, Andrew & Ada Stewart, canal basin, Andrew Stewart, father, p.38.

Alexandria (Arlington) County, Virginia Death Records, 1853-1896

STEWART, Richard, (f), M, 7 OCT 1874, Roach's farm, consumption, 18y, Susan Cocks, Richmond Co., farming, unmarried, James Smith, head of family, p.34.

STEWART, Winnie, (f), F, 25 JAN 1879, Jefferson Dist., old age, 90y, --, Va., widow, -- Stewart, son, p.39.

STODARD, Mary, (f), F, 13 AUG 1889, Alexa. Co., dropsy, 50y, --, Md., consort of Isaac Stodard, I. Stodard, husband, p.51.

STOMEL, Julius, W, M, 16 APR 1891, Alexa. Co., hemorrhage, 60y, --, Germany, clerk, consort of Gertshe Stomel, Gertshe Stomel, wife, p.53.

STONE, John, W, M, 10 NOV 1868, Alexa., shot, 14y, unknown, Alexa., errand boy, single, S.J. Reid, coroner, p.25.

STONEY, Henry, (f), M, [no date] 1858, --, pauper, John Stephenson.

STOOPS, James, Jr., W, M, 12 AUG 1859, Alexa., drowned, 16y, James & M. Stoops, Alexa., James Stoops, Sr., father.

STOOPS, James S., W, M, 26 SEP 1859, Alexa., consumption, 47y, --, Alexa., cabinet maker, consort of E. Stoops, M.L. Penn, neighbor.

Stranger, W, M, [no date] 1858, --, pauper, John Stephenson.

Stranger, W, M, [no date] 1858, --, pauper, John Stephenson.

Stranger, W, M, [no date] 1858, --, pauper, John Stephenson.

STRIDER, Edwin W., W, M, 24 JUN 1855, Alexa., infl. of brain, 2y, John & E. Strider, Alexa., J.S. Strider, father, p.13.

STUART, Charles T., W, M, 30 NOV 1853, Alexa., dysentery, 57y, C. & S. Stuart, King Geo. Co., consort of Ann L. Stuart, Albt. Stuart, son, p.4.

STUART, James, (f), M, 20 NOV 1866, Alexa., diarrhea, 8y, Chas. H. & Annie Stuart, Chas. Co. Md., single, Chas. H. Stuart, father, p.21.

STUMMETS, Maria J., W, F, 12 SEP 1889, Washington, D.C., cancer of stomach, 33y, --, Va., consort of David Stummets, D. Stummets, husband, p.51.

SULLIVAN, Ida, W, F, JUN 1866, Alexa., dysentery, 2y, Margt. & Edwd. Sullivan, Alexa., merchant, single, Edwd. Sullivan, father, p.20.

SUMMERS, Maria, W, F, 10 APR 1853, Alexa., pneumonia, 45y, J. & -- Zimmerman, Fairfax Co., consort of John Summers, John Summers, husband, p.2.

SUMMERS, Richd., W, M, SEP 1855, Alexa., spasms, 6y, W. & M. Summers, Alexa., W. Summers, father, p.12.

SUMMERS, Susannah, W, F, 18 MAR 1855, Alexa., pneumonia, 65y, A. & A. Young, D.C., consort of J.A. Summers, J.W. Summers, son, p.14.

SUTHARD, Chas., W, M, 13 SEP 1858, Alexa., blind sudden, 32y, consort of Mary Suthard, M. Suthard.

SWAIN, Catherine, W, M, 10 SEP 1859, Alexa., consumption, 25y, --, Alexa., consort of J.G. Swain, J.G. Swain, husband.

SWAIN, Cora, W, F, 23 JUN 1867, Alexa., fever, 4m, F. & Louisa Swain, Alexa., None, single, F.G. Swaine [sic], father, p.23.

SWAIN, Jane A., W, F, 3 JUL 1854, Alexa., consumption, 30y, -- & -- Reed, Fairfax, consort of S.G. Swain, S.G. Swain, husband, p.6.

SWAIN, Stephen D., W, M, [no date] 1856, summer complaint, 11m29d, Stephen & Mary, p.17.

SWAINE, E.M., W, F, 3 MAY 1853, Alexa., consumption, 29y, H. & E. Day, Alexa., consort of Stephen Swaine, S. Swaine, husband, p.2.

SWANN, Frances B., W, F, 3 NOV 1886, Jefferson Dist., old age, 71y, Wm. T. & Frances, Alexa. Co., single, T.W. Swann, brother, p.48.

SWANN, Jane E., W, F, 4 MAR 1858, Alexa., consumption, 22y, Thomas E.

Alexandria (Arlington) County, Virginia Death Records, 1853-1896

Swann, Alexa., T.S. Blacklock.
SWANN, Mary H., W, F, 6 SEP 1895, Alexa. Co., old age, 75y, --, Alexa. Co., widow, S.A. Colbert, daughter, p.61.
SWANN, Mary, W, F, 8 JUN 1859, Alexa., consumption, 21y6m, Capt. Thomas Swann, Alexa., T.S. Blacklock, bro. in law.
SWANN, T.W., W, M, 28 OCT 1858, Alexa., fits, 26m, T.W. & H.M. Swann, Alexa. Co., T.W. Swann.
SWANN, Thos. W., W, M, 1 JUL 1895, Alexa. Co., old age, 77y, --, Alexa. Co., farming, consort of Mary Swann, S.A. Colbert, daughter, p.61.
SYPHAX, Ada, (f), F, 3 APR 1885, Alexa. Co., --, 6m, Ennis G. & Emma, Emma Syphax, mother, p.47.
SYPHAX, Archie, (f), M, SEP 1894, Alexa. Co., consumption, 3y, E.G. & Emma, Alexa. Co., E.G. Syphax, father, p.59.
SYPHAX, Lydia, (s), F, 8 DEC 1859, Alexa., old age, 80y, --, Austin Syphax, grandson.
SYPHAX, Otis, M, 3 MAR 1879, Arlington Dist., brain fever, 1y, Ennis G. & Emma Syphax, Arlington Dist., Ennis G. Syphax, father, p.40.
SYPHAX, Rosey, (f), F, 26 MAY 1873, Arlington Twp., dysentery, 3m, Cornelius Syphax, Arlington, p.33.

T

TACEY, Jefferson, W, M, 14 JAN 1880, Mid Pike, consumption, 50y, Geo. W. & Jane Tacey, Alexa. Co., Treasurer of Alexa., consort of Maud Tacey, Maud Tacey, wife, p.41.
TALBOTT, Bayne S., W, M, 30 JUL 1868, Alexa., summer complaint, 4m25d, E.S. & S. Talbott, Maine, none, single, E.S. Talbott, father, p.25.
TARLTON, Theodore, W, M, [no date] 1857, --, 5m, --, Alexa., Henry Tarlton, father.
TATE, Gerard, (f), M, SEP 1853, Alexa., apoplexy, 70y, Alexa., consort of Henrietta Tate, H. Tate, widow, p.4.
TATSAPAUGH, Edwin, W, M, [no date] 1856, gastric fever, 35y, --, printer, Julia Tatsapaugh, p.16.
TATSAPAUGH, John, W, M, 6 FEB 1855, Alexa., liver disease, 67y, P. & -- Tatsapaugh, Alexa., merchant, consort of Jane E. Tatsapaugh, J.P. Tatsapaugh, son, p.10.
TATSAPAUGH, Susan, W, F, 12 MAY 1855, Alexa., suicide, 30y, H. & -- Tatsapaugh, Alexa., C. Neale, coroner, p.14.
TATSAPAUGH, W.H., W, M, 19 AUG 1859, Alexa., consumption, 34y, --, Alexa., upholsterer, R.H. Tatsapaugh, brother.
TATSAPAUGH, [blank], W, F, 12 MAY 1855, Alexa., unknown, 2d, -- Alexa., Susana Tatsapaugh, Alexa., C. Neale, coroner, p.14.
TAYLER, Emily C., W, F, 2 MAR 1859, Alexa., teething, 1m2d, J.T. & Mary J. Tayler, Alexa., J.T. Tayler, father.
TAYLER, Richard L., W, M, 30 OCT 1859, Alexa., tumor of stomach, 29y, --, Md., tailer, consort of M.J. Tayler, M.J. Tayler, wife.
TAYLOR, A.A.B., W, F, 29 DEC 1854, Alexa., unknown, 50y, A. & S.P. Waugh, P. Wm. Co., consort of J.T. Taylor, J.T. Taylor, husband, p.9.
TAYLOR, Chas. E., W, M, 3 JUL 1857.
TAYLOR, Chas. R., W, M, 20 OCT 1867, Alexa., fever, 23y, R.J. & J.A. Taylor, stabler, none, single, Julia A. Taylor, mother, p.24.
TAYLOR, Chas. W., W, M, 11 AUG 1885, Alexa. Co., consumption, 40y, --, farming, consort of Cora E. Taylor, F.H. Taylor, brother, p.47.
TAYLOR, Eugene, W, M, 30 AUG 1858, Alexa., --, 1m, R.L. & Eugene Taylor,

Alexandria (Arlington) County, Virginia Death Records, 1853-1896

Alexa., R.L. Taylor.

TAYLOR, Geo., (s) of George Ward, M, 7 MAR 1856, --, Charles Ward, p.16.

TAYLOR, George, W, M, 13 DEC 1883, Alexa. Co., --, 11m, Thos. & Virginia Taylor, Alexa. Co., Thomas Taylor, father, p.44.

TAYLOR, Ida, W, M, 14 JUL 1857, Alexa., consumption, 2y, C.C. & Anna Taylor, Alexa.

TAYLOR, John S., (f), M, 24 AUG 1867, Alexa., measles, 4y, J. & R. Taylor, Alexa., none, single, Rosetta Taylor, mother, p.24.

TAYLOR, Joseph, W, M, 31 AUG 1887, Alexa. Co., --, 3d, [Thos. & Virginia], --, Thos. Taylor, father, p.49.

TAYLOR, Mary J., W, F, 6 JUL 1880, Ballston, dysentery, 60y, --, S.C., single, Geo. H. Mortimore, next door neighbor, p.41.

TAYLOR, Morris, (f), M, 20 SEP 1881, near brick barn, --, 4m, Quincey & Elizth. Taylor, near brick barn, Quincey Taylor, father, p.43.

TAYLOR, R.J., W, M, 17 NOV 1855, Alexa., accident, 41y, J. & P. Taylor, Fairfax, consort of J.A. Taylor, J.A. Taylor, widow, p.11.

TAYLOR, Rebecca, W, F, 16 JAN 1856, dropsy, 75y, --, W. Clipstine, p.16.

TAYLOR, Richard C., W, M, 6 OCT 1895, Alexa. Co., --, 8y28d, F.H. & Sarah, Alexa. Co., Sarah Taylor, mother, p.61.

TAYLOR, Robt., W, M, 23 DEC 1880, Washn. Road toll gate, diphtheria, 4y8m, Thos. & Virginia Taylor, Alexa. Co., Thos. Taylor, father, p.41.

TAYLOR, Susannah B., W, F, 7 OCT 1856, --, J.H. & M. Taylor, J.H. Taylor, p.17.

TAYLOR, Virginia C., W, F, 18 MAR 1858, Alexa., catarrh fever, 1y12d, S.B. & Virginia Taylor, Alexa., S.B.T.

TAYLOR, Walter, W, M, 30 SEP 1886, Jefferson Dist., --, 3m15d, Thos. & Virginia, Alexa. Co., Thos. Taylor, father, p.48.

TAYLOR, Willie, W, F, 10 SEP 1857, Alexa., consumption, --, C.C. & Anna Taylor, Alexa.

TEMPLE, Henry, (f), M, 18 JUN 1886, Arlington Dist., hemorrhage, 26y, John & Jane, Alexa. Co., labor, single, John Temple, father, p.48.

TENNESON, Charles, W, M, 29 NOV 1868, Alexa., suicide, 27y, Sam'l. Tenneson, Alexa., none, single, Sam'l. Tenneson, father, p.25.

TENNYSON, J.B., W, M, 26 FEB 1859, Alexa., scarlet fever, 8y, Saml. & Margt. Tennyson, Alexa., Saml. Tennyson, father.

TERRELL, [blank], (f), F, DEC 1896, Alexa., --, 3d, Taliaferro & Susan, Alexa. Co., Taliaferro Terrell, father, p.63.

TERRY, Benjamin, M, 10 JUL 1879, Arlington Dist., teething, 2y, Scipio & Mary J. Terry, Arlington Dist., Scipio Terry, father, p.40.

TERRY, Cora, (f), F, 11 APR 1893, Alexa. Co., --, 8m11d, Scipio & Anna, Alexa. Co., Anna Terry, mother, p.57.

TERRY, Mary J., F, 30 JUN 1880, F. Village, colic, 41y, Benjamin & Maria Holmes, King & Queen Co., housekeeping, consort of Scipio Terry, Scipio Terry, husband, p.41.

TERRY, Sarah, (f), F, 21 NOV 1895, Alexa. Co., --, 14y, Scipio & Ann, Alexa. Co., Ann Terry, mother, p.61.

TERRY, Scipio, (f), M, 2 FEB 1893, Alexa. Co., --, 6y7m, Scipio & Anna, Alexa. Co., Anna Terry, mother, p.57.

THOMAS, Benja., W, M, 17 SEP 1856, suicide, 45y, --, England, p.17.

THOMAS, Dartha, F, 8 NOV 1879, Washington Dist., child birth, 35y, --, Va., housekeeping, consort of Richard Thomas, Richard Thomas, husband, p.40.

THOMAS, Hayward, (f), M, 31 MAR 1888, Culpeper, whooping cough, 4m, Joseph & Edwena, Joseph Thomas, father.

THOMAS, Henry, (f), M, 16 NOV 1895,

Alexandria (Arlington) County, Virginia Death Records, 1853-1896

Wash. D.C., paralysis, 55y, Frank & Eliza, Md., labor, consort of Lucy Thomas, Lucy Thomas, wife, p.61.

THOMAS, Mary, W, F, 28 FEB 1856, bilious fever, 9y, Henry & Jane Cryss, Jane Cryss, p.16.

THOMAS, Wm., W, M, 23 MAR 1857, Alexa., consumption, 30y, --, shoemaker.

THOMPSON, Emeline, W, F, 14 NOV 1853, Alexa., pneumonia, 53y, Geo. & J. Slacum, Alexa., Saml. Thompson, dec., J.W. Burke, son in law, p.1.

THOMPSON, Lucy Adelaide, W, F, 8 JUN 1894, Alexa. Co., cholera, 5m, Edward F. Thompson, Alexa. Co., Edward F. Thompson, father, p.59.

THOMPSON, Sophia, W, F, 24 AUG 1859, Alexa., teething, 1y3m, James & Salina Thompson, Alexa., James Thompson, father.

THOMPSON, [blank], W, M, 13 NOV 1895, Alexa. Co., consumption, 5m, John L. & Nanna, Wash. D.C., Nanna Thompson, mother, p.61.

THORNTON, Delia, (f), F, DEC 1891, Alexa. Co., old age, 80y, --, widow, Eliza Chinn, neighbor, p.53.

THORNTON, John, W, M, 4 SEP 1859, Alexa., drowned, --, unknown, sailor, Alexa. Gazette, newspaper.

THORNTON, Sarah, (f), F, APR 1867, Alexa., old age, 90y, --, housekeeper, married, Caroline Thornton, daughter, p.24.

THORNTON, William, (f), M, 2 JUN 1866, Alexa., heart disease, unknown, unknown, unknown, laborer, single, constable, coroner, p.20.

TIBBS, Matilda, (f), F, 15 JUN 1876, near East Ft. Craig, fits, 35y, Enoch & Scarlet White, Fauquier Co., widow, Wm. H. Augusta, son in law., p.36.

TIBBS, Susan, (f), F, 3 MAR 1867, Alexa., consumption, 11y, A. & M. Tibbs, Greene Co., none, single, Matilda Tibbs, mother, p.24.

TICER, James, W, M, APR 1854, Alexa., accidental, 18y, L. & M. Ticer, Alexa., L. Ticer, father, p.7.

TILDEN, William, W, M, 6 SEP 1872, Arlington Dist., congestive chill, 43y, unknown, England, mason, married, Randolph Birch, friend, p.32.

TINKLER, William E., W, M, 7 JUL 1856, Alexa., teething, 1y8m, Edward & Charlotte, Alexa., Edward Tinkler, head of family, p.15.

TINNEY, Alfred, (f), M, 14 AUG 1890, --, kidney trouble, 60y, --, Fauquier Co., labor, consort of Julia Tinney, Julia Tinney, wife, p.52.

TINNEY, Gertie, (f), F, 26 DEC 1880, near Sissonville, pneumonia, 3m, Alfred & Julia Tinney, King & Queen Co., Alfred Tinney, father, p.41.

TINNEY, Lewis, (f), M, 18 DEC 1877, near Nelson's, teething, 2y, Julia & Alfred Tinney, near Nelson, widower, Julia Tinney, mother, p.37.

TITUS, Samuel, W, M, JUN 1889, Wash. D.C., old age, 74y, --, Va., farmer, consort of Martha Titus, J.E. McNair, son in law, p.51.

TODD, William, W, M, 27 DEC 1867, Alexa., kicked by a horse, 43y, M. & J. Todd, Alexa., laborer, single, Mary Todd, mother, p.24.

TOOLS, John, (f), M, JUL 1886, Jefferson Dist., disease of kidney, 55y, --, Va., labor, consort of Julia Tools, Julia Tools, wife, p.48.

TOPLEY, Lemuel, W, M, 6 OCT 1885, Alexa. Co., fall, 49y, Alexr. & Susanna, Pa., consort of Anna A. Topley, A.A. Topley, wife, p.47.

TOPLEY, Ruth E., W, F, 7 DEC 1890, Wash. D.C., --, 4y9m, Lemuel & Anna, Alexa. Co., Anna Topley, mother, p.52.

TORREYSON, Willie D., W, M, 28 NOV 1873, Arlington Twp., cholera infantum, 8m, W.H. & M.E. Torryson [sic], Pa., p.33.

Alexandria (Arlington) County, Virginia Death Records, 1853-1896

TRAMMELL, Sarah, W, F, 20 MAR 1858, Alexa., disease of kidney, 46y, --, Alexa., consort of Geo. W. Trammell, G.W. Trammell, husband.

TRAVERS, Angeline, W, F, 9 MAY 1886, Arlington Dist., consumption, 29y, --, Va., consort of John L. Travers, J.L. Travers, husband, p.48.

TRAVERS, Augustus W., W, M, 17 JUN 1889, Alexa. Co., strained, 32y, Jno. W. & Rachel Travers, Va., laborer, consort of Annie Travers, A. Travers, wife, p.51.

TRAVERS, Henry W., W, M, 16 AUG 1887, Alexa. Co., consumption, 53y, --, King & Queen Co., Ann Travers, wife, p.49.

TRAVERS, Mary E., W, F, JUN 1854, Alexa., dysentery, 1y6m, J.W. & R. Travers, Alexa., J.W. Travers, father, p.9.

TRAVERS, Mary F., W, F, JUL 1890, --, intermitting fever, 1y, John L. & Bell M., Alexa. Co., John L. Travers, father, p.52.

TRAVERS, [blank], W, F, 15 NOV 1881, near Ft. Barry, --, 1m, John L. & Angeline Travers, near Ft. Barry, J.L. Travers, father, p.43.

TRAVIS, Lucretia, W, F, 18 JAN 1859, Alexa., croup, 3y2m, Thos. Sr. & Henrietta Travis, Alexa., Henry Brown, bro. in law.

TRAVIS, Lucy, W, F, 10 JAN 1859, Alexa., --, 6m, Thos. & Lucy Travis, Alexa., Thomas Travis, father.

TRAVIS, Mary, W, M, FEB 1866, Alexa., unknown, 3y18d, Bridget & John Travis, Richmond, single, John Travis, father, p.21.

TREAKLE, Emma J., W, F, 15 AUG 1867, summer complaint, 17m, Jane & Wm. Treakle, Alexa., waterman, single, Jane Treakle, mother, p.24.

TREAKLE, H.C., W, M, SEP 1854, Alexa., infln. of brain, 6d, W. & J. Treakle, Alexa., W. Treakle, father, p.7.

TREAKLE, James W., W, M, 5 MAR 1853, Alexa., unknown, 5m, W. & J. Treakle, Alexa., W. Treakle, father, p.4.

TRIPLETT, Alice A., W, F, 7 JUN 1859, Alexa., --, 9y, Wm. & Catherine Triplett, Alexa., Catherine Triplett, mother.

TRIPLETT, Eliza, W, F, 18 APR 1854, poor house, paralytic, 40y, -- Richardson, Westd. Co., W.H. Triplett, John Stephenson, keeper, p.9.

TRIPLETT, Henry, W, M, 26 DEC 1867, Alexa., dissipation, 30y, --, Alexa., clerk, widower, Fred Colbert, friend, p.24.

TRIPLETT, Lavinia M., W, F, 19 OCT 1853, Alexa., pneumonia, 3y3m7d, T. & M. Triplett, Ky., Thornton Triplett, father, p.1.

TROUT, [blank], W, M, 17 FEB 1858, Alexa., suicide, 30y, --, Baltimore, machinist, coroner.

TROYMAN, Julius, (f), M, AUG 1891, Alexa. Co., Bright's disease, 70y, --, Va., consort of Amanda Troyman, A. Troyman, wife, p.53.

TUBMAN, Ida, W, F, 28 AUG 1858, Alexa., scarlet fever, 3y9m, Jas. & L. Tubman, Alexa., Jas. Tubman.

TUBMAN, Peter, W, M, 31 AUG 1857, Alexa., --, Chr. Neal, coroner.

TUBMAN, William, W, M, 4 AUG 1859, Alexa., intermittent fever, 28y, --, Alexa., clerk, consort of J. Fannie Tubman, J. Fannie Tubman, wife.

TUCKER, Elizabeth, W, F, 12 NOV 1868, Alexa., asthma, 71y, H. & E. Leonard, Charles Co., none, married, Mrs. Lucas, daughter, p.25.

TUCKER, G.W., W, M, 20 DEC 1890, --, fell & broke neck, 50y, --, Vermont, physician, single, J.N. Tunston, neighbor, p.52.

TUNSTON, Elijah, (f), M, 28 NOV 1894, Alexa. Co., --, 8m14d, John & Mary, Alexa. Co., Mary Tunston, mother, p.59.

TUNSTON, Elijah A., (f), M, 28 NOV 1893, Alexa. Co., --, 8m, J.F. & Mary, Alexa. Co., J.F. Tunston, father, p.57.

TURLE, Chs., W, M, 24 MAY 1853,

Alexandria (Arlington) County, Virginia Death Records, 1853-1896

Alexa., scarlet fever, 7m, J. & M. Turle, Alexa., John Turle, father, p.5.
TURLEY, Harriett J., (f), F, 9 FEB 1894, Alexa. Co., --, 8m, Andrew J. & Nora L., Alexa. Co., Nora L. Turley, mother, p.59.
TURLEY, Mable L., (f), F, 5 JUN 1889, Alexa. Co., brain fever, 9m, A.J. & Nora Turley, Va., A.J. Turley, father, p.51.
TURNER, Jane, F, 16 NOV 1879, Washington D.C., --, 35y, --, Va., housekeeping, consort of Albert Turner, Albert Turner, husband, p.40.
TURNER, Lucy A., (f), F, 15 JUN 1876, near cemetery, cold, 6m, Albert & Jane Turner, near cemetery, Albert Turner, father, p.36.
TURNER, Pamelia, W, F, 26 JAN 1859, Alexa., unknown, 41y, --, consort of W.W. Turner, W.W. Turner, husband.
TURNER, W.B., W, M, 29 OCT 1855, Alexa., [deabells?], 19y, -- Turner, Md., clerk, J.F. Carlin, friend, p.10.
TWINE, William, (s) of Mrs. Cazenove, M, SEP 1853, Alexa., spasms, 1y, P. & M. Twine, Fairfax Co., slave, Maria Twine, mother, p.5.
TYLER, J.W., W, M, 9 AUG 1855, Alexa., dysentery, 10m, G. & E.M. Tyler, Alexa., E.M. Tyler, mother, p.12.

U

UNDERWOOD, W.H., W, M, 7 AUG 1859, Alexa., inflammation [of] bowels, 3y, J.W. & Mary Underwood, Alexa., J.W. Underwood, father.
UNDERWOOD, W.H., W, M, 4 MAY 1859, Alexa., --, 2y8m6d, W.H. & S.E. Underwood, Alexa., W.H. Underwood, father.
Unknown, W, M, 1 NOV 1855, Alexa., unknown, 2y, found, C. Neale, coroner, p.14.
Unknown, W, M, 10 JUL 1856, froze to death, --, coroner, p.16.

UPSHER, Abraham, (f), M, 11 DEC 1881, Brown's Bend, cold, 17y, Archie & Mary Upsher, Alexa. Co., single, Mary Upsher, mother, p.43.
UPSHER, Mary, (f), F, OCT 1881, Brown's Bend, cold, 13y, Archie & Mary Upsher, Alexa. Co., single, Mary Upsher, mother, p.43.

V

VACCARI, Fred., W, M, 4 JUL 1858, Alexa., inflammation [of] bowels, 8y, --, Leghorn, Italy, consort of Rose Vaccari, R. Vaccari.
VANDEGRIFT, Joseph, W, M, 3 JUL 1865, Nelson Co., fell from horse, 17y, Catherine & H.A., Jersey and Philadelphia, Co. engineer, single, H.W. Vandegrift, father, p.19.
VANDERFRIFT, Wm. H., (f), M, AUG 1875, Jefferson Mag. Dist., p.35.
VANSANT, Elizabeth, W, F, 25 APR 1856, suddenly, 58y, --, James Vansant, p.16.
VANSTORY, [blank], (f), F, OCT 1875, Alexa. Co., consumption, 65y, --, Tenn., p.35.
VanVOAST, Sarah D., W, F, 16 JUL 1873, Arlington Twp., old age, 67y, Geo. & Charity Conzell, Arlington, p.33.
VEANY, Florance, (f), F, 1 MAR 1896, Alexa. Co., consumption, 4y, Cornelius & Lidia, Fairfax Co., Cornelius Veaney, father, p.63.
VEITCH, Andrew W., W, M, MAR 1893, Wash. D.C., cancer, 40y, Wm, & Sarah, Alexa. Co., farmer, consort of S. Emma Veitch, W.R. Birch, father in law, p.57.
VEITCH, Bessie I., W, F, [12] SEP 1890, District of Columbia, --, 7m, R.L. & Mary E., Dist. of Columbia, R.L. Veitch, father, p.52.
VEITCH, [Jesse] H., W, M, 22 MAR 1890, Alexa. Co., pneumonia, 21y, Geo. W. & Maggie, Alexa. Co., clerk, single, G.W.

Alexandria (Arlington) County, Virginia Death Records, 1853-1896

Veitch, father, p.52.

VEITCH, Jas. H., W, M, 19 JUN 1872, Arlington Dist., congestion [of] brain, 7m, Richard A. & Matilda, Arlington, farmer, parents, father, p.32.

VEITCH, Nellie May, W, F, 10 AUG 1879, Arlington Dist., water on the brain, 7y, John W. & Mary A. Veitch, Arlington Dist., John W. Veitch, father, p.40.

VEITCH, Raymond L., W, M, JUL 1887, Alexa. Co., --, 28d, Robt. L. & Elizabeth, Alexa. Co., R.L. Veitch, father, p.49.

VEITCH, Sarah, W, F, OCT 1892, --, old age, 85y, --, Alexa. Co., widow, J.W. Veitch, son, p.55.

VEITCH, W.P., W, M, 2 FEB 1856, --, 45y, --, Alexa., tailor, Mary Veitch, p.16.

VEITCH, Wm. C., W, M, 2 AUG 1878, opp. Crist's, heart disease, 74y, Alexr. & Barbra Veitch, Alexa. City, farmer, consort of Sarah Veitch, Sarah Veitch, wife, p.38.

VERMILLION, James, W, M, 12 SEP 1859, Alexa., mania-à-potu, 39y, --, Ireland, laborer, Dr. D.M. French, physician.

VERNON, George [sic], W, M [sic], 5 JUL 1867, Alexa., paralysis, 39y, Jesse & -- Spencer, Alexa., housekeeper, married, Jas. Vernon, husband, p.24.

VICKERS, Margaret, W, F, 6 FEB 1853, Alexa., old age, 74y, J. & S. Dowell, P. William Co., Tho. Vickers, E. Driscoll, niece, p.4.

VINE, Edgar, (s), [M], Alexa., old age, 90y, --, Alexa., R.T. Wilson.

VIOLETT, H.E., W, F, 17 NOV 1855, Alexa., consumption, 33y, S. & E. Baggott, Alexa., consort of E.R. Violett, S.O. Baggett, brother, p.12.

VIOLETT, Ida Field, W, F, JUL 1866, Alexa., white swelling, 6y6m, Geo. & Sallie Fields, Alexa., Bart Delphy, grandfather, p.20.

VIOLETT, John Stuart, W, M, APR 1866, Alexa., diphtheria, 4y, Robert & Emma Violett, Alexa., Bart Delphy, grandfather, p.20.

VIOLETT, Robert, W, M, 7 MAR 1866, Alexa., mania-à-potu, 25y, Chloe Violett, Alexa., painter, married, Bart Delphy, father in law, p.20.

VIOLETT, Steward, W, M, 16 MAY 1865, Alexa., diphtheria, 4y, Robt. & Emma Alexa., cooper, single, Barth. Delphy, grandfather, p.19.

VORCE, Sarah, W, F, 22 JUL 1879, Jefferson Dist., enlargement of liver, 47y, T. & Julia Baldwin, N.Y., housekeeping, consort of Nelson Vorce, Nelson Vorce, husband, p.40.

W

WADDY, Eliza, W, F, 22 JUN 1857, Alexa., cancer, 30y, --, Alexa., consort of Tho. Waddy, T. Waddy.

WADDY, J.D.S., W, M, 14 JUN 1853, Alexa., cholera morbus, 5y, T. & E. Waddy, Alexa., Thos. Waddy, father, p.1.

WADDY, James C., W, M, 20 DEC 1859, Alexa., teething, 11m, James E. & Mary Waddy, Alexa., James E. Waddy, father.

WADDY, [blank], W, F, 26 MAY 1866, Alexa., unknown, 2d, Thos. & Annie Waddy, Alexa., Annie Waddy, mother, p.21.

WADE, James H., W, M, 2 MAY 1854, Alexa., diseased brain, 11y, R.H. & J. Wade, Alexa., R.H. Wade, father, p.7.

WALKER, Eddie, W, M, 8 SEP 1889, Alexa. Co., typhoid fever, 2y8m15d, Ernest & Lucy Walker, Va., Ernest Walker, father, p.51.

WALKER, Emma E.B., W, F, 20 SEP 1858, Alexa., consumption, 22y, James & C. Walker, Alexa., Jas. Walker.

WALKER, Geo. L., W, M, 5 MAY 1878, near Walker's Chapel, teething, 3m8d, Robt. & Margret Walker, near Walker's Chapel, Robt. Walker, father, p.38.

WALKER, Lotta D., (f), F, 15 JUL 1887,

Alexandria (Arlington) County, Virginia Death Records, 1853-1896

Alexa. Co., --, 5m11d, Philip & Sadie E., Alexa. Co., p.49.
WALKER, Margaret, (f), F, SEP 1894, Alexa. Co., chills, 28y, Wm. & Lucy, Alexa. Co., Agnes Johnson, mother in law, p.59.
WALKER, Nellie L., (f), F, 13 SEP 1888, Alexa. Co., --, 10d, Philip & S.E. Walker, --, Philip Walker, father.
WALKER, [not named], (f), F, 14 APR 1894, Alexa. Co., --, 9d, Walter & Victoria, Alexa. Co., Walter Walker, father, p.59.
WALKER, [not named], (f), F, 16 JAN 1893, Alexa. Co., --, 9d, Walter A. & Victoria, W.A. Walker, father, p.57.
WALL, William, W, M, 1 NOV 1865, Alexa., old age, 81y, unknown, Ireland, R.R. conductor, widower, Augustus Wall, son, p.19.
WALLACE, Garfield, (f), M, JUL 1881, near Syphax's, --, 5m, Nelson & Margaret Wallace, Alexa. Co., N. Wallace, father, p.43.
WALLACE, Polly, (f), F, 2 OCT 1891, Nauck, old age, 80y, --, Va., widow, Delphia Wallace, daughter, p.53.
WALLACE, Willie, (f), M, AUG 1875, Alexa. Co., summer sickness, 5m, Nelson Wallace, Alexa. Co., p.35.
WALLACE, [blank], (f), M, JUN 1884, F. Vill[age], --, 1m, Nelson & Margret, Alexa. Co., Nelson Wallace, father, p.45.
WARD, George, (f), M, 3 JAN 1890, Alexa. Co., gripe, 20y, John W. & Elizabeth, Alexa. Co., labor, J.W. Ward, father, p.52.
WARD, Harriet, (f), F, JUL 1895, Alexa. Co., --, 37y, John & Mialia, Madison Co., consort of Abraham Ward, J.W. Ward, father in law, p.61.
WARD, John T., W, M, 16 JUN 1853, Alexa., scarlet fever, 6y, W.H. & L. Ward, Md., cartman, W.H. Ward, father, p.2.
WARD, Julius, (f), M, 8 SEP 1893, Alexa. Co., consumption, 25y, John W. & Elizabeth, labor, single, John W. Ward, father, p.57.
WARD, Laura, W, [F], 20 AUG 1856, bilious fever, 24y6m, Freeman Mansfield, William Ward, p.16.
WARD, Morris M., (f), M, 13 OCT 1881, F. Village, --, 7m23d, John & Ella Ward, Alexa. Co., John Ward, father, p.43.
WARDER, John E., W, M, 19 NOV 1853, Alexa., unknown, 1y9m, R. & M.A. Warder, Alexa., M.A. Warder, mother, p.3.
WARDER, Mary E., W, F, 1 JAN 1859, Alexa., whooping cough, 5m29d, R.H. & M.E. Warder, Alexa., R.H. Warder, father.
WARE, Matthew, (f), M, DEC 1892, Alexa. Co., heart failure, 48y, --, Va., laborer, consort of Pricilla Ware, P. Ware, wife, p.55.
WARE, Pricilia, (f), F, JAN 1896, Alexa. Co., rheumatism, 45y, --, Middlesex Co., housework, widow, Fred Goldman, son, p.63.
WARING, Mary E., W, F, AUG 1891, Clarke Co., drowned, 4y, Geo. W. & M.E., Clarke Co., G.W. Waring, father, p.53.
WARNER, John, (s), M, 1 MAY 1859, Alexa., dropsy, 75y, --, Va., Robert Brockett, master.
WARNER, William, (f), M, 6 DEC 1854, poor house, consumption, 30y, -- Warner, Alexa., John Stephenson, keeper, p.10.
WASHINGTON, Adaline, (f), F, 25 JUL 1868, Alexa., summer complaint, 14m, Wm. & R. Washington, Alexa., none, single, Rebc. Washington, mother, p.25.
WASHINGTON, Albert, (f), M, 29 OCT 1866, Alexa., unknown, 4y, Albert & Emily Washington, Warrenton, laborer, Albert Washington, father, p.21.
WASHINGTON, Amelia, (f), F, 3 SEP 1879, Arlington Dist., confinement, 23y6m, Dan'l. & Elen Cocklin, S.C.,

Alexandria (Arlington) County, Virginia Death Records, 1853-1896

housekeeping, consort of James Washington, James Washington, husband, p.40.

WASHINGTON, Daniel, (f), M, 18 SEP 1879, Arlington Dist., --, 20d, James & Amelia Washington, Arlington Dist., James Washington, father, p.40.

WASHINGTON, Effie, W, F, 25 DEC 1858, Alexa., scarlet fever, 3y6m20d, Geo. & Sallie Washington, Alexa., George Washington.

WASHINGTON, Ella, (f), F, 26 AUG 1892, Alexa. Co., --, 19y, John & Ella Carter, Wash. D.C., consort of Jas. Washington, Ella Carter, mother, p.55.

WASHINGTON, Emily, (f), F, DEC 1867, Alexa., childbirth, --, Alexa., none, married, Celia Sheppard, friend, p.24.

WASHINGTON, Emily, (f), F, DEC 1866, Alexa., confinement, 30y, Fanny & Edward Davis, Warrenton, laborer, married, Alfred Washington, husband, p.21.

WASHINGTON, Emma, (f), F, 17 OCT 1881, F. Village, malaria fever, 2y10d, George & Sarah Washington, Alexa. Co., Geo. Washington, father, p.43.

WASHINGTON, Fielding, (f), M, 1 APR 1895, Alexa. Co., consumption, 56y, --, Orange Co., labor, consort of Lucinda Washington, L. Washington, wife, p.61.

WASHINGTON, George, (f), M, 6 MAR 1892, Alexa. Co., consumption, 22y5m, Jas. & Luvenia, Va., laborer, single, Jas. Washington, father, p.55.

WASHINGTON, George, (f), M, 1 JAN 1867, Alexa., pneumonia, 40y, --, Alexa., none, married, Celia Sheppard, friend, p.24.

WASHINGTON, George, (f), M, 5 AUG 1887, Alexa. Co., paralyzed, 70y, --, Alexa. Co., Robt. Monroe, Overseer [of the] Poor, p.49.

WASHINGTON, James, (f), M, FEB 1893, Alexa. Co., old age, 76y, --, single, Sarah Washington, daughter in law, p.57.

WASHINGTON, James E., (f), M, 16 MAR 1886, Arlington Dist., consumption, 13y, Geo. & Martha, Alexa. Co., Geo. Washington, father, p.48.

WASHINGTON, John, (f), M, 15 MAY 1868, Alexa., drowned, 12y, G. & C. Washington, Alexa., none, single, C. Washington, mother, p.25.

WASHINGTON, Mariah, (f), F, MAR 1867, Alexa., --, 11m, Jas. & M. Washington, Culpeper Co., laborer, single, M. Washington, mother, p.24.

WASHINGTON, Mary, (f), F, 22 APR 1867, Alexa., congestive chill, 70y, --, Talbot Co. Md., housekeeper, married, R. Washington, daughter in law, p.24.

WASHINGTON, Milton, (f), M, 18 DEC 1894, Alexa. Co., spasms, 7d, John & Henrietta, Alexa. Co., John Washington, father, p.59.

WASHINGTON, O[r]lando, W, M, 23 OCT 1857, Alexa., pneumonia, 3y11m, Geo. & Sallie Washington, Alexa., merchant.

WASHINGTON, Walter, (f), M, 4 NOV 1881, F. Village, malaria fever, 4y, George & Sarah Washington, Alexa. Co., Geo. Washington, father, p.43.

WASHINGTON, [blank], (f), F, JUL 1867, Alexa., --, 8m, E. & A. Washington, Alexa., none, single, Celia Sheppard, friend, p.24.

WATCHMAN, John, W, M, 24 JUN 1855, Alexa., choleic, 4m, T. & D. Watchman, Alexa., T. Watchman, father, p.13.

WATERMAN, Mary, W, F, 30 JUN 1855, Alexa., eurycephalous, 1y7m, S. & C. Waterman, Alexa., S. Waterman, father, p.11.

WATERS, Dorothea, W, F, 17 OCT 1854, Alexa., Bright's disease, 65y, Benj. Waters, O. Fairfax, physician, p.10.

WATERS, Jonathan, (f), M, JUL 1893, Alexa. Co., --, 50y, --, labor, W.A. Walker, neighbor, p.57.

WATERS, Julia, (f), F, 30 SEP 1879, Jefferson Dist., fever, 29y, John & Kitty

Alexandria (Arlington) County, Virginia Death Records, 1853-1896

Thomas, Warrenton, housekeeping, consort of William Waters, Kitty Thomas, mother, p.40.

WATERS, William, W, M, 10 SEP 1855, Alexa., unknown, 13y, S. & W. Waters, Stafford Co., locksmith, Edd. Carr, bro. in law, p.11.

WATERS, [not named], (f), F, 30 MAY 1891, Alexa. Co., --, 10d, J. & Georgianna Waters, Alexa. Co., J. Waters, father, p.53.

WATKINS, Washington, (f), M, 10 JUL 1879, Georgetown D.C., --, 26y, Washington & Rachel, Md., labor, single, Rachel Watkins, mother, p.40.

WATSON, Charlotte, (f), F, 19 OCT 1894, Wash. D.C., --, 44y, --, Va., Margaret Holmes, daughter in law, p.59.

WATTLES, H.S., W, M, 9 JUN 1858, Alexa., scarlet fever, 5m, C.W. & H.S. Wattles, Alexa., C.W. Wattles.

WATTLES, Nathaniel, W, M, 12 JUL 1856, summer complaint, 10m3d, H.S. & Caroline, H.S. Wattles, p.17.

WATTS, Hattie, (f), F, 25 OCT 1873, Arlington Twp., burned to death, 6y, Louis & Ann Watts, Loudoun, p.33.

WATTS, Lulie, (f), F, 25 OCT 1873, Arlington Twp., burned to death, 1y, Louis & Ann Watts, Loudoun, p.33.

WATTS, Willie, (f), M, 25 OCT 1873, Arlington Twp., burned to death, 4y, Louis & Ann Watts, Loudoun, p.33.

WEBB, Martha, (f), F, 15 NOV 1868, Alexa., consumption, unknown, Elizabeth Jenkins, unknown, unknown, married, Ellen Webb, daughter, p.25.

WEBB, Mary, (f), F, MAR 1866, Alexa., Alexa., consumption, 40y1m, Richard Carter, Stephensburg, laborer, married, Alfred Webb, father, p.20.

WEBSTER, Jesse, (f), M, AUG 1895, Alexa. Co., shot, 20y, John & Georgianna, Loudoun Co., labor, single, Wm. Webster, brother, p.61.

WEBSTER, William, W, M, 17 JUL 1856, congestion of the bowels, 35y11m25d, John & Sarah, John Webster, head of family, p.17.

WEIR, Dr., W, M, 8 MAY 1857, Alexa., consumption, 50y, --, Alexa., physician, Miss Thruston.

WELCH, Catherine, W, F, SEP 1853, Alexa., spasms, 1m, J. & M. Welch, Alexa., John Welch, father, p.3.

WELCH, Jas. S., W, M, 14 AUG 1889, Alexa. Co., congestion [of] bowels, 76y, Ed. & Lettece Welch, Va., miller, consort of Harriet J. Welch, H.J. Welch, [wife], p.51.

WELCH, John F., W, M, 15 SEP 1853, Alexa., killed, 16y, J. & A. Welch, Alexa., stone cutter, John Welch, father, p.2.

WELCH, M., W, M, 1 MAY 1854, Alexa., chills & fevers, 23y, W. & E. Welch, Ireland, B. Dailey, sister, p.7.

WELCH, Mary, W, F, OCT 1853, Alexa., spasms, 2m, J. & M. Welch, Alexa., John Welch, father, p.3.

WELLS, John, (f), M, 11 JUN 1879, Arlington Dist., brain fever, 39y, --, Md., farming, consort of Mary Wells, Mary Wells, wife, p.40.

WELLS, John A., (f), M, 14 JUL 1879, Arlington Dist., spasms, 3m6d, John & Mary Wells, Arlington Dist., Mary Wells, mother, p.40.

WELLS, Martena, W, F, 10 MAY 1893, Alexa. Co., old age, 95y, --, widow, W.L. Beach, grandson, p.57.

WELLS, Richard N., W, M, 20 OCT 1858, Alexa., scarlet fever, 2y6d, Jas. & Sarah Wells, Alexa., Jas. Wells.

WELLS, Richard N., --, M, 6 NOV 1859, Alexa., scarlet fever, 4y, Joseph & Amanda Wells, Alexa., Joseph Wells, father.

WELLS, Rosesetta, (f), F, 1 APR 1877, near Freedmen's Village, consumption, 27y, Louisa & Sam'l. Howard, Md., housework, widow, John Wells, husband,

Alexandria (Arlington) County, Virginia Death Records, 1853-1896

p.37.
WELLS, [blank], (f), F, 30 MAY 1878, Georgetown Road, --, 9d, John & Mary Wells, Geo'town Road, John Wells, father, p.38.
WESLEY, Lizzie, (f), F, 20 JUN 1872, Arlington Dist., consumption, 27y, unknown, Va., laborer, Charles Wesley, Geo. Mortimore, undertaker, p.32.
WESLEY, Mary, (f), F, 25 JUL 1872, Arlington Dist., unknown, 10y, Charles & Lizzie, Va., --, Geo. Mortimore, undertaker, p.32.
WEST, Albert, (f), M, JUL 1855, Alexa., small pox, 23y, -- West, Alexa., soap boiler, B. Thomas, employer, p.12.
WEST, Alberta A., (f), F, 14 APR 1891, Alexa. Co., pneumonia, 10m, Geo. T. & Mary West, Alexa. Co., G.T. West, father, p.53.
WEST, Benjamin F., W, M, 25 AUG 1853, Portland, Maine, typhoid fever, 21y, J. & P. West, Alexa., U.S. Coast Survey, John West, father, p.4.
WEST, Cornelius, (f), M, 14 DEC 1888, Alexa. Co., --, 45y, --, Md., labor, consort of Jane West, Jane West, wife.
WEST, James W, M, 22 JUN 1892, Alexa. Co., --, 8m, Henry & Mary, Alexa. Co., Mary West, mother, p.55.
WEST, Jerry, W, M, 11 MAR 1856, Alexa., drowned, 49y, --, E. Snowden, editor, p.15.
WEST, John, W, M, 1 JUL 1855, Alexa., unknown, 6m, J. & E. West, Fairfax, E. West, mother, p.12.
WEST, Mary E., (f), F, 6 OCT 1885, Alexa. Co., --, 19y, Cornelius & Mary J., Alexa. Co., Cornelius West, father, p.47.
WEST, Mary Jane, (f), F, [no date] 1875, Alexa. Co., croup, 2m, p.35.
WEST, Rosetta, (f), F, OCT 1885, Alexa. Co., --, 6y2m, Cornelius & Mary J., Alexa. Co., Cornelius West, father, p.47.
WEST, [blank], (f), F, NOV 1885, Alexa. Co., --, Cornelius & Mary J., Alexa. Co., Cornelius West, father, p.47.
WESTLEY, Charles, (f), M, 15 JUL 1873, Arlington Twp., consumption, 35y, p.33.
WETHERS, Harry, W, M, [no date] 1887, Alexa. Co., 2m15d, James E. & Pricilla, Alexa. Co., Pricilla Wethers, mother, p.49.
WHALEN, Ann, W, F, [no date] 1855, Alexa., consumption, 30y, G. & -- Arrington, P. Wm. Co., John Whalen, Susan Arrington, sister in law, p.13.
WHALEN, Thos., W, M, 29 OCT 1866, Alexa., summer complaint, 1m14d, Elizth. & Jas. Whalen, Alexa., James Whalen, father, p.21.
WHALEY, Geo., W, M, 18 AUG 1894, Alexa. Co., consumption, 41y, Washn. & Elizabeth, Pa., consort of Rachel Whaley, Rachel Whaley, wife, p.59.
WHEAT, Robert Wilson, W, M, 22 APR 1865, Alexa., consumption, 50y, Benoni & Mary, Md., mer., married, J.J. Wheat, brother, p.19.
WHEAT, Willie, W, F, 17 OCT 1857, Alexa., pneumonia, 1m14d, Benoni & Matilda Wheat, Alexa., merchant.
WHEATLEY, [blank], W, F, AUG 1854, Alexa., 2d, Jas. S. & J. Wheatley, Alexa., Jas. Wheatley, father, p.7.
WHEELER, John, W, [M], 13 JUN 1858, Alexa., cholera infantum, 10m, John Wheeler, Alexa., John Wheeler.
WHITE, Geo. W., (f), M, 21 DEC 1893, Alexa. Co., consumption, 61y, --, Fauquier Co., labor, single, M.B. Gambrill, employer, p.57.
WHITE, Hanna M., W, F, 19 MAY 1891, Alexa. Co., diarrhea, 52y, --, London, England, clerk, consort of T.W. White, T.W. White, husband, p.53.
WHITE, Nolle, (f), M, JAN 1866, Alexa., unknown, 2y, Susan & Malaca White, Alexa., laborer, Susan White, mother, p.21.
WHITE, Vachel, W, M, NOV 1857, Alexa., consumption, 58y, --, shoemaker, Mrs.

101

Alexandria (Arlington) County, Virginia Death Records, 1853-1896

White.
WHITEHEAD, Birtha L., W, F, 28 JUN 1896, Alexa. Co., brain fever, 2y, John M. & Josephine, Alexa. Co., single, John M. Whitehead, father, p.63.
WHITEHEAD, Elizabeth, W, F, 24 APR 1889, Alexa. Co., consumption, 35y, --, Va., housekeeper, consort of J.H. Whitehead, W.J. Whiteing [sic], husband, p.51.
WHITEWELL, Augusta, W, F, 7 JAN 1859, Alexa., disease of heart, 27y, --, Va., George Duffey, friend.
WHITING, Arthur, --, 8 SEP 1858, Alexa., scarlet fever, 3y, Fairfax & Margaret Whiting, Fairfax Whiting, father.
WHITING, Eliza, (f), F, 31 MAR 1853, Alexa., unknown, 35y, -- Pitcher, Bermuda Island, John Whiting, Milly Jones, mother in Law, p.4.
WHITING, Robert W., (f), M, 18 JUN 1891, Alexa. Co., cholera infantum, 1y10m23d, R.W. & Roberta Whiting, Alexa. Co., Roberta Whiting, mother, p.53.
WHITING, Robt. W., (f), M, 24 NOV 1889, Alexa. Co., consumption, 34y, Albert & Maria Whiting, Va., Treas. Va. Institute, consort of Roberta Whiting, Roberta Whiting, wife, p.51.
WHITTINGTON, Ann, W, F, 17 OCT 1854, Alexa., dysentery, 80y, John & Martha Bassford, Md., Thomas Whittington, H.B. Whittington, son, p.6.
WHITTINGTON, G.H., W, M, 12 JUN 1859, Alexa., --, 5m, Geo. T. & Jane L. Whittington, Alexa., Geo. T. Whittington, father.
WHITTLESEY, Elizabeth, W, F, 19 JUN 1868, Alexa., cancer, 62y, J. & A. Peel, Wilmington, N.C., --, married, O.C. Whittlesey, son, p.25.
WHITTLESEY, L., W, M, 14 JAN 1868, Alexa., kidney disease, 72y, Jos. & M. Whittlesey, Wash., Conn., teacher, married, O.C. Whittlesey, son, p.25.
WIBIRT, Stephen B., W, M, 9 MAY 1882, Col. Pike, --, 58y, --, N.Y., Supt. of Schools, consort of Margret Wibirt, W.H. Wibirt, son, p.44.
WILCOX, Lew. Samuel, W, M, JUN 1853, Alexa., consumption, 35y, unknown, Washington City, revenue service, Mrs. Wilcox, M. Maddux, hotel keeper, p.1.
WILDIER, Adline, (f), F, 10 APR 1884, F. Vill[age], --, 4y11m15d, Isiah & Martha, Alexa. Co., Isiah Wildier, father, p.45.
WILDIER, Dora, (f), F, 3 MAY 1882, near F. Vill[age], small pox, 6y2d, Isiah & Martha Wildier, F. Vill[age], Martha Wildier, mother, p.44.
WILKINS, John, W, M, 28 DEC 1859, Alexa., consumption, 38y, --, Northumberland, consort of Eliza J. Wilkins, Eliza J. Wilkins, wife.
WILKINSON, Jane, W, F, 6 JUL 1865, Alexa., heart disease, 34y, Joseph & Mary, Ireland, laborer, consort of Jas. Wilkinson, Jas. Wilkinson, husband, p.19.
WILKINSON, John, W, M, 12 JUL 1865, Alexa., brain fever, 1y1m, James & Jane W., Ireland, laborer, single, James Wilkinson, father, p.19.
WILLETT, Archie, W, M, 22 NOV 1890, Alexa. Co., --, 3m21d, Geo. P. & Jane E., Geo. P. Willett, father, p.52.
WILLIAMS, Ann E., W, F, 7 JUN 1859, Alexa., --, 4y, Geo. & Maria Williams, Alexa., George Williams, father.
WILLIAMS, Ann, W, F, 3 NOV 1859, Alexa., convulsions, 28y, --, Md., D.M. French, physician.
WILLIAMS, Bazil, W, M, 14 DEC 1854, Alexa., carbuncle, 78y, B. Williams, Fairfax, farmer, David Williams, nephew, p.9.
WILLIAMS, Clara, (f), F, 13 MAY 1895, Alexa. Co., consumption, 8y, Lewis & Sarah, Pr. Wm. Co., labor, Sarah Williams, mother, p.61.
WILLIAMS, Clarence, (f), M, 18 JUL 1883, Alexa. Co., --, 1y, Jas. & Harriet Williams, Alexa. Co., Jas. Williams,

Alexandria (Arlington) County, Virginia Death Records, 1853-1896

father, p.44.

WILLIAMS, Daniel, (f), M, 18 FEB 1880, canal basin, consumption, 40y, --, Middlesex Co., laborer, Harriet Williams, Ada Steward, sister in law, p.41.

WILLIAMS, Dolly, W, F, OCT 1855, Alexa., old age, 90y, R, Williams, son, p.11.

WILLIAMS, E.P., W, F, 6 MAY 1858, Alexa., scarlet fever, 20d, Robt. & Ann Williams, Alexa., Robt. Williams.

WILLIAMS, Edwd., W, M, JUL 1854, Alexa., unknown, 3m, R. & M. Williams, R. Williams, father, p.6.

WILLIAMS, Ella, (f), F, 15 MAY 1879, Jefferson Dist., croup, 2y, --, Jefferson Dist., Maria Coleman, grandmother, p.40.

WILLIAMS, Frank, (f), M, 9 MAY 1895, Alexa. Co., drowned, 22y, Daniel & Catherine, Alexa. Co., labor, single, Emma Williams, sister, p.61.

WILLIAMS, Geo., W, M, 27 DEC 1855, poor house, consumption, 60y, -- Williams, Pa., J. Stephenson, keeper poor house, p.14.

WILLIAMS, Harriet, (f), F, 27 SEP 1896, Alexa. Co., killed, 47y, Henry & Martha, Alexa. Co., housework, consort of J.F. Williams, J.F. Williams, husband, p.63.

WILLIAMS, Harriet, (f), F, 26 AUG 1888, Jefferson [Dist.], malaria, 65y, --, widow, Wm. Bain, son in law.

WILLIAMS, Harry, (f), M, 9 DEC 1893, Alexa. Co., --, 1y, James & Harriet, Alexa. Co., James Williams, father, p.57.

WILLIAMS, Harry Lee, (f), M, 9 DEC 1892, Alexa. Co., pleurisy, 9m, Jas. & Harriet Williams, Alexa. Co., Jas. Williams, father, p.55.

WILLIAMS, Ida J., W, F, 6 SEP 1867, Alexa., congestive chill, 4y8m, Geo. & M. Williams, Alexa., none, single, M. Padgett, friend, p.24.

WILLIAMS, James, (f), M, 1 DEC 1876, near Slaters, smoked to death, 45y, --, Caroline Co., husband of Isabella Williams, Isabella Williams, wife, p.37.

WILLIAMS, John T., W, M, 23 AUG 1866, Alexa., cholera, 49y, Thos. & Winnie Williams, Alexa., painter, married, Thos. Williams, son, p.21.

WILLIAMS, John Thomas, (f), M, OCT 1873, Arlington Twp., unknown, 1y1m, John & Margaret Williams, Arlington, p.33.

WILLIAMS, Julia, (f), F, 2 APR 1881, Georgetown, D.C., heart disease, 30y, Spencer & Matilda Hyson, Va., Albert Hyson, brother, p.43.

WILLIAMS, Julia, (f), F, 25 NOV 1876, near slaters, 4y, Jas. & Isabella Williams, Alexa. Co., Isabella Williams, mother, p.37.

WILLIAMS, Lewis, (f), M, 26 DEC 1895, Alexa. Co., consumption, 48y, Harry & Charlott, Pr. Wm. Co., labor, consort of Sarah E. Williams, Sarah Williams, wife, p.61.

WILLIAMS, Lillie, (f), F, AUG 1884, Hall's Hill, --, 2m, Mollie Williams, Alexa. Co., Jamie Williams, grandmother, p.45.

WILLIAMS, Lucy, (f), F, AUG 1892, Alexa. Co., consumption, 20y, Wm. & Louisa, Alexa. Co., Louisa Williams, mother, p.55.

WILLIAMS, Lucy, (f), F, 24 AUG 1868, Alexa., water on brain, 10m, M. & Kate Williams, Alexa., none, single, M. Williams, father, p.25.

WILLIAMS, Mary, (f), F, 31 MAY 1895, Alexa. Co., --, 7y, Lewis & Sarah, Pr. Wm. Co., Sarah Williams, mother, p.61.

WILLIAMS, Minia, (f), F, 2 JUL 1868, Alexa., consumption, 21y, Jac & Agnes Williams, Alexa., laborer, married, Jacob Williams, father, p.25.

WILLIAMS, Ora, (f), M, 8 NOV 1892, Alexa. Co., --, 13y, --, Alexa. Co., Sarah Williams, aunt, p.55.

WILLIAMS, Rachel, (f), F, 1 AUG 1876, near Ft. Richardson, consumption, 40y, Thos. & Nellie Harrison, Prince Geo. Co.

Alexandria (Arlington) County, Virginia Death Records, 1853-1896

Md., housework, consort of William Henson, William Henson, husband, p.37.
WILLIAMS, Sarah, W, F, SEP 1855, Alexa. Co., typhoid fever, 18y, C.W. & E. Williams, P. William Co., David Williams, brother, p.10.
WILLIAMS, Winefred, W, F, 17 AUG 1854, Alexa., dropsy, 56y, R. & E. Roxbury, Fairfax Co., Thomas Williams, T. Williams, husband, p.9.
WILLIAMS, [blank], (f), F, 22 NOV 1879, Jefferson Dist., --, 7d, Alberta Williams, Jefferson Dist., Patsey Turner, next door neighbor, p.40.
WILLIE, Willie [sic], W, M, 7 SEP 1859, Alexa., burnt with camph., 5y, --, Md., D.M. French, physician.
WILLIS, Ellen, (f), F, OCT 1873, Arlington Twp., unknown, 2d, Edward & Ellen Willis, Arlington, p.33.
WILLIS, Maud, (f), F, NOV 1896, Alexa. Co., --, 11m, Henry & Rose, Rose Willis, mother, p.63.
WILSON, Alex., (f), M, JUN 1890, Alexa. Co., --, 40y, --, Laura Cox, Keeper of Poor House, p.52.
WILSON, Andrew, (f), M, 7 AUG 1878, Washington Road, consumption, 40y, --, Hanover Co., labor, consort of Rose Wilson, Rose Wilson, wife, p.38.
WILSON, Cora, (f), F, 14 JUN 1880, near Pelham's, cold, 2y3m, Henry & Louisa Wilson, Henry Wilson, father, p.41.
WILSON, John, W, M, MAY 1890, Alexa. Co., pneumonia, 63y, --, England, gardener, consort of Bridget Wilson, Jos. Wilson, son, p.52.
WILSON, Julia, (f), F, JUN 1889, Alexa. Co., brain fever, 2y, W.G. & M.A. Wilson, Va., W.G. Wilson, father, p.51.
WILSON, L., W, F, JUL 1868, Alexa., brain fever, 6m, C. & F. Wilson, Alexa., none, single, M. Wilson, mother, p.25.
WILSON, Louise, (f), F, 6 JUN 1891, Alexa. Co., consumption, 35y, Elias & Julia, Va., housework, consort of Henry Wilson, H. Wilson, husband, p.53.
WILSON, Richard H., (f), M, 15 DEC 1878, Sissonville, teething, 2y, Henry & Louisa Wilson, Sissonville, Louisa Wilson, mother, p.38.
WILSON, Walter G., (f), M, 24 JUN 1892, Alexa. Co., pneumonia, 46y, Edward & Mary J., Culpeper Co., farmer, consort of Mildred A. Wilson, M.A. Wilson, wife, p.55.
WILSON, [blank], (f), F, 30 MAR 1879, Jefferson Dist., --, 4d, James & Maggie Wilson, Jefferson Dist., James Wilson, father, p.40.
WINDSOR, Eliza, (f), F, 10 MAY 1880, F. Village, --, 23y11m, Geo. & Martha Windsor, Alexa. Co., housework single, Moore Windsor, brother, p.41.
WINDSOR, [blank], (f), M, 18 AUG 1879, Jefferson Dist., --, 3d, Moore & Lizzie Windsor, Jefferson Dist., Moor[e] Windsor, father, p.40.
WINFIELD, [blank], (f), M, 24 SEP 1892, Alexa. Co., 1d, Wm. & Louisa, Va., Louisa Winfield, mother, p.55.
WINSEL, Anna C., W, F, 5 NOV 1857, Alexa., pneumonia, 1y1m11d, John & Barbara Winsel, Alexa., John Winsel, father.
WINSELL, Barbara, W, F, 12 SEP 1858, Alexa., childbirth, 30y, --, consort of John Winsell, John Winsell.
WINSELL, [blank], W, F, 12 SEP 1858, Alexa., --, 1d, Jas. & Barbara Winsell, Alexa., Jas. Winsell.
WINSTON, Anmarilla, (f), F, 9 OCT 1878, F. Village, --, 2m2d, Wm. N. & Luvenia Winston, F. Village, Wm. N. Winston, father, p.38.
WINSTON, Molly W., (f), F, 7 OCT 1887, nr. F. Vill[age], --, 1m20d, Wm. N. & Luvenia, Alexa. Co., W.N. Winston, father, p.45.
WINSTON, Susan, W, F, 9 DEC 1859, Alexa., diarrhea, 30y, --, Va., Dr. Isaac Winston, father.

Alexandria (Arlington) County, Virginia Death Records, 1853-1896

WINTERS, Charlotte, (f), F, 3 APR 1854, poor house, old age, 90y, -- Winter, unknown, John Stephenson, keeper, p.9.

WISE, George, W, M, 3 APR 1856, rheumatism, 78y, --, J.L. Kinzer, p.16.

WISE, Richd. H., W, M, 26 APR 1855, Alexa., --, 4y, G.A. & H.J. Wise, Alexa., G.A. Wise, father, p.12.

WISE, Wm., (f), M, NOV 1879, Arlington Dist., consumption, 35y, --, Arlington Dist., labor, Wm. H. Lomax, overseer of poor, p.40.

WOLZ, Geo. C., W, M, 13 APR 1894, Alexa. Co., 3y2m8d, Geo. M. & Carrie, Alexa. Co., Geo. M. Wolz, father, p.59.

WOOD, A.M., W, F, 11 SEP 1853, Alexa., consumption, 25y, J. & M.A. Hall, consort of A. Wood, A. Wood, husband, p.1.

WOOD, Anna, (f), F, 25 AUG 1879, Arlington Dist., tress, 6m, Isaac & Leither Wood, Arlington Dist., Leither Wood, mother, p.40.

WOOD, Catherine, (f), F, 16 AUG 1877, near conv. camp, old age, 100y, Elisie Wood, Md., Eliza Wood, daughter in law, p.37.

WOOD, Idva, (f), F, OCT 1895, Alexa. Co., --, single, Isaac Wood, father, p.61.

WOOD, John, (f), M, 18 JAN 1877, near conv. camp, consumption, 36y, Cath. & Edward Wood, Md., labor, Eliza Wood, sister, p.37.

WOOD, John, W, M, [no date] 1858, Alexa., scarlet fever, 5y, John D. & Mary E. Wood, Alexa., John Wood.

WOOD, Leafy, (f), F, AUG 1895, Alexa. Co., --, Isaac & Leafy, consort of Isaac Wood, Isaac Wood, husband, p.61.

WOOD, Mary, W, F, 14 JUL 1857, Alexa., old age, 76y, --, consort of Richd. Wood, Mrs. Edelin, daughter.

WOOD, Nelson, (f), M, 20 DEC 1883, Alexa. Co., dropsy, 39y, --, Ky., labor, consort of Mary Wood, Mary Wood, wife, p.44.

WOOD, Robt., (f), M, SEP 1875, Jefferson Mag. Dist., consumption, 23y, p.35.

WOOD, Washington, (f), M, MAR 1894, Alexa. Co., consumption, 45y, --, Patsy Wood, wife, p.59.

WOOD, William H., (f), M, 1 MAY 1877, near conv. camp, teething, 6m, Lether & Isac, near conv. camp, Lether Wood, mother, p.37.

WOOD, [blank], (f), M, 7 MAR 1878, Dr. King's farm, --, 11d, Nelson & Lucy Wood, Dr. King's farm, Nelson Wood, father, p.38.

WOOD, [Capt.] Isaac, W, M, 27 SEP 1865, Alexa., apoplexy, 63y, unknown, Md., harbor master, married, Walter Waddy, son in law, p.19.

WOODFIELD, Chas. Thos., W, M, 25 JUL 1866, Alexa., unknown, 2y18m, Wm. H. & Mary Woodfield, Alexa., mechanic, Mary E. Woodfield, mother, p.21.

WOODHOUSE, Annie M., W, F, 17 NOV 1859, Alexa., consumption, 24y, --, Prince Wm. Co., consort of Wm. W. Woodhouse, W.W. Woodhouse, husband.

WOOLLS, Rozana, W, F, 14 AUG 1854, Alexa., typhoid fever, 35y, J. & S. McGuire, N. York, W. Woolls, W. Wools, husband, p.7.

WOOLLS, Stephen, W, M, 10 JUN 1865, Alexa., apoplexy, 72y, unknown, England, Gent., widower, Wm. Wools, son, p.19.

WORMLEY, Bertha, (f), F, 15 FEB 1884, nr. F. Vill[age], --, 11m, John W. & Josephine, Alexa. Co., J.W. Wormly [sic], father, p.45.

WORMLEY, Phillip, (f), M, 16 NOV 1880, Washn. D.C., kicked by mule, 22y6m, Nelson & Ellen Wormley, labor, single, Nelson Wormley, father, p.41.

WORTHUM, [blank], W, F, 7 MAY 1853, Alexa., unknown, 4d, W.R. & M.A. Worthum, Alexa., W.R. Worthum, father, p.5.

WRENN, Mary, W, F, 5 JAN 1873, Arlington Twp., consumption, 14y, Philip

Alexandria (Arlington) County, Virginia Death Records, 1853-1896

& Susanna Wrenn, Prince William Co., p.33.

WRENN, Philip, W, M, 11 DEC 1875, Alexa. Co., typhoid fever, 51y, father of Sam Wren, Alexa. Co., p.35.

WRIGHT, Ann, (f), F, 31 MAY 1878, Prospect Hill farm, cold, 40y, --, Orange Co., housework, widow, M.J. Smith, daughter, p.38.

WRIGHT, Herbert, (f), M, 28 OCT 1890, Alexa. Co., --, 22d, Wm. & Luvenia, Alexa. Co., Wm. Wright, father, p.52.

WRIGHT, Jane, (f), F, MAY 1884, nr. F. Vill[age], fits, 27y, --, Abraham Sauers, next door neighbor, p.45.

WRIGHT, Jas. T., W, M, NOV 1892, Wash. D.C., --, 65y, --, Va., farmer, single, Geo. Shorter, neighbor, p.55.

WRIGHT, Margaret, (f), F, 25 AUG 1873, Arlington Twp., --, 30y, Lewis Wright, D.C., p.33.

WRIGHT, Rose, (f), F, 17 MAR 1878, Georgetown Road, teething, 1y, Benj. & Jane Wright, Geo'town Road, Benj. Wright, father, p.38.

WRIGHT, Samuel, (f), M, 23 AUG 1881, F. Village, consumption, 46y, Sam'l. & Susan Wright, Va., Susan Sumerville, daughter, p.43.

WUNDER, [Dr.] Henry S., W, M, 23 DEC 1866, Washington, D.C., dropsy, 75y2m21d, Christopher & Mary Wunder, Germantown, Pa., physician, married, Geo. O. Wunder, son, p.20.

WYLIE, Andrew, W, M, 9 APR 1859, Alexa., --, 11y8m, Andrew & Mary C. Wylie, Alexa., Andrew Wylie, father.

Y

YEATS, Henrietta, (f), F, 12 JAN 1881, near Geo. Reed's, old age, 70y, --, Manda Lewis, granddaughter, p.43.

YOUNG, Albert, W, M, 27 AUG 1857, --, head affection, 9m, A. & L.C. Young, carpenter.

YOUNG, Emma, (f), F, 19 JUN 1875, Jefferson Mag. Dist., p.35.

YOUNG, James E., W, M, OCT 1892, Wash. D.C., pneumonia, 49y11m, John M. & Eliza W., Wash. D.C., single, W.A. Young, brother, p.55.

YOUNG, John, W, M, 20 AUG 1858, Alexa., broken neck, 29y, --, consort of Susannah, S. Young.

YOUNG, Nicholas, (f), M, SEP 1880, Alexa. City, killed, 30y, Daniel & Maria Young, Alexa. Co., labor, single, Maria Washington, mother, p.41.

YOUNG, Peter, (f), M, 16 SEP 1893, Alexa. Co., --, 53y, --, Alexa. Co., labor, consort of Eliza Young, Eliza Young, wife, p.57.

Z

ZIMMERMAN, A., W, F, OCT 1855, Alexa., consumption, 75y, consort of J. Zimmerman, J.M. Clapdore, son in law, p.11.

ZIMMERMAN, Adam, W, M, 1 FEB 1856, Alexa., pneumonia, 58, --, Md., butcher, Tinch E. Zimmerman, p.14.

ZIMMERMAN, M.A., W, F, 14 JUN 1854, Alexa., scrofula, 14y, W. & A. Zimmerman, W. Zimmerman, father, p.9.

ZIMMERMAN, Reubin, W, M, 31 MAY 1859, Alexa., dysentery, 47y, --, Alexa., merchant, consort of Mary Zimmerman, Benj. Waters, father in law.

ZIMMERMAN, Thornton, W, M, 17 NOV 1856, Alexa., stricture, 27y, --, Md., p.15.

Alexandria (Arlington) County, Virginia Death Records, 1853-1896

Not Identified

[blank], W, M, 16 DEC 1857, --, measles, 1y3m4d.
[blank], (s) of Jane Slaughter, F, 31 AUG 1854, Alexa., unknown, 1d, H. & M. Branson, Alexa., M. Branson, mother, p.7.
[blank], (s) of W.N. Birkley, 5 MAY 1854, Alexa., pneumonia, 1y, unknown, Alexa., O. Fairfax, physician, p.10.
[blank], (s) of R.H. Hunton, M, OCT 1854, Alexa., unknown, 2m, -- & Mary, Alexa., J.A. Barbee, hirer, p.6.
[blank], (s) of Elizabeth Gordon, 27 APR 1854, Alexa., scrofula disease of the brain, 8y, unknown, Alexa., O. Fairfax, physician, p.10.
[blank], (s) of L. Peyton, M, AUG 1853, Alexa., unknown, 3d, William & Mahaley, Alexa. Co., slaves, S. Summers, owner, p.5.
[blank], (s) of Col. W.F. Lee, M, Alexa., 76y, --, Alexa. Co., Col. W.F. Lee.
[blank], (s) of Col. W.F. Lee, M, 1y, --, Alexa. Co., Col. W.F. Lee.
[blank], (s) of B.W. Hunter, F, --, 50y, --, Alexa. Co., B.W. Hunter.
[blank], (s) of B.W. Hunter, F, --, 76y, Philip & Catharine Parks, Alexa. Co., B.W. Hunter.
[blank], (s) of Col. W.F. Lee, F, 2y, --, Alexa. Co., Col. W.F. Lee.
[blank], (s) of Col. W.F. Lee, F, 60y, --, Alexa. Co., Col. W.F. Lee.
[blank], (s) of Col. Minor, [no date] 1857, Alexa. Co.
[blank], (s) of J.N. Harper, --, 10 APR 1858, Alexa., 6m, --, J.N. Harper, owner.
[blank], An unknown infant, W, --, 2 JAN 1857, Alexa., --, Chr. Neal, coroner.
[blank], Delilah, (s) of J.N. Harper, F, 10 APR 1858, Alexa., --, 36y, --, J.N. Harper, owner.
[blank], Elizabeth, (s) of Joseph Gregg, F, [no date] 1854, Alexa., congt. fever, 9m, slave, Alexa., Joseph Gregg, master, p.6.
[blank], Elizabeth, (s) of J.S. Peach, F, AUG 1858, Alexa., water of brain, 8m, --, J.S. Peach, owner.
[blank], Ellice, (f), M, [no date] 1875, Arlington Mag. Dist, p.35.
[blank], Emma Louise, W, F, 7 AUG 1857, --, brain fever, 1y11m, Jacob & Sarah Bruen.
[blank], Fanny, (s) of James Garroll, F, AUG 1855, Alexa., child bed, 18y, slave, Fairfax, J. Garroll, owner, p.12.
[blank], Frank, (s) of R.S. Ashby, M, DEC 1854, Alexa., pleurisy, 3y, -- & Martha, Fauquier, R.S. Ashby, master, p.6.
[blank], Gerald, (s) of R. Crupper, --, 15 NOV 1858, Alexa., old age, 80y, --, Robt. Crupper, owner.
[blank], Hannah, (s), F, 8 AUG 1859, Alexa., consumption, 34y, --, Alexa., G.L. Stewart, master.
[blank], Harriett, (s), F, SEP 1859, Alexa., consumption, 25y, --, Alexa., Benj. Waters, master.
[blank], Infant, no name, --, 12 APR 1857, Alexa., --, Chr. Neal, coroner.
[blank], Jacob, (s) of Mrs. Burfoot, M, 28 MAR 1853, Alexa., consumption, 52y, --, Alexa., slave, H.T. Thompson, hirer, p.3.
[blank], Jane, (f), F, 30 DEC 1859, Alexa., burned, 63y, --, Alexa., Lucy, daughter.
[blank], Jenny, (s) of Bazil Hall, F, 26 FEB 1858, Alexa., hung, 45y, --, Alexa. Co., E. Sangster, sheriff.
[blank], Jim, (s) of H. Bontz, M, APR 1853, Alexa., whooping cough, 1y, slave, Alexa., H. Bontz, owner, p.2.
[blank], Liticia, (s) of Tho. Coffer, F, FEB 1854, Alexa., burnt, 13y, Fairfax, T.C. Atkinson, hirer, p.9.
[blank], Louisa, (s) of J.N. Harper, --, NOV 1858, Alexa., --, 22y, --, J.N. Harper, owner.
[blank], Lucretia, (s) of J.H. McVeigh, F, AUG 1853, Alexa., scarlet fever, 9y,

Alexandria (Arlington) County, Virginia Death Records, 1853-1896

slaves, Prince William Co., J.H. McVeigh, owner, p.1.

[blank], Luke, (s), M, 20 DEC 1856, murdered, 72y, --, paperer, John Stephenson, p.17.

[blank], Malinda, (s), F, 20 NOV 1858, Alexa., summer complaint, 10y, --, A. McLeish, owner.

[blank], Mary Jane, (s) of B.C. Mason, F, NOV 1853, Alexa., kidney affection, 12y, slaves, Alexa., B.C. Mason, owner, p.4.

[blank], Nelly, (s) of Isaac Whinston, F, 14 JAN 1856, --, burnt to death, 10y, --, Isaac Whinston, p.16.

[blank], No Name, (f), M, 2 JUN 1866, Alexa., heart disease, unknown, unknown, unknown, constable, coroner, p.21.

[blank], Patsey, W, F, [no date] 1857.

[blank], Richard, (f), M, 2 JUN 1853, Alexa., spasms, 1y, unknown, Alexa., J.L. Smith, friend, p.1.

[blank], Robert, (s) of B.C. Mason, M, SEP 1853, Alexa., consumption, 22y, slaves, Alexa., B.C. Mason, owner, p.4.

[blank], Sarah (s) of W. King's estate, F, 23 NOV 1853, Alexa., unknown, 6y, Sarah --, Alexa., J. Guisendaffer, friend, p.2.

[blank], Talliaferro, (s) of T. Caton, M, [no date] 1857.

[blank], Thaddeus, (s) of W. Birch, M., APR 1853, Alexa. Co., unknown, 2y, -- & Honesty, Alexa., W. Birch, owner, p.5.

[blank], W, F, --, born dead, --, Catharine Parks.

[blank], W, M, 14 SEP 1867, ---, single, S.N. Chipley, T.A. Stoutenburg, coroner, p.24.

[blank], Willie, (s) of A. McLeish, M, 15 NOV 1858, Alexa., summer complaint, 10y, --, A. McLeish, owner.

[not named], (f), M, APR 1887, Alexa. Co., --, 3d, --, Henry Drummond, friend, p.49.

Other Books by Wesley E. Pippenger:

Alexandria (Arlington) County, Virginia Death Records, 1853-1896

Alexandria City and Arlington County, Virginia Records Index: Vol. 1

Alexandria City and Arlington County, Virginia Records Index: Vol. 2

Alexandria County, Virginia Marriage Records, 1853-1895

Alexandria Virginia Marriage Index, January 10, 1893 to August 31, 1905

Alexandria, Virginia Marriages, 1870-1892

Alexandria, Virginia Town Lots, 1749-1801
Together with the Proceedings of the Board of Trustees, 1749-1780

Alexandria, Virginia Wills, Administrations and Guardianships, 1786-1800

Alexandria, Virginia 1808 Census (Wards 1, 2, 3, and 4)

Alexandria, Virginia Death Records, 1863-1896

Alexandria, Virginia Hustings Court Orders, Volume 1, 1780-1787

Connections and Separations: Divorce, Name Change and Other Genealogical Tidbits from the Acts of the Virginia General Assembly

Daily National Intelligencer *Index to Deaths, 1855-1870*

Daily National Intelligencer, *Washington, District of Columbia Marriages and Deaths Notices (January 1, 1851 to December 30, 1854)*

Dead People on the Move: Reconstruction of the Georgetown Presbyterian Burying Ground, Holmead's (Western) Burying Ground, and other Removals in the District of Columbia

Death Notices from Richmond, Virginia Newspapers, 1841-1853

District of Columbia Ancestors, A Guide to Records of the District of Columbia

District of Columbia Death Records: August 1, 1874-July 31, 1879

District of Columbia Foreign Deaths, 1888-1923

District of Columbia Guardianship Index, 1802-1928

District of Columbia Interments (Index to Deaths)
January 1, 1855 to July 31, 1874

District of Columbia Marriage Licenses, Register 1: 1811-1858

District of Columbia Marriage Licenses, Register 2: 1858-1870

District of Columbia Marriage Records Index, 1877-1885

District of Columbia Marriage Records Index
October 20, 1885 to January 20, 1892: Marriage Record Books 21 to 30

District of Columbia Probate Records, 1801-1852

District of Columbia: Original Land Owners, 1791-1800

Early Church Records of Alexandria City and Fairfax County, Virginia

Georgetown, District of Columbia 1850 Federal Population Census (Schedule I) and 1853 Directory of Residents of Georgetown

Georgetown, District of Columbia Marriage and Death Notices, 1801-1838

Husbands and Wives Associated with Early Alexandria, Virginia (and the Surrounding Area), 3rd Edition, Revised

Index to Virginia Estates, 1800-1865
Volumes 4, 5 and 6

John Alexander, a Northern Neck Proprietor, His Family, Friends and Kin

Legislative Petitions of Alexandria, 1778-1861

Pippenger and Pittenger Families

Proceedings of the Orphan's Court, Washington County, District of Columbia, 1801-1808

The Georgetown Courier *Marriage and Death Notices: Georgetown, District of Columbia, November 18, 1865 to May 6, 1876*

The Georgetown Directory for the Year 1830: to which is appended, a Short Description of the Churches, Public Institutions, and the Original Charter of Georgetown, and Extracts of the Laws Pertaining to the Chesapeake and Ohio Canal Company

The Virginia Gazette and Alexandria Advertiser:
Volume 1, September 3, 1789 to November 11, 1790

The Virginia Journal and Alexandria Advertiser:
Volume I (February 5, 1784 to January 27, 1785)

Volume II (February 3, 1785 to January 26, 1786)

Volume III (March 2, 1786 to January 25, 1787)

Volume IV (February 8, 1787 to May 21, 1789)

The Washington and Georgetown Directory of 1853

Tombstone Inscriptions of Alexandria, Volumes 1-4

www.ingramcontent.com/pod-product-compliance
Lightning Source LLC
Chambersburg PA
CBHW070503100426
42743CB00010B/1739